D1613046

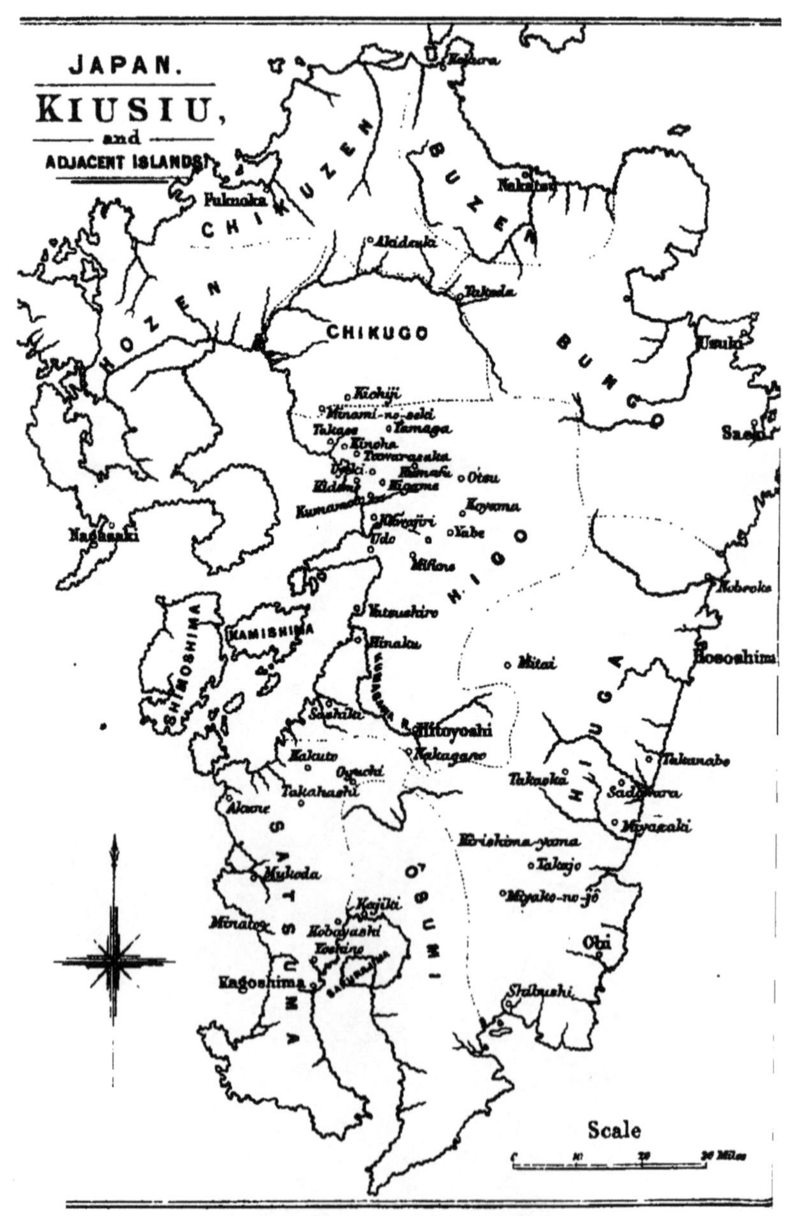

Published by John Murray Albemarle Street London

THE SATSUMA REBELLION.

AN EPISODE OF

MODERN JAPANESE HISTORY.

BY AUGUSTUS H. MOUNSEY, F.R.G.S.,

HER BRITANNIC MAJESTY'S SECRETARY OF LEGATION AT ATHENS;
RECENTLY HER BRITANNIC MAJESTY'S SECRETARY OF LEGATION IN JAPAN;
AUTHOR OF "A JOURNEY THROUGH THE CAUCASUS AND
THE INTERIOR OF PERSIA."

WITH MAPS.

LONDON:
JOHN MURRAY, ALBEMARLE STREET.
1879.

LONDON:
PRINTED BY WILLIAM CLOWES AND SONS,
STAMFORD STREET AND CHARING CROSS.

PREFACE.

Although the Satsuma Rebellion attracted little notice in Europe, where public attention was, at the time of its occurrence, completely absorbed by the Eastern Question, it fills a remarkable chapter in the annals of Japan, and seems destined to mark an epoch in the history of that country, as being, to all appearances, the last serious attempt that will be made to revive some of the institutions of its feudal system.

The causes of this Rebellion date from the year of the Restoration, 1868; and an examination of them shows the importance of the questions at issue between the two parties to the conflict, and supplies a considerable mass of new and interesting information relative to the internal politics of Japan, and the motives and aims of its principal statesmen.

Its course, extending over a period of more than seven months, illustrates the severity of the struggle; whilst its romantic incidents bring out in bold relief the character of Saigô, the Satsuma leader; whose dramatic career and tragic death have earned for him, amongst his countrymen, the title of a 'Great Hero of the East,' and can hardly fail to interest English readers.

Hence it is that the story of this Rebellion has appeared to me worthy of record.

The materials for this story were collected from the most authentic sources, documentary and oral, during the latter part of my residence at Tôkiô, where I had frequent opportunities of acquiring information from Japanese who had taken an active part in its suppression; and in putting them into a readable form, I soon became aware that my work would not be easily intelligible to general readers unless it were preceded—

Firstly, by a brief sketch of the Restoration of 1868, in regard to which I should state that the chapter containing this sketch is simply an epitome of the publications of the ablest writers on this subject;

Secondly, by an account of the part played by the Satsuma clan in preparing the way for the Restoration and bringing it about;

And, Thirdly, by a narrative of the individual action in public affairs of the prominent men in the Satsuma clan up to the outbreak of the Rebellion.

I have accordingly adopted this plan, and I avail myself of the opportunity afforded to me by this Preface, to express the hope that any repetition which may have resulted from its adoption may be considered unavoidable by my readers, especially by those of them who are already acquainted with Japanese history.

The method of spelling and accentuating Japanese words which I have adopted is that which has been followed for many years by the British officials in Japan, and by most European scholars residing there.

It is based on the principle of pronouncing the vowels as on the Continent, and the consonants as in England.

Thus, *a*	is pronounced	as	*a* in father.
,, *e*	,,	,,	*ay* in may.
,, *i*	,,	,,	*i* in machine.
,, *o*	,,	,,	*o* in so.
,, *u*	,,	,,	*u* in full.

After *s*, *ts*, and *dz*, the sound of *u* is often almost inaudible.

As to the consonants, it is here only necessary to remark that *g* in the middle of a word is pronounced in the Tôkiô dialect like *ng* in sing. Thus, Nagasaki becomes Nangasaki.

In regard to one word—the name of the capital of Japan—I have departed from the form still employed by British officials, for the following reasons:

Previous to the year 1868 the capital of the Shôguns was called Yedo, but after the Restoration, and when the Mikado removed his court to that city, its name was changed to Tôkiô, or eastern capital, in contradistinction to Kiôto, or western capital. Since that event the Japanese have universally used the new name, and it has also been adopted by most of the foreign legations in their official communications with the Japanese government, as well as by the American and some European nations.

It seems probable, therefore, that the old name, Yedo, will soon become obsolete amongst the Japanese, and that the new one, Tôkiô, will eventually have to be adopted by the British public.

I have consequently thought it advisable to use the latter name, wherever mention is made of the capital after 1868, in the hope that I may thus contribute to some extent to render Tôkiô familiar to English ears.

AUG. H. MOUNSEY.

CASTLETOWN,
February 28, 1879.

CONTENTS.

PART I.

THE RESTORATION OF 1868.

CHAPTER I.

The ancient form of government in Japan—The feudal system —Three political orders in the state—Kugé, Daimiô, and Heimin—The Tokugawa Shôguns; decline of their authority —Abolition of the Shôgunate and establishment of the present form of government . . . . . . *Pages* 1–12

PART II.

THE PART PLAYED BY THE SATSUMA CLAN IN PREPARING THE WAY FOR THE RESTORATION AND BRINGING IT ABOUT.

CHAPTER II.

The principality of Satsuma—Its capital, Kagoshima—The Daimiô House of Shimadzu—Independent character of the Satsuma clan—Shimadzu Saburô, his hereditary hatred of the Tokugawa family—Bombardment of Kagoshima—Satsuma's part in the overthrow of the Shôgunate—Aims of the leaders of the clan 13–23

PART III.

THE INDIVIDUAL ACTION IN PUBLIC AFFAIRS OF THE PROMINENT MEN OF THE SATSUMA CLAN UP TO THE OUTBREAK OF THE REBELLION IN 1877.

CHAPTER III.

Saigô Takamori—His connection with the "Kennô" school of politicians and consequent banishment to Ôshima—His recall and appointment as administrative head of the Satsuma clan—His military and political services—Ôkubo Toshimitsu—Terashima Munenori—First sign of divergence of opinion between the leaders of the Satsuma clan—Disaffection in the principality . . . . *Pages* 24–34

CHAPTER IV.

Iwakura Tomomi—His mission to Kagoshima and its results—State of things in Satsuma—Views of the leaders of the Tosa and Chôshiu clans—Saigô's political programme—He accepts the post of councillor of state 34–47

CHAPTER V.

Abolition of the Daimiates—Composition of the ministry which enforced this measure—Saigô's participation in it—Shimadzu's disapproval of it—The government attempts to conciliate Satsuma—Difference of opinion in the Cabinet in regard to Japan's relations with Korea—War or peace 47–59

CHAPTER VI.

Motives of the war party—The peace party prevails—Revolt in Hizen—Further attempts to conciliate Satsuma—The Formosan expedition—Shimadzu memorialises the Mikado with a view to upset the government—He resigns, but is induced to enter the Mikado's household 59–76

CHAPTER VII.

Disquieting state of Satsuma—Saigô's "private schools"—The Kagoshima arsenal—Treaty of commerce concluded with Korea—Satsuma's dissatisfaction with the peaceful result of the Korean expedition and with the abolition of the practice of wearing swords—Shimadzu returns to Kagoshima—Position of parties in Japan—Development of the "private schools" . . . . *Pages* 76–87

CHAPTER VIII.

The Pension Commutation Act—Discontent of the Samurai—Rising in Higo, and massacre of part of the garrison of Kumamoto—Mayebara's insurrection in Chôshiu—Quiescent attitude of Satsuma—Conciliatory treatment of Satsuma pensioners—Shimadzu's and Saigô's views of the national policy 87–104

PART IV.

THE REBELLION.

CHAPTER IX.

Relative position and resources of the Imperial government, and of Satsuma—The cabinet—Army and navy—Post and telegraphs—Saigô's character and prestige—His lieutenants—Military strength and other material resources of Satsuma 105–120

CHAPTER X.

The students of the "private schools" oppose the removal of ammunition from Kagoshima—Admiral Kawamura sent to pacify them—Failure of his mission—Story of the plot to assassinate Saigô—Civil war proclaimed . . . 121–139

CHAPTER XI.

Saigô and his army march out of Kagoshima, invest Kumamoto and advance to Minami-no-seki—Position and movements of the Mikado's forces—Prince Arisugawa-no-Miya appointed commander-in-chief — Repulse of the rebels — Occupation and abandonment of Kagoshima by the Imperialists. *Pages* 139–154

CHAPTER XII.

Siege of Kumamoto—Battle of Tawarazaka—Attitude of the Tosa clan—Relief of Kumamoto 154–167

CHAPTER XIII.

Position of affairs after the relief of Kumamoto—Attempts at mediation—Plans of the rebel leaders—Importance to both parties of the possession of Kagoshima 167–180

CHAPTER XIV.

Course of the civil war in the north—Division of the rebel army into three corps—Amnesty proclamations—The Imperialists take Hitoyoshi, and enter Satsuma—Merciless character of the war 181–189

CHAPTER XV.

Course of the war in the south—Failure of the rebels to retake Kagoshima—They retire to the province of Hiuga, and are pursued by overwhelming forces—Miyako-no-jô taken by the Imperialists—Japanese war stratagems—Effects of the fall of Miyako-no-jô 190–201

CHAPTER XVI.

Battle of Nobeoka—Desperate position of the rebels—Saigô's irruption through the Imperialist lines—Panic at Tôkiô—Saigô enters Kagoshima—Retires to Shiroyama—Is surrounded by the Imperialists—Assault of Shiroyama—Death and burial of Saigô and his Samurai 202–217

CHAPTER XVII.

Termination of the Rebellion—State of public feeling in regard to Saigô—Rewards for the services of the army and navy—Festival in honour of the fallen—Punishment of the rebel prisoners . . . . *Pages* 217–230

CHAPTER XVIII.

CONCLUSION.

Cost of the Rebellion, in men, property, and money—Japanese finance—The national debt—Land-tax—Pension Commutation Act—Effect of the Rebellion on the financial position of the country 231–250

CHAPTER XIX.

Political effects of the Rebellion, as regards the province of Satsuma and the agitation for constitutional changes in Japan—Memorial of the Tosa reformers—Assassination of Ôkubo—Institution of local and elective assemblies . . 250–274

APPENDIX 275–294

MAP OF KIUSIU . . . . *Frontispiece.*

MAP OF JAPAN . . . . *at the end.*

NOTICES OF THE CRESTS ON THE BINDING OF THIS BOOK.

THE Mikado has two crests. The first of them, the uppermost on the front side of the binding, is a representation of the *Kiku* or *Chrysanthemum*, and is usually delineated by sixteen petals, conjoined and rounded at the outer extremities, issuing from a small circle in the centre. Some Japanese state that this is not the Chrysanthemum, but is intended as a representation of the sun, so as to bear some connection with the red sun on the National Flag. This theory seems unworthy of credence, as the *Kiku* is frequently represented as a double flower; that is, with the rounded extremities of sixteen other petals, showing from below, in the interstices at the ends of those drawn in the foreground. The *Kiku* is found as a mark on the hilts of the swords forged by the Emperor Gô Toba, who ascended the throne in 1186.

The second of the Imperial Badges is a representation of the leaf and flower of the *Kiri* or *Paulonia Japonica*. It displays three leaves and three flowers. The central stem bears seven buds, and those on the sides five each. Many other families bear the *Kiri* badge, but, as a general rule, the buds are but five in number on the central stem and three on each of the others. This rule regarding the difference in the number of buds is not, however, observed very strictly.

The lowest crest is that of the *House of Shimadzu, Daimiô of Satsuma*, and represents the ring of a horse's bridle-bit.

The crest on the reverse side of the binding is that of the Tokugawa family. It is composed of three leaves of the hollyhock within a circle, the points of the leaves meeting in the centre, and is said to have been adopted, in 1529, by the father of Iyéyasu.

THE

SATSUMA REBELLION.

PART I.

THE RESTORATION OF 1868.

CHAPTER I.

The ancient form of government in Japan—The feudal system—Three political orders in the state—Kugé, Daimiô, and Heimin—The Tokugawa Shôguns; decline of their authority—Abolition of the Shôgunate and establishment of the present form of government.

THE ancient form of government in Japan was briefly as follows: The Mikado was the most absolute of sovereigns. His authority rested, as it does to this day, on the firm belief of his subjects in his direct lineal descent from the gods who created Japan and the rest of the world—a belief which was not only a religious dogma, but also the very foundation of the political fabric. Hence the whole country was his, and all its inhabitants owed him implicit obedience. He governed by means of the nobles of his court who were called Kugé and were chiefly offshoots of the Imperial family. These nobles monopolised all the great offices of the state, and from their ranks were formed the two great governing councils which dealt respectively with all matters appertaining to the gods and their worship, and with all political affairs. They also filled the principal posts in the eight departments entrusted with the executive government of the country.

In this form the supreme authority remained with the Mikado up to the twelfth century, when the feudal system arose in Japan. The governing power then began to pass gradually into the hands of the great feudal families, and finally in 1603 became vested in the baronial family of Tokugawa, the successive members of which enjoyed the title of Shôgun and virtually ruled the country for more than two centuries and a half. The Mikado and his court continued to exist after this change—the former being still universally acknowledged as the divine ruler of the country and the dispenser of all good, the latter retaining, in the estimation of all classes, the precedence which their high birth and long monopoly of the State dignities had conferred upon them; but both the Mikado and the Kugé were mere shadows of their ancestors. The Shôguns possessed all the real power, and though nominally they could decide no important internal question without the assent of the sovereign to whom they owed their investiture, they were generally strong enough to impose their will upon him.

Equal in rank with the Shôguns, but subject to them, were the Daimiô, most of whom were originally military adventurers, who had conquered their provinces in the middle ages of Japanese history by the sword, and exercised independent authority within the limits of their domains, but were bound to perform certain acts of homage to the Shôgun. The government of the latter was composed of those Daimiô on whose loyalty to his dynasty he could rely, and the subordinate posts were filled by the Samurai of his own and his allied clans.

The Samurai were the two-sworded retainers of the Daimiô, descendants of the men who had won their lords' provinces for them, and had been rewarded by grants of land. They formed the military strength of the nation and were at the same time its most educated class.

There were thus three political orders in the State. The Kugé, who, though impoverished by the loss of the lands from which they had in olden times drawn their revenues, still maintained their ancient prèstige, and still held their nominal dignities; the Daimiô, who had enriched themselves with the Kugé's property and reigned as quasi-independent princes over their clans, but were subject to the Shôgun, and often cringed before the Kugé in order to obtain some empty title or inferior office about the imperial court; and the Samurai, or vassals of the Daimiô, who were the backbone of the nation.

The first of these orders numbered about 150 families, the second nearly * twice that

* The total number of Daimiô was 268. Eighteen of these, the oldest and most powerful of their class, were called Kokushiu, and chief amongst them were the Daimiô of Satsuma, Chôshiu, and Tosa. 129 of them formed another class called Go-Fudai and were looked upon as supporters of the Tokugawa Shôguns,

26? 18
127
121 · Outside feudatories

number, and the third about 400,000 households. Below them was the agricultural and artisan population numbering about thirty millions * and called Heimin, whose position was similar in many respects to that of serfs, and who had no political status whatever. Above all these classes were the Mikado, the secluded divinity of Kiôto, still theoretically the source of all authority; and the Shôgun, the real depository of power and the actual and acting governor of the country.

Such was the position, in general terms, of the governing powers and classes under the Shôguns of the Tokugawa family.

---

by whom they were created and with whose family forty of them were connected by the ties of blood.

* No reliable data have yet been discovered relative to the population of Japan in olden times and opinions are much divided in regard to this subject. Some authorities maintain that the empire was as densely inhabited two and a half centuries ago as it is at present; some state that the population retrograded until within the last twenty years; and others assert that it has increased by seven or eight millions since A.D. 1600. The question has not yet been thoroughly examined, and conjecture and inference appear to be the bases of all these opinions, the last of which is, I am inclined to think, the most correct. The latest census returns give the entire population of the empire at thirty-four millions in round numbers.

These Shôguns had maintained peace throughout Japan for 250 years, but there is no doubt that their authority had begun to wane long before Perry and his squadron appeared off its coasts in 1853 and demanded the conclusion of a treaty with the United States of North America. For a long time previously many of the most powerful Daimiô had been discontented with the state of subjection in which they were held by the Shôguns, and, in the opinion of those who have most attentively studied the internal politics of the country, a revolution of some sort or other would have occurred before long, even without the advent of foreigners and the establishment of treaty relations with them. These events merely ripened the already acquired convictions of many leading men in the different clans as to the necessity of some radical changes in the form of government, and hastened their execution.

The Japanese nation was at this time united in wishing to maintain its traditional policy of national seclusion; and there is no doubt that the Shôgun was surprised and awed into the signature of the treaties of 1858 with the

Western Powers of Europe by the successes of the British and French arms in China. In signing these treaties he assumed a power,* and also a title, that of Tycoon, which did not belong to him. He thus not only placed himself in direct opposition to the Mikado and his court, but also increased the feelings of enmity and jealousy with which many of the Daimiô and their clans had long regarded his dynasty. The Mikado refused to ratify the treaties, and

* All foreign authors make this statement, but doubts have been recently raised as to its correctness, and I am informed by Mr. Satow, Japanese Secretary to H.M.'s Legation at Tôkiô, the best authority on such questions, "that neither constitutional law or practice prohibited the Shôgun from entering into treaty relations with foreign powers." In support of this view Mr. Satow states that when Iyéyasu (the first of the Tokugawa Shôguns) granted extensive trading privileges to the Dutch and English, he does not appear to have consulted the Mikado, and that none of the decrees issued by Iyéyasu's successors against the Christians and Portuguese ran in the Mikado's name. Mr. Satow adds that the revival of the idea of reinvesting the Mikado with sovereign rights was due to a History of Japan, published about 1700 by the second Prince of Mito, a grandson of Iyéyasu; to the histories of Rai Sanyô, who wrote about the beginning of this century; and to the leaders of the modern pure Shintôists. I must, however, remark that in preparing and carrying out the restoration, the Mikado's party held that the Shôgun's assumption of the right of making treaties with foreign powers was just as much a usurpation on his part as was his exercise of authority in purely internal affairs.

repeatedly ordered the closing of the open ports and the expulsion of the barbarians. The Shôgun was unable to fulfil these orders, and his inability to do so became a powerful weapon against him in the hands of his opponents. The southern Daimiô indeed regarded and used it as the surest means of obtaining their aims and desires. Their half-concealed hatred took the form of open opposition to the Shôgun and, rallying round the Mikado's throne, they demanded, at first, his reduction to their own level and, finally, the abolition of his office as well as the expulsion of foreigners.

For some years the Shôgun was able to maintain his position by adopting a temporising policy towards the court of Kiôto, promising to cancel the treaties, but of course failing to fulfil his promises. But his authority was daily decreasing in the country, whilst the difficulties which he had created for himself in his relations with the representatives of foreign powers by concealing his real position and assuming that of temporal emperor, or Tycoon of Japan, became proportionately greater. At length in 1865, the

Shôgun was obliged not only to admit his inability to expel the barbarians, but also to inform the Mikado that his throne would be imperilled and his person in danger if he delayed any longer to give his assent to the treaties. These representations were successful and the Mikado at last ratified the treaties. The Shôgun died suddenly a few months later (September 1866) from unnatural causes, it is said.

His successor Kéiki, a man of the most vacillating and irresolute character, accepted office with much reluctance and with the conviction that the days of the Shôgunate were numbered; but the despondent feelings which he then entertained were speedily though only temporarily dissipated by the death of the Mikado, in February 1867, and by the accession to the throne of the reigning Emperor Mutsuhito, then a minor fifteen years of age. Over this youthful monarch, who did not possess the inveterate prejudices of his father against foreigners, Kéiki hoped to gain complete influence and thus retain the power if not the name of his present office. But the south-western Daimiô, who had now the aid of some of the Kugé, were more than ever decided on abolishing the Shôgunate, and their league had gained such strength in the autumn of 1867, that it then became evident that the final struggle between the two parties was not far distant. The Shôgun himself, who is said to have had great repugnance to risking his cause in the field, seems to have been anxious to avoid hostilities. The conviction he had entertained on assuming his office now presented itself to his mind with increased force, and the strength of his opponents made it clear to him that the dual system of government which had existed so long was henceforward impossible. Accordingly, in November 1867, he went from Ôzaka, where he had been for some time resident, to Kiôto, the capital of the Mikado, and there surrendered his title and authority into the hands of his liege lord, stipulating, however, at the same time that the Daimiô should be assembled to decide in concert with him and by a majority of votes, on the future constitution of the empire. The Mikado accepted his resignation and summoned the Daimiô to Kiôto, but charged the Shôgun to carry on the administration of the country *ad interim.*

Thus a peaceful solution of the constitutional question at issue might possibly have been arrived at, if the southern and western clans had not been determined to proceed to extremities and destroy for ever the power of the Tokugawa family.

On the 3rd of January 1868, before the assembly of Daimiô could meet, the troops of five of the chief of these clans seized the palace at Kiôto and after expelling the Shôgun's adherents got possession of the Mikado's person. They thereupon caused his Majesty to issue a decree abolishing the Shôgunate, and further declared their intention of depriving the late holder of this office of his revenues. The Shôgun retired to Ôzaka, and there his adherents, whose deepest interests were menaced by this threat, forced him to have recourse to arms. In the battle which ensued at Fushimi, a village between Kiôto and Ôzaka, they were defeated by the troops of the leagued clans who fought under the standard and in the name of the Mikado.

The Shôgun thereupon departed to Tôkiô,

refused to sanction further hostilities against the Mikado and was soon afterwards allowed to retire into the private life in the country which he still enjoys. His partisans continued the civil war for some months, but were finally crushed in October 1868.*

The office of Shôgun was abolished, and the victors, chief amongst whom were the Satsuma, Chôshiu and Tosa clans, established the government, modelled after that which existed up to the twelfth century, which has since ruled the country in the Mikado's name. The principal authors of the Restoration recognised the impossibility of annulling the treaties with the nations of Europe; opposition to their consequences was discountenanced by the new government in its own interest; and the agitation for the expulsion of foreigners subsided.

* i.e. on the mainland. The Shôgun's fleet, which had obtained possession of Hakodaté in the island of Yezo, did not surrender until 1869.

PART II.

THE PART PLAYED BY THE SATSUMA CLAN IN PREPARING THE WAY FOR THE RESTORATION AND BRINGING IT ABOUT.

CHAPTER II.

The principality of Satsuma—Its capital, Kagoshima—The Daimiô House of Shimadzu—Independent character of the Satsuma clan—Shimadzu Saburô, his hereditary hatred of the Tokugawa family—Bombardment of Kagoshima—Satsuma's part in the overthrow of the Shôgunate—Aims of the leaders of the clan.

SATSUMA, as collectors of porcelain and those who are conversant with the history of our early relations with Japan are aware, is the name of a principality situated at the southern extremity of Kiushiu, one of the four large islands which, with numberless islets, form the Empire of Japan. This island is an important portion of Japan on account of its geographical position, as it faces the central part of China and is only about 100 miles from the southern shores of Korea. It is generally rugged and mountainous, though there are here and there plains of considerable extent, and is divided into the provinces of Hizen, Chikuzen, Buzen, Chikugo, Higo, Bungo, Satsuma, Hiuga, and Ôsumi. The two latter, from ancient times fiefs of the Daimiô of Satsuma, together with the province of their own name, form the principality of Satsuma, which, with the adjacent provinces of Higo and Bungo, was the scene of the late rebellion.

The capital of the principality is Kagoshima, which is said to be one of the most ancient towns in Japan. It is situated on the west side of the deep gulf of Kagoshima and opposite to it, at a distance of about two miles, is the island of Sakurajima, surmounted by a picturesque volcanic mountain 3600 feet high. The town, which contains 87,000 inhabitants, covers a large space of ground, but there is nothing particularly striking in it except the quarter in which the residences of the Samurai are situated. There the streets are broad and lined with houses set back from the road and surrounded with gardens, above the enclosing walls of which orange, maple and wax trees throw their branches. Near the centre of the town is a large open space, used as a parade ground, and behind it rises a hill, covered to its summit with beautiful foliage and vegetation, and called Shiroyama. The chief industries of Kagoshima are the manufacture of cotton, silk, pottery and glass, and the arsenal there is one of the largest in the empire. The principality is famous for its tobacco and horses; rice, tea, camphor and cedar-wood are amongst the number of its products.

The family of Shimadzu, which has ruled this principality for several centuries, is one of the richest and most influential in Japan, its assessed revenue of 770,800 koku* of rice being only exceeded by that of the Prince of Kaga, viz., 1,022,700 koku. Its members have always been the most strenuous opponents to the establishment of a centralised government for the whole of Japan, and have been equally hostile to any interference in the internal affairs of their territory. As long ago as 1590, when Taikô Sama attempted to make himself master of the

* 1 Koku = 331 lbs. Average value 17*s.* 7*d.*

empire, he was obliged to raise an army numbering, it is said, 150,000 men in order to subdue the 50,000 troops that Satsuma could then place in the field. The Daimiô of the province of that day, though defeated, was allowed to retain his former position and power; and again, when Iyéyasu succeeded in establishing the universal sway of the Tokugawa dynasty, he thought it prudent to leave the Shimadzu family in possession of all the lands they had previously acquired and held by force of arms, though he felt himself strong enough to transfer many of the other Daimiô from their original seats to other parts of the country. The armed classes of Satsuma, famed amongst all the clans for their military prowess, were especially characterised by a spirit of independence and an impatience of control to which their distance from the seat of government no doubt greatly contributed. Hence both the princes and the people came to consider themselves superior to the inhabitants of all the other provinces, all intercourse with which they strictly watched by carefully guarding the boundaries of the principality.

Their province formed more than any other an *imperium in imperio*, and the old saying that each of its inhabitants considered himself a Satsuma man first and then a Japanese, continued to be perfectly true up to the date of the recent Rebellion.

The present head of the House of Shimadzu is a nephew of the late Daimiô, who died in 1858. As he was then an infant and has not yet shown any inclination to devote his attention to politics, his father, Shimadzu Saburô (more correctly called Shimadzu Hisamitsu) has acted as representative of the clan since that year. This nobleman had, during his brother's reign, passed a secluded life, occupying himself chiefly with the study of Chinese and Japanese literature, in most branches of which he had become proficient. But as soon as he was called upon to manage the affairs of his clan, he took an active part in the general politics of his country. His hereditary hatred of the Tokugawa family caused him to join the party which had for some years advocated the restoration of the Mikado and the expulsion of foreigners. The same reason also induced him in 1862 to propose to the Imperial Court that a special envoy should be despatched to Yedo, to induce the Shôgun to come down to Kiôto in order to discuss and adopt active measures for the expulsion of foreigners, in concert with the nobles of the Mikado's court. This proposal being approved, Shimadzu Saburô obtained permission to accompany the envoy and assist him in his mission, and in the early part of 1862 he marched to Yedo with a following of 600 armed men. In undertaking this journey he had, it appears, other objects in view of a more personal nature than the above. One of these was to procure the repeal of the ordinance which compelled all the Daimiô to pass a considerable portion of their time every year in Yedo and to leave their families in that city as hostages during their absence from it. Another was to obtain the assent of the Shôgun's government to his appointment to a very high post at the Mikado's court. Neither of these requests was granted at the time, and it is said that during the whole of his stay in Yedo, Shimadzu was refused admittance to the Shôgun's presence. This treatment naturally augmented the feelings of hatred and jealousy entertained by the Satsuma clan against the Tokugawa family, and Shimadzu and his adherents returned homewards burning with resentment and the desire for revenge. On their way and shortly after leaving Yedo, they met and attacked a party of Englishmen riding along the high road, and this incident brought the names of Satsuma and Kagoshima prominently before the British public. For the reparation at once demanded by the British Government for this outrage not being promptly and fully accorded by the government of the Shôgun, which averred that it had no power to arrest the authors of it when once they had returned to their own province, Kagoshima was bombarded and burnt by a British squadron.

The Shôgun's government was probably not displeased to see the pride of this powerful clan thus humbled. It was well aware that, long before the arrival of foreigners in Japan, the idea of restoring the supreme power in the State to the Mikado had taken deep root in the minds of the educated classes of the south-western clans and that

Satsuma, heading the movement, was making active preparations, avowedly against the foreign barbarians, but really against its own power; that Satsuma, in short, aimed at reducing the Shôgun to the position of its own and all other Daimiô, as vassals of the Court of Kiôto. It therefore regarded the British expedition against Kagoshima as a measure calculated to strengthen its own position by weakening the chief member of the league which it foresaw would eventually be formed against its power; and hence, far from taking umbrage at the despatch of the British squadron, the Shôgun's government offered to send a Japanese steamer with a high official on board to accompany it, in the hope that the expedition would result in rendering Satsuma more submissive to its own authority.

This expectation was not, however, fulfilled. For the bombardment of Kagoshima convinced the leaders of the Satsuma clan that the world contained other nations more powerful and more civilised than Japan and that their existence must be considered in calculating the political future of their own country. It proved to them that, whether the subjects of these nations were to be received as friends or driven away as enemies, Japan must present to them a united front. Such a union they now saw more clearly than ever could only be attained by the destruction of the Shôgunate and the restoration of the Mikado.

Thus actuated by the twofold motives of patriotism and clannish hatred of the Tokugawa family and its allies, the Satsuma men took a very active part in the events which occurred between the years 1862 and 1868. It was principally owing to their efforts that the league of the south-western clans against the Shôgunate was finally cemented, and their troops formed a considerable portion of the force which by a *coup de main* drove the Shôgun's adherents out of the palace at Kiôto and obtained possession of the Mikado's person.

It was from Satsuma that first came the proposal to abolish the office of the Shôgun, and in this and other ways the clan placed itself so prominently at the head of the league against the Shôgun that the latter's government formally declared war against it and at once burnt and pillaged its Yashiki * in Ôzaka and Yedo. At the battle of Fushimi, in the fighting which took place in July 1868 at Uyéno, and which resulted in the surrender of the whole of the city of Yedo to the Imperialists, and in the subsequent pursuit and defeat of the Shôgun's adherents, Satsuma troops greatly distinguished themselves, being always foremost in the fight and bearing the brunt of the battle. In short, the services rendered by the clan to the Imperial cause were of such importance that they were acknowledged at the time in a letter of the following tenor, which the Mikado addressed to Shimadzu Saburô:

"For many years past you have been the
" chief upholder of my cause. The defeat of
" the rebels at Fushimi in 1868, which was the
" greatest blow to the Shôgun's power and
" which caused a general change in the feeling
" of the country, was mainly brought about by
" your troops. You sent them also to the
" north-east and, gaining one victory after
" another, you have conquered the insurgents

* Mansions of the Daimiô, to which were attached dwellings for their retainers and extensive grounds.

" and brought about the present peace. It is
" owing to your efforts that I am restored to
" my present position, and I regard you as the
" pillar of our country. In acknowledgment
" of your meritorious service, I reward you
" with an annual pension of 100,000 koku of
" rice and raise your rank."

The Satsuma leaders had, therefore, good grounds for looking forward to prominent positions in the future government of the country, under the new order of things, as the natural and well-merited reward of their services. Some of them, indeed, it may be presumed from subsequent events, aimed more at acquiring for themselves the executive authority of the extinct Shôgunate, without its name, than at making the Mikado the real and effectual depositary of the supreme power.

PART III.

THE INDIVIDUAL ACTION IN PUBLIC AFFAIRS OF THE PROMINENT MEN OF THE SATSUMA CLAN UP TO THE OUTBREAK OF THE REBELLION IN 1877.

CHAPTER III.

Saigô Takamori—His connection with the "Kennô" school of politicians and consequent banishment to Ôshima—His recall and appointment as administrative head of the Satsuma clan—His military and political services—Ôkubo Toshimitsu—Terashima Munenori—First sign of divergence of opinion between the leaders of the Satsuma clan—Disaffection in the principality.

CHIEF amongst the Satsuma leaders was Saigô Takamori.* Born at Kagoshima in 1826, of simple Samurai parents, he was educated chiefly at Kiôto, and as a young man appears to have been in constant communication with a school of politicians

* Kichinosuké was the name by which he was familiarly called. Takamori was his historical name. Every Japanese of Samurai birth has in like manner two names. The historical name is generally of four syllables and is called Nanori.

composed of men of different clans, which desired either the expulsion of foreigners or, if this were impossible, such a change in the constitution as would give the chief clans a voice in the nation's relations with them and would, above all, relieve these clans from arbitrary subjection to a ruler who was not the sovereign of the country, but merely a subject of the Mikado. Fully imbued with these principles, Saigô, on his return home from Kiotô, speedily rose by his own ability to considerable influence in his clan and with the then reigning Daimiô. The latter, an able and intelligent man, agreed with him in thinking that force alone would bring about a change in the constitution of the country, and by his advice attempted to make timely preparations for it, by maintaining and developing the military spirit and organisation of his clan.

As time went on, the members of this school came to see that their objects could only be attained by the overthrow of the Shôgunate and the restoration of sovereign authority to the Mikado; and they assumed, as their motto, the word "Kennô" i.e. "Duty towards the Emperor."

The Shôgun's government used every means in its power to suppress their teaching, and in 1858 it succeeded in arresting most of the members of this school, amongst them being Gasshô, a priest of Kiôto and an intimate friend of Saigô. After a brief interval of imprisonment, Gasshô managed to escape and made his way to Saigô's house in Satsuma. There taking counsel together, these two men came to the conclusion that their cause was desperate and agreed to drown themselves rather than fall into the hands of the Shôgun's emissaries, whom they knew to be on their track. Accordingly, as they were being conveyed one night across the bay from Kagoshima to the island of Sakurajima, they both jumped overboard. The boatmen picked them up, but the priest was dead, and Saigô, already insensible, was with difficulty recalled to life. Thereupon the Satsuma authorities, fearing lest the Shôgun's government should accuse them of harbouring its enemies and yet determined to save Saigô, banished him to Ôshima, a small island off the southern coast of the principality.

His residence there no doubt afforded him

leisure to ponder over the affairs of his country, and it is not improbable that he there became convinced of the impossibility of expelling foreigners and restoring Japan to its previous state of isolation—a conviction which was confirmed by the subsequent bombardment of Kagoshima, after which event, according to Adams,* the Satsuma clan were foremost in discarding the feelings of contempt with which foreigners were then generally regarded, and in endeavouring to acquire the advantages of European superiority in the arts of peace and war.

However this may be, his exile, far from curing him of his hatred of the Shôgun's government, appears to have strengthened this feeling. The soundness of the advice he had always given to his master relative to the necessity of reforming the military system of the clan and maintaining its forces in an efficient state, was fully proved by the bombardment of Kagoshima, and in 1863, Shimadzu Saburô recalled him from banishment and placed him at the head of the administration of the principality. He at once resumed an

* History of Japan, vol. i. p. 328.

active part in the general politics of the empire, and his new position of chief councillor of the Satsuma chieftain gave his opinions and words great weight with the other clans.

It was chiefly through his influence and agency that the south-western Daimiô and Samurai were induced to forget their old feuds and unite in the league, above referred to, against the Tokugawa family. He commanded in person the Satsuma contingent at the battle of Fushimi, and marching thence with the forces of the league was employed as military adviser by Prince Arisugawa, the commander-in-chief, in arranging terms of peace with the Shôgun, from whom, by his tact and conciliatory manner, he succeeded in obtaining peaceable possession of the castle of Yedo. Saigô also accompanied Prince Arisugawa in his expedition to Echigo, where a number of rebels kept the field till the summer of 1868, and he took part in the defeat, in October of the same year, of the last remnant of the Shôgun's adherents who still maintained themselves on the mainland.

These services were acknowledged by the Mikado in a letter of the following tenor:

"You have been the strongest upholder of "my cause, and you have for years been "zealously endeavouring to secure my re-"storation. By your skill as military com-"missioner in obtaining possession of Yedo "Castle, in gaining the victories of Echigo, "and by your diligence in all affairs connected "with my service, you have gained for me "the peace I enjoy to-day. I honour your "actions, and as a reward therefore decree to "you a pension of 2000 koku of rice."*

Nor was it in military affairs alone, that Saigô rendered valuable services to his sovereign. The Restoration of the latter was due firstly to the feelings of jealousy and enmity which the clans had long cherished against the Tokugawa Shôguns, and secondly to the prestige of the Mikado's name, to the religious reverence with which the sacred person of the descendant of the Sun goddess had been regarded for centuries. But this power could not long subsist on these moral grounds alone,

* Saigô at first refused this reward, and finally only accepted it on being expressly commanded to do so by the Mikado. He applied it, as will be seen later, to the foundation and maintenance of the "private schools."

and it soon became evident that it must be supported by material force. This necessity was well understood by the men who had been most instrumental in bringing about the Restoration, and they met it by taking advantage of the enthusiasm engendered amongst the clans by that event. By the power of this feeling they induced the Daimiô to take a step, which, like the circumstances under which it was taken, has no precedent in the recorded history of any other country in the world. This step was nothing more nor less than the voluntary surrender to the Mikado of their hereditary fiefs and revenues in order that they might be used in giving stability to a central government, to be administered by the sovereign with the aid of cabinet ministers and a national council, in restoring, in short, with certain modifications, the ancient form of government referred to in the first pages of this work.

In proposing and carrying out this measure, Saigô, now more influential than ever in the councils of the Satsuma clan, took a very prominent part, and was soon afterwards appointed to an important post in the ministry of war.

Other members of the Satsuma clan had already been named to influential appointments in the new government, and amongst these was Ôkubo Toshimitsu, whose name is associated with all the important changes subsequently carried out by the Mikado's government.

Ôkubo was born about the same time as Saigô, of a humble Samurai family, and, like all Satsuma men, early imbibed a strong feeling of hatred and jealousy of the Tokugawa Shôguns. He too joined the ranks of the school of politicians who looked longingly forward to the restoration of the governing power to the Mikado, and is said to have shown great tact in conducting the negotiations which went on between these politicians and a small number of the Kugé who entertained similar views. He likewise took a prominent part in the affairs of his clan. In 1868, immediately after the abdication of the Shôgun, it was Ôkubo who proposed and succeeded in carrying out the removal of the capital from Kiôto to Yedo and the abandonment by the Mikado of the excessively reverential ceremonial which had surrounded him for centuries, but which

Ôkubo justly considered incompatible with the future he foresaw for Japan. He was at once made a councillor of state, and during his long tenure of office, which only terminated with his assassination in 1878, he was the most vigorous of the reforming spirits in the government, the perservering and strenuous opponent of the conservatism (to be presently noticed) of Shimadzu and Saigô. Another Satsuma man, Terashima Munenori, was at the same time made under secretrary in the department for foreign affairs, of which he is still the head, and subordinate posts under the central government were given to many others.

These were the most prominent men of the clan at the time of the Restoration, and up to the year 1869 they appear to have acted in concert. After that date they became divided into two parties, whose tendencies and aims were no longer identical. Shimadzu Saburô and Saigô appear henceforth as the representatives of the special and separate interests of their clan, whilst Ôkubo, Terashima, and a large number of their clansmen, who held subordinate posts in the different ministries, became more and more identified with the central government. A divergence of opinion as to the future policy and aims of the clan arose amongst its members, and the disunion thus created was destined to grow and increase each year until it ended in a death-struggle between the two parties.

The first manifest sign of this change occurred in November 1870, when the Satsuma troops, who had remained in Tôkiô * since the Restoration as a guard for the central government, petitioned the Mikado to be relieved from this service. Their leaders declared that the exertions of the clan during the civil war, the debts it had contracted towards foreigners for arms and munitions, and a succession of bad harvests had greatly embarrassed the finances of their province; and that it was unable any longer to meet the expense of sending garrison troops to the new capital. Shimadzu and Saigô presented the petition, but it does not appear to have been supported by either Ôkubo or Terashima, and there is little doubt that the real grounds of the request which it contained were the discontent and disappointment of the two

* The new name given to Yedo after the Restoration.—*Vide* Preface.

former statesmen at finding that the part in the government of the country allotted to them was infinitely less than what they considered they had a right to expect.

These feelings were fully shared by the troops and by the majority of the clan. The former, having obtained leave to depart, at once returned to their homes, and their half-concealed discontent then broke forth into open complaints. The disaffection in Satsuma became, indeed, so wide spread and was considered so serious, that the government deemed it necessary to send a special embassy to Kagoshima to appease the wounded pride of the clan.

CHAPTER IV.

Iwakura Tomomi—His mission to Kagoshima and its results—State of things in Satsuma—Views of the leaders of the Tosa and Chôshiu clans—Saigô's political programme—He accepts the post of councillor of state.

For the purpose indicated in the conclusion of the preceding chapter, the government selected Iwakura Tomomi, one of the ablest and most distinguished of the few Kugé whose names had become connected with the politics of their country. Brought up at

Kiôto, he became one of the personal attendants of the Mikado when only twenty years old, and a story is told of him which shows that, even at that early age, he possessed the decision of character of which he has given many subsequent proofs.

At that time the sum of money allowed by the Tokugawa government for the support of the Mikado was very small; and one day when his Majesty ordered one of his attendants to bring him some paper, in order that he might write down some poetry which he had just composed, he was told that there was no paper in the palace and no money to buy it with. This state of penury being reported to Iwakura, he at once demanded an audience of the governor of Kiôto, and made strong representations to him regarding the miserable pittance doled out for the maintenance of the court, remarking that, although the governor held his office from the Shôgun's government, he was first of all a subject of the Mikado, and bound, therefore, to provide for his Majesty's welfare. The governor, impressed by the firmness of Iwakura's tone and words, immediately advanced money from his own purse, and wrote to Yedo to urge the necessity of increasing the allowance for the imperial court. To show that by this step Iwakura exposed himself to disagreeable consequences, it is only necessary to state that the name of the governor of Kiôto was at once placed on the list of men of doubtful loyalty by the Yedo government.

Iwakura, together with Sanjô Sanéyoshi, the present prime minister, subsequently became the most active of the Kugé in advocating the cause of the Mikado, and in bringing about his restoration; and on the formation of the new government in 1868, he was appointed to the office of Gijô (superior to that of councillor of state) and had a pension of 5000 koku conferred upon him for his services.

He started in January 1871, accompanied by Ôkubo, and took with him a sword which he was to present, in the Mikado's name, to the shrine of the late Daimiô of Satsuma, who had been canonised after death, and whose memory was revered and loved by the people. He succeeded in allaying the discontent of the clan for the time being, and the result of his mission was that the three clans of Satsuma, Chôshiu, and Tosa, agreed to send fresh troops to Tôkiô to maintain the authority of the Mikado's government, and form the nucleus of a permanent force, which was now seen to be of primary importance by his Majesty's advisers. For time had plainly shown them that a centralised system of administration could not exist on the precarious support of the clans, and that if the unity of the empire was to become a fact, the creation and maintenance of a regular army, recruited indiscriminately from all classes of the people, and from all parts of the country, were absolutely necessary.

Iwakura himself must have seen convincing proofs of this during his visit to Satsuma; for, though on his return he professed to believe in the loyalty of Shimadzu and Saigô, he seems to have been considerably surprised and perturbed by the state of things then existing in their province. The whole principality was divided into districts, each of which was subjected to a stern military organisation. All its resources were devoted to the maintenance of its armed forces and the Samurai, or two-sworded men, numbering at least 30,000 men, were being constantly drilled and exercised. At the capital, Kagoshima, there was great activity in these exercises. The large arsenal, established before the Restoration and provided with a cannon foundry and powder mills, was still in the hands of Satsuma men. They also held the fortifications on the island of Sakurajima, commanding the harbour of Kagoshima, which had been erected some years previously, with the view of being used either against foreigners or against the Shôgun's government.

An English gentleman, who visited the province about this time, heard loud complaints on all sides against the members of the central government. They were accused of imposing an intolerable burden of taxation on the country, of living in unbridled luxury, and of squandering the wealth of the nation on superfluous buildings and undertakings of all sorts. Accusations too vague to veil the real cause of discontent, viz. the disappointment of the clan at not being invested with the preponderating influence in the government of the empire, which it considered to be the fitting reward of its great services during the revolution. The same gentleman was even told that the prince would shortly start for Tôkiô, with four or five regiments to make fresh representations on the subject, and that, if these did not suffice to bring about a change, more serious measures would be adopted. Shimadzu Saburô held supreme power in his principality, and all Satsuma men obeyed his orders, and his alone. The surrender of his lands and provincial authority was then, and appeared to be intended to remain, merely nominal. Satsuma was as feudal as ever.

Iwakura, as above stated, succeeded in the object of his mission, but his success was not due either to the prestige which surrounded him as an envoy of the Mikado or to his own influence and tact. It appears that before acceding to his proposals, Saigô, acting for Shimadzu, consulted the confederates of his clan in former days. To use the words of a chronicler of the day: "Saigô came to the chief men in "Tosa and Chôshiu, and said: The Tôkiô "government is incompetent and bad; let

" us, the three great clans who set it up and
" who have hitherto acted in harmony to-
" gether, proceed to reform and change it.
" But the chief man of Tosa answered, and
" Chôshiu agreed with him: Whatever may
" be the reasons for your dissatisfaction with
" the imperial government, the line of action
" towards it, which you propose, is altogether
" behind the times. It was all very well for
" our three clans to combine and overturn
" the usurping Shôgun, but the same course
" would be utterly indefensible towards the
" true and only constitutional government.
" Your proposal ignores the altered position
" of the clans, which are no longer separate
" political units, but simply parts of the
" integral realm of His Majesty the Tennô.*
" If you wish to improve the government,
" the constitutional road is open to you.
" Petition His Majesty, and offer your ser-
" vices." It is said that in making these proposals, Saigô had the promised support of several other clans, but however this may be, he
professed himself convinced by the arguments
of Tosa, and sent the desired quota of Satsuma

* The official appellation of the Emperor, compounded of Ten, heaven, and ô, another form of Kô, a term applied to sovereigns.

troops to join with those of Chôshiu, Tosa, and eight other provinces, in preparing the way for the establishment of a regular army.

Soon after this, viz. in May 1871, Saigô, who had remained in Satsuma since his return there in November 1870, came up to Tôkiô, and in the following month of June there appeared in the newspapers a somewhat remarkable political programme, which, though never proved to proceed from his pen, was generally believed at the time to contain a statement of his views, on the government of the country. Like most other Japanese manifestoes, it is diffuse and not always consistent, but throws some light on the party politics of the country, and is therefore given here in extenso :—

"All officials of the central government to "be sent back to their original clans. Their "number to be reduced, and only clever men "re-elected.

"A distinct line of policy to be laid down "and adhered to, regardless of changes in the "personnel of the government; based upon "the polity of Japan in the middle ages, but "regard being had to the constitution of "western states.

"The administration of law and the military "system to be uniform in all provinces of the "empire. The number of troops to be fixed "in accordance with the amount of money that "can be permanently devoted to the army.

"All government measures, small and great, "to be well discussed and considered and then "enacted. Free expression to be allowed to "individual opinion, but rulers must take "decided resolutions on all things, and "enforce them.

"The principle of finance is simply this: to "estimate the annual income, and proportion "expenditure to it. The yearly revenue from "taxation to be taken as the starting-point; "one-tenth to be set aside for the sovereign's "private expenses; the expenses of administra-"tion, the charges for the army and navy, &c., "all to have their share which ought not to be "exceeded; when the system has thus been "established, then production may be en-"couraged, and provision made for times of "emergency.

"The issue of paper currency to be cur-"tailed. A law of circulation and converti-"bility of the same to be established. A reserve

"fund to be created, the formation of joint-
"stock companies to be encouraged, the rules
"of foreign commerce to be defined, and the
"balance of trade made to incline in our
"favour.

"A lasting system in all these things to be
"established, which need not be changed for
"a thousand years.

"The imperial court is but a name: *let the*
"*great clans give it at least* 10,000 *of their best*
"*troops with their families, let these be inscribed*
"*for ever on the muster-rolls of the imperial*
"*court*, and let these troops form the nucleus of
"the troops to reduce evil-doers to obedience.

"The duties of all officials to be well defined,
"and let them be responsible for their proper
"execution.

"The government should be one and united.
"The rule limiting the exercise of functions by
"the same person to four years to be abolished.
"A system of permanent appointments to be
"introduced in its stead.

"*The sovereign must possess the power in*
"*measures of* government and legislation, of
"reward and punishment, conferring grants,
"and ordering confiscations; and *must not let it*

" *depart out of his hands in the least.* He must
" not prohibit a rise or fall in the price of rice,
" of gold and silver, and of all other articles of
" commerce, which must be left to the natural
" course of events. The government has only
" to reform what is wrong and to punish
" those who do wrong. It must facilitate the
" transport of corn, money, &c. This is an
" immutable law of all time.

" Laws must be obeyed. That which can be
" done without danger or hurt must be well
" considered. When once the law is issued, it
" must be obeyed in spite of grumblings and
" opposition.

" Laws are instruments for protecting the
" 'little people,' who, since the world began,
" have always been seventy or eighty per cent.
" of the world's population. The laws should
" therefore be in accordance with the feelings
" of the 'little people.'

" No class to be favoured above another.
" All to be governed uniformly.

" The treaties to be strictly observed. If any-
" thing beyond them is demanded of us, we
" must point out what is just, and then defend
" it to the last.

"Japan ought to be prepared for defence "and offence. We must not attempt to civilise "Japan too quickly, and must do first what our "resources permit. We *must abandon all steam "machinery and railroads*, &c., and work dili-"gently to perfect our military system. Let "us not try to do one hundred things at once, "but have patience and go on by degrees. "Looking upon the present state of politics, I "do not *think the centralisation system can be "carried on for long*. It would be impossible to "recount the quantity of disadvantages that "would result. The system must be calmly "discussed."

There is no doubt much sound sense in this programme, and it contains some advice which was very appropriate at the time, more especially that regarding the establishment of a lasting system of laws; for the government seemed intent on destroying, root and branch, the whole administrative fabric of the past without having any fixed plans for the future. They were wavering between half-a-dozen forms of government, and the country was flooded and the people were harrassed with a multitude of decrees and enactments, often vexatious in their tendency, and sometimes contradictory in their sense. Saigô's views relative to finance, the convertibility of the paper currency, and the necessity of adapting the laws to the wants and feelings of the "little people," are also most just. On the other hand, it appears from this document that he held very conservative opinions on many points. He wished the supreme power to be vested exclusively in the hands of the Mikado himself, and to repose permanently on the support of the three great clans. He was also opposed to railroads and other such like European appliances; to the introduction, in short, of Western civilisation.

Such were the views and opinions of the Satsuma clan at this time, as far as its leaders thought it advisable to publish them. But it does not appear that their adoption in toto was to be the condition of a continuance of its support of the central government. The clan accepted less than it asked, and was satisfied for the time being with the reconstruction of the cabinet and ministerial departments, which took place soon afterwards (August 11, 1871), and was to a great extent due to its influence.

In this cabinet Saigô accepted the post of Sangi, or Councillor of State, and it was no sooner installed than it proceeded (August 29) to carry out the most radical of all the changes that have been made in the constitution, viz. the abolition of the clans.

CHAPTER V.

Abolition of the Daimiates—Composition of the ministry which enforced this measure—Saigô's participation in it—Shimadzu's disapproval of it—The government attempts to conciliate Satsuma—Difference of opinion in the Cabinet in regard to Japan's relations with Korea—War or peace.

IT has been stated above that the clans voluntarily restored their respective territories and administrative authority to the Mikado in March 1869. Since then their chiefs, the Daimiô, had been allowed to retain both the one and the other, and the administration of the country had continued to move in its old feudal groove. By the decree of August 29, 1871, the Daimiôs' authority was formally abolished. Their administrative powers were vested in officials appointed by the Mikado, irrespective of their place of birth and clanship, and their revenues were reduced to one-tenth of the assessed value of the revenues of their respective provinces.

When this change became known in Europe, politicians and statesmen were deeply impressed by its magnitude. The feudal system of Japan had been described to them as being exactly similar to what existed in medieval Europe, and they had likewise been told that the authority of the Mikado had been in complete abeyance for a couple of centuries. Whence then, they asked, came the power to ordain such a revolution? Still greater was their surprise when they learnt that this change had been carried out without opposition. How came it, they then inquired, that a system, which in Europe had only been eradicated by gradual and cautious steps and after long wars, was peaceably upset by a stroke of the pen and in a day in Japan.

We know more of the country than we did in those days, and we have now learnt that most of the Daimiô had for long ceased to resemble the great feudal barons of Europe, and that they were mere puppets in the hands of their councillors, the Karô or chief men of each clan. These men, no doubt, foresaw that the mass of the new officials must be selected from their own ranks, which contained the only men acquainted with the details of administration. Their masters, on the other hand, were not at all displeased to get rid of the merely formal part they took in the public affairs of their Daimiates, and considered that the diminution in their incomes under the new system would be compensated by the regularity with which they would be paid in future.

The latter point is of considerable importance in treating of this great constitutional change, and a very erroneous impression regarding it has resulted from the use, by several writers on Japan, of the words "revenue" and "assessment" as synonymous terms. To show how far this was from being the case, it is only necessary to instance a province where the assessment was 30,000 koku. The amount of taxes, i.e. revenue raised in this province, was only 16,000 koku. Of this sum 8000 koku were appropriated to the payment of the pensions and allowances of the retainers of the clan, 4000 were applied to administrative purposes, and merely the remaining 4000 came into the lord's hands for the maintenance of himself and his family. If there happened to be a bad harvest, all three quotas were naturally diminished. Now, under the new system, the Daimiô of this province was to receive one-tenth of the assessment, i.e. 3000 koku annually, regularly paid and subject to no reductions; and as he was to be freed from all claims on his purse on the part of his clansmen, and could in future spend the whole of his income for his own exclusive and private use, it is doubtful whether he was a loser at all in a pecuniary sense.

This instance of the difference between assessment and revenue was by no means an uncommon one, and thus, whilst the Daimiô were compensated for the loss of their provincial state and power, by fixed incomes, the regular payment of which was guaranteed by the state, and by complete liberty as to their manner of life, their retainers counted on an enlargement of their sphere of action and looked forward, not without good grounds, to becoming the administrators of national instead of district affairs.

If these facts be borne in mind; if the difference between the feudal system of Japan and that of the middle ages in Europe be well weighed; and if it be clearly understood that all the authors of the transformation of the system of government, viz. the Mikado, the Daimiô, and the most influential of the clansmen, were interested in the change, the surrender of their baronial authority by the Daimiô, which only became a reality when the decree for the abolition of the clans was issued, in August 1871, was less marvellous than it has hitherto been described. It was no doubt a very remarkable and unprecedented event, but, when viewed in connection with the above circumstances, it fails to excite the same feelings of wonder and surprise which it created at the time. Those who are acquainted with Asiatic nations will probably be much more inclined to indulge in such feelings when they consider the extent to which this most easternly nation, secluded for centuries from all communication with the rest of the world, has adopted Western civilisation in the short space of one decade.

The abolition of the Daimiates was decreed, as above stated, on the 29th of August 1871, and the government which decreed it, as reconstructed on the 11th of that month, was composed as follows: The offices of prime and vice-prime minister were filled by Sanjô Sanéyoshi and Iwakura Tomomi, who still hold them. They are Kugé,* had both taken an active part in preparing the Restoration and had been appointed to their present posts immediately after it. They and four councillors of state formed the cabinet, the councillors being Saigô, representing Satsuma; Kido Takayoshi, from the province of Choshiu; Itagaki Taisuke, from Tosa; and Ôkuma Shigenobu, from Hizen. The heads of the different ministries, the chief of whom were then Ôkubo, minister of finance, and Gotô Shojiro (Tosa), minister of public works, were only admitted to the council at this time, when the affairs of their respective departments were discussed, and had no voice in the general policy of the government. It is therefore evident that Saigô played an important part in the adoption of the constitutional change just referred to. He appears,

* This title, as well as that of Daimiô, was abolished by imperial decree in 1869. They were replaced by that of Kwazoku = Noble. The appellation Samurai, or two-sworded men, was at the same time changed into Shizoku.

however, to have acted on this occasion without the approval of Shimadzu Saburô; for, when it came to be enforced, the latter openly expressed his disapproval of its results as well as of the ideas of the government on many other matters. As he enjoyed the confidence of a very large number of the military class, and was regarded by it as the protector of its interests, it was of great importance to the government to obtain his support; and with a view to this end, the Mikado, attended by Saigô, paid a visit to the Satsuma chieftain at Kagoshima, in July 1872. It appears that Shimadzu then expressed his conservative views very frankly, and that he told his sovereign that in his opinion the country was being ruined by the adoption of European civilisation and that Saigô was much to be blamed for supporting such a policy. Neither the Mikado nor his cabinet seem to have been influenced by these opinions, but it was, no doubt, in consequence of this expression of them and by order of Shimadzu that, when the railway from Yokohama to Tôkiô was opened by the Mikado in person, in October of the same year, Saigô and the young Prince of Satsuma were conspicuous by their absence from the ceremony, which was attended by all the other ministers and dignitaries of the state. Their conduct was in accordance with the views expressed in Saigô's programme above quoted, and was much remarked at the time as indicative of disunion between the Satsuma leaders and the other members of the cabinet.

An open breach did not, however, occur at this time, and in April 1873, the government at last, and after much negotiation, prevailed on Shimadzu Saburô to visit Tôkiô. At the same time they offered him a high post in the government if he would consent to modify his opposition to their projected changes. Shimadzu arrived in the capital about the end of that month, accompanied by several hundred armed retainers, all wearing the old costume of the country, and their two swords; and their appearance caused no little sensation in Tôkiô, where many of the Samurai had already availed themselves of the permission granted to them by the Imperial Decree of September 1871, to lay aside their weapons, and where many of the people had adopted a hybrid European dress. In order to conciliate him, Saigô was named commander-in-chief of the Mikado's land forces in May, but this appointment failed to produce the desired effect on this obstinate and conservative noble. Shimadzu remained firm in his opposition to the progressive measures of the government, and in June, finding that his advice was unheeded, asked leave to return home. The Mikado refused this request, and ordered him to remain in the capital until the return from Europe of Iwakura and the members of his mission.* This took place in September of the same year, and resulted in a split in the cabinet, the avowed cause thereof being a question arising out of the state of Japan's relations with the kingdom of Korea.

The Koreans have been looked upon by the Japanese in the light of tributaries from very remote times. The greater part of their

---

* Iwakura, accompanied by Ôkubo and Itô, had left Tôkiô in December 1871, on a mission to the United States and to the principal courts in Europe—the object of which was to endeavour to obtain a revision of the treaties between them and Japan.

country was invaded and conquered A.D. 203* by the martial Empress Jingô Kôgu, and for centuries afterwards Korean envoys used to pay homage at Kiôto on the accession to the throne of each successive Mikado. During the intestine wars of the middle ages, the Koreans took advantage of Japan's weakness to discontinue this practice, and for some time there was no communication between the two countries except through the head man of Tsushima, an island midway in the channel which separates them, who maintained a small trading settlement at Sorio. Taikô Sama, whose immoderate ambition aimed at the subjection and incorporation of China as well as of Korea, overran the latter country in 1592, and might possibly have retained his hold upon it, had not China sent an army against his forces and compelled them to retire to its southern extremity. Reinforcements were sent by Taikô, but his death in 1598 put a stop to further hostilities. A truce was concluded and the Japanese

* According to Japanese Chronology, which is unreliable regarding all events previous to the seventh century of our era.

army returned home with much spoil and, it is said, with the ears of 10,000 Koreans. Envoys accompanied them, and since that date the government of Séoul continued to send congratulatory missions to each of the Shôguns of the Tokugawa dynasty on his accession. After the restoration of 1868, it refused, however, to acknowledge the Mikado as emperor of Japan, or to have any official relations with his government, which it held to be in league with the Western barbarians. It treated with contumely the Mikado's envoys who were sent to re-establish direct intercourse between the two countries, and reduced the small Japanese community at Sorio to the position formerly held by the Dutch at Decima. The attitude of the Koreans toward this settlement became indeed so menacing in 1873, that the Japanese government withdrew all but very subordinate officers from that place.

This state of things caused wide-spread indignation amongst the Samurai, with whom "War with Korea" became a popular cry, and occupied the serious attention of the cabinet. Its members were agreed in thinking that

Japan, which they all held to be destined to play a great part in Asiatic politics, could not tolerate the attitude assumed by Korea, and that decisive action of some sort or other must be taken in the question. But they were not united as to the nature of this action. Some of them agreed that the government and the country would be wanting in self-respect if they allowed themselves to be defied with impunity by a nation which they had always considered inferior to their own; that the past conduct of the Koreans merited chastisement, and that any further negotiations with them would be useless if unsupported by an armed force. Others of the ministers were, on the other hand, opposed to coercive measures of a violent nature at this time. There was, in short, a war and a peace party in the cabinet. Saigô headed the former, and was supported by four of the councillors of state (whose number had now been increased to nine), viz.: Yeto-Shimpei, Itagaki-Taisuke, Soyejima (minister of foreign affairs), and Gotô Shojiro; whilst Iwakura, immediately after his return from Europe, became the chief of the peace party, which declared that the country was unprepared for war, and that financial ruin would be the result of undertaking it.

For both of these parties there were, behind the question openly at issue between them, other objects of far more importance in their eyes than the humiliation of Korea and the assertion of Japanese power. These objects will be considered in the opening pages of the following chapter.

CHAPTER VI.

Motives of the war party—The peace party prevails—Revolt in Hizen—Further attempts to conciliate Satsuma—The Formosan expedition—Shimadzu memorialises the Mikado with a view to upset the government—He resigns, but is induced to enter the Mikado's household.

THE Mikado's government having finally abolished the Daimiô and contented them by leaving them the absolute use of one-tenth of their former revenues, had now to provide in some way for their retainers, the powerful class of the Samurai. These men, numbering with their families nearly 2,000,000 of souls, had for centuries enjoyed hereditary pensions of rice, the payment of which had, under the feudal system, been charged to the revenues of their respective provinces, but was, on the abolition of the clans, taken over by the central government. To continue these pensions at their original rate and to furnish the requisite funds for the creation and maintenance of a standing army and for all the other novel requirements of a centralised administration, was a task which the treasury could not perform, and a burden which the country could not bear. The government therefore decided on capitalising all the pensions of the Daimiô and Samurai, and now offered to all those amongst them who desired to commute their pensions, marketable government bonds bearing interest at rates varying according to the original amount of each pension. This operation was therefore voluntary on the part of the Samurai, but they foresaw that it would, in all probability, ere long be made compulsory, and that when this was effected, they would not only suffer great and immediate pecuniary loss, but would also eventually cease to be the governing class of the country.

Another measure which had been strongly

advocated by Ôkubo, and recently enacted by the government, in opposition to the wishes of the war party, was specially distasteful to Shimadzu and Saigô, and greatly influenced their conduct at this juncture. This measure was a conscription law making service in the army or navy obligatory on the adult males of all classes of the population, and evidently intended to destroy all clannish feeling, cohesion, and power, and to result eventually in the disarmament of all the Samurai.

Now the war party did not at all desire this result, and Shimadzu and Saigô especially foresaw that the reduction of this class to the level of the Heimin would deprive them, probably for ever, of the means of giving a concrete form to their theories of the proper system of government for Japan.

Ever since the Restoration, they and their clan had in vain claimed a preponderating influence in the new government, and in an invasion of Korea, or any other warlike expedition, they thought they discerned a sure means of attaining this object, as well as of reversing the government policy in regard to the Samurai pensions and the conscription. Saigô, now commander-in-chief of the Mikado's land forces, no doubt expected to be placed at the head of the expedition, and, as the regular army was not yet sufficiently organised, Samurai would necessarily form the bulk of his troops. The fighting men of Satsuma and of several of the south-western provinces were clamouring for war, and with their aid he no doubt counted on a short and victorious campaign, and on returning home with such prestige and material support, that he would be enabled to dictate his own terms to the Tôkiô government, i.e. turn out of office Sanjô, Iwakura, and their party, and make himself and his partisans the rulers of the country.

The peace party saw through this design, and their chief, Iwakura, was able to baffle it. The cabinet decided against the project for invading Korea, and thereupon the war party resigned office. The government forbade its members to leave Tôkiô, but Saigô and Yetô returned at once, in spite of this order, to their respective provinces. The former, nevertheless, retained his title of commander-in-chief, although a good many Satsuma officers sent in their resignations at this time, probably by his orders.

Almost coincident with the return of Saigô and Yetô to their homes, disorders broke out in Hizen, and shortly afterwards, in January 1874, an attempt was made to assassinate Iwakura by a band of Samurai, who attacked him whilst driving from the Mikado's palace, and only failed to attain their object on account of the darkness of the night. In the same month an insurrection of the Samurai of Hizen occurred, Yetô placing himself at their head. The cry of the insurgents was, "War with Korea, restoration of the Daimiô, and expulsion of foreigners;" but the real cause of the rising was undoubtedly the disaffection existing amongst the military class at the prospect of losing their pensions. The government, therefore, fearing lest Saigô and his followers might make common cause with these men, sent Shimadzu, who had remained in Tôkiô, to Kagoshima to restrain the clan. What inducements they gave him to undertake this mission, it is impossible to say, and we have no certainty as to the cause of the quiescent attitude maintained by Satsuma at this juncture. Some Japanese politicians explain it by saying that her leaders did not consider her yet strong enough to declare war against the government, but others attribute her conduct to a completely different cause. They state that, after the refusal of Chôshiu and Tosa to join them in upsetting the Tôkiô government, in December 1870, Saigô and Shimadzu became convinced that Satsuma must count on its own resources alone to effect this object; that it therefore became their policy to weaken those clans which were likely to oppose their projects; and that the Satsuma leaders originated and brought about the outbreak in Hizen for this purpose. This opinion is not wanting in plausibility, and its adoption gives us the most intelligible explanation of Satsuma's motives in holding aloof from this and also from the subsequent risings of the Samurai of Higo and Chôshiu, in October 1876.

Whatever the cause, Satsuma did not move —and the government, which had now an army of 15,000 men, disciplined by European officers, soon succeeded in suppressing the revolt. It was finally crushed by the recapture of the town of Saga by Ôkubo, and Yetô and eleven of his adherents were executed.

No sooner was peace restored in Hizen than the government became anxious to have Shimadzu and Saigô back in the capital, their presence there being considered a guarantee for the good behaviour of their clan. The Mikado, therefore, sent a mission to Kagoshima to persuade them to return. Saigô refused, but Shimadzu, after parleying for three weeks with the Imperial envoy, obeyed the summons.

His political views and opinions do not appear to have been at all changed by the recent events, nor do the previous refusals of the government to be guided by his counsels seem to have in the least diminished his convictions as to their absolute wisdom and ultimate adoption. For it was about this time that he drew up a memorial of them, of which more will be said below, for presentation to the Mikado. The two prime ministers, to whom this document was first communicated, dissuaded him from prosecuting the matter further at this time, and it seems that the means they employed for this purpose were the offer of the title of Sa-daijin, the second in point of rank in the government, and a promise to make war on Formosa.

A pretext for such a war had been afforded by the murder, on more than one occasion, by some of the wild aboriginal tribes of that island of some shipwrecked Japanese and Loochooans, and the object of the expedition was stated to be the chastisement of these tribes and the acquirement of guarantees for the future security of Japanese ships and seamen. Some negotiations had taken place with China relative to the claims of that country to Formosa, and the government of Peking was reported by the Japanese agent there to have declined all responsibility for the acts of the tribes in question. All risk of the possibility of complications with China being thus removed, the Japanese government decided on obtaining satisfaction themselves.

The punishment of these savages was of course a secondary object with them in this decision, the chief motives for which were a desire, springing from the vanity of the national character, to obtain prestige by some warlike expedition, the necessity for opening some escape-pipe for the discontent prevalent amongst the Samurai, and the necessity, equally great, of soothing the Satsuma clan, and diverting their attention from home politics.

Saigô's brother, who had greatly distinguished himself during the war of the Restoration and more especially at the battle of Uyéno, was accordingly appointed to the chief command, and many of the troops were Satsuma men. The expedition sailed from Nagasaki in May 1874, and was composed of about 3000 men; a less numerous force than would have been requisite for an invasion of Korea, but yet sufficiently large to include a good many of the hottest heads in the Samurai class. Thus the government hoped that they would by this enterprise conciliate Satsuma, and yet avoid putting too much power in her hands. They thought also that it would afford them a plausible reason and a good opportunity for increasing the regular army, to such an extent as to be efficient, not only for national defence, but also for controlling the Samurai class.

As far as the declared object of the expedi-

F 2

tion was concerned, it was successful, since the Formosan tribes were defeated in several encounters and the Japanese troops returned home in triumph in December 1874, whilst Ôkubo, who had been sent on a special mission to Peking with reference to this affair, succeeded in obtaining a money indemnity from the Chinese government for the expense incurred by Japan.

As regards its other motives, the expedition had not the like success; Saigô, indeed, is said to have disapproved of it from the first, saying that it was merely a sop to appease the Satsuma appetite for fighting, and an inadequate reward for her quiescent attitude during the Hizen revolt. Great complaints, too, were made at Kagoshima at the treatment of the invalided and wounded of the clan, who on their return from Formosa were turned adrift at Nagasaki, and allowed to find their way home as best they could. As, however, his clansmen had greatly contributed to the success of the expedition, Shimadzu appears to have thought that he, their chief, ought now to be listened to with more attention by the Tôkiô government.

In April 1875, he accordingly formally presented the Memorial of his views, above referred to, to the prime minister. This document which was addressed to the Mikado was a very lengthy one, the greatest part of it being filled with a recapitulation, from Shimadzu's point of view, of the services which he had rendered to the Imperial family.

It stated that he had been of great use to the late Emperor, from 1862 to 1864, in the negotiations between the court and the military class, which led to the league against the Shôgun, and that when summoned by the present Emperor, in 1867, he had at once gone to Kiôto in the hope of being able to assist in the Restoration.

Unfortunately he was seized by kakké,* palsied in his legs, and thus disabled from taking any active part in the events of 1868.

In the spring of 1869, a letter in the Emperor's own hand, containing many expressions of praise, was sent to him. He repaired to Kiôto to offer his thanks, and

* A disease endemic in certain low-lying towns of Japan, and analogous to a complaint known in India, Ceylon and South Brazil, under the name of Beriberi. The Japanese name Kakké is derived from two words signifying "an affection of the legs."

received an advancement in rank. His disease again attacked him and he was obliged to retire from office and return home. In the winter of 1870, Iwakura brought him an Imperial letter summoning him to the capital. He was too ill to go himself, but caused Saigô to proceed thither in the summer of 1871. During the autumn of the same year the clans were abolished, and about the same time all sorts of injurious innovations were introduced at court and throughout the land. "He (Shimadzu) was ill and could only grind "his teeth with rage. The above was the "work of various clan retainers, who set "their lords at nought, and of five or six of "his former clansmen."

The memorial then went on to say that at the time of the Mikado's visit to Kagoshima (in the summer of 1872) Shimadzu had protested against all this and begged for the dismissal of his former retainers. He had at the same time submitted a memorandum of his opinions on public affairs to the prime minister, and was asked to proceed to the capital shortly afterwards, in order to give verbal explanations regarding them, but was too ill to do so.

In 1873, he was again summoned to the capital, and went. He sent in his explanations, but for thirty days received no answer. He was finally told that, of the fourteen clauses of his memorandum, those relating to sumptuary, educational, and military regulations could not be adopted. He then asked for leave to return home, but was told to remain in Tôkiô till the return of Iwakura. This took place in September 1873. In October, Saigô and Itagaki resigned on account of the Korean affair. In December Shimadzu was appointed to the cabinet, but, as his views were not adopted, declined the post offered to him.

In January 1874, the Hizen insurrection took place, and Saigô being reported to be implicated in it, Shimadzu obtained leave to go home and bring Saigô back with him.

Saigô refused to come, and he (Shimadzu) could not force him to do so. Two Imperial messengers then came to Kagoshima, and escorted him to Tôkiô. On his arrival he was appointed to office, and discussed with Sanjo and Iwakura the question of "dismissing corrupt officials." His advice was not taken, and he wanted to resign, but was persuaded by the court to retain his post. "As yet, however (up to May 1874),* your "Majesty has not shown the slightest sign of "adopting his foolish ideas, and the Imperial "line of action is day by day falling away, the "military class are losing their fidelity, the "farmers and merchants are oppressed by "tyrannical laws, while foreign doctrines are "widely spreading, and the minds of the people "are perturbed. If this goes on, ruin must "ensue. Alas! Shimadzu's former retainers, "now in office, make common cause with "corrupt officials. If they disobey the head "of their former clan, how can they remain "faithful to their sovereign? They are "greedy after wealth and position. Your "servant can do nothing to prevent all this. "His sickness and dotage are coming upon "him, he begs to resign the appointments "of Sa-daijin and second rank. Let him do "this, and let your Majesty cast on him the "responsibility of the adoption of his ideas."

* i.e. when the memorial was shown to Sanjô and Iwakura, and when its author was persuaded by them to let it lie dormant for the time being.

The so-called clauses, i.e. the innovations against which Shimadzu protested, now increased to twenty, were as follows :—

1. The substitution of foreign dress for the old ceremonial court costume of the sovereign.

2. The use of the solar calendar.

3. The adoption of foreign dress in the state departments.

4. The engagement of foreigners for the service of the state and the adoption of their ideas.

5. The want of ability in the Emperor's instructions.

6. The multitude of sycophants around the Emperor.

7. The near approach of common soldiers to the sovereign's person.

8. The multitude of insolvent and dissipated officials.

9. The non-prohibition of the idle pleasures of the nobles.

10. The adoption of foreign rules and models in schools.

11. The excessive strictness of the regulations in Tôkiô.

12. The non-appointment of a fencing-master for the Emperor.

13. The erection of unnecessary buildings, regardless of the state of the treasury.

14. The adoption of foreign drill.

15. The useless increase of worthless officials.

16. The non-prohibition of the extension of evil doctrines (Christianity).

17. The permission to intermarry with foreigners.

18. The creation of a board of religion, which confuses Buddhism and Shintôism together.

19. The union of the departments of the interior and the treasury.

20. The adoption of the foreign manner of dressing the hair, the abandonment of the practice of wearing two swords, and the disregard shown to Japanese who keep to old customs in these two respects.

In conclusion Shimadzu says: "On the " above points I wish to receive a clear ex- " planation from your Majesty, and, without " regard to the aversion to my views shown " by others, I beg to make this enquiry."

It is needless to make much comment on the curious document of which the above is an epitome. It is manifest from it that the object of the chief of the Satsuma clan in overthrowing the Shôgunate was certainly not the introduction into Japan of European institutions and customs. It is equally manifest that Shimadzu had not modified in a single iota the reactionary views he had held ever since the Restoration; that he was still the proud haughty noble of the feudal days; that he was blind to the altered condition of all Japan outside the Island of Kiushiu, and ignorant of the increase of stability already attained by the central government; for there is no doubt that Shimadzu expected that his representations, which were supported by Itagaki, who had again entered the ministry as councillor of state at the close of the Formosan war, would result in the dismissal of the whole of Sanjô's and Iwakura's cabinet, and the appointment of himself, Saigô, and their friends, to office.

In this expectation Shimadzu was, to his surprise, disappointed. At the instance of Ôkubo he was informed that his views could not be entertained, and he thereupon sent in his resignation of the post of Sa-daijin. It was accepted without hesitation by the government, which now felt itself strong enough to show that it feared neither Satsuma nor the Samurai. Its members did not, however, yet wish to provoke an open breach with either the one or the other, and again had recourse to a temporising policy. In November 1875, they succeeded in inducing Shimadzu to accept a high though merely honorary post in the Mikado's household, and in the following month they revived the idea of sending a mission to Korea and of invading that country, if their demands were not peaceably granted.

CHAPTER VII.

Disquieting state of Satsuma—Saigô's "private schools"—The Kagoshima arsenal—Treaty of commerce concluded with Korea—Satsuma's dissatisfaction with the peaceful result of the Korean expedition and with the abolition of the practice of wearing swords—Shimadzu returns to Kagoshima—Position of parties in Japan—Development of the "private schools."

THE motives of the government in reviving the idea of sending a mission to Korea were similar to those which had caused the Formosan expedition, viz. to divert the attention of the Samurai, and especially those of Satsuma from home politics.

The state of the principality was such as to give increased anxiety to the Tôkiô government. Its independent position and opposition to all interference in its affairs on the part of the central government have been noticed above. No change had taken place in either of these respects since the Restoration. In the other provinces the work of administrative centralisation and unification had been progressing, and Imperial officers, selected without respect to their clanship or place of birth, had assumed the direction of affairs in them. Satsuma alone refused to have anything to do with officials who were not natives of the province, and there everything went on as if the feudal system were still in force, the only difference being that particularist opinions were becoming more pronounced, and the military spirit and training were being daily more developed.

When Saigô retired from office in 1873, and returned home, he employed his time and the pension granted to him by the Mikado for his services during the war of the Restora-

in founding and maintaining, at Kagoshima, an institution which, to avoid exciting the susceptibilities of the central government he named "Shi-gakkô" or the "private school." This institution was nothing more nor less than a military academy, and amongst its chief supporters were Shinowara Kunimori, Kirino Toshiaki, and Ôyama Tsunayoshi, names which will often recur in this story. At this time (December 1875) it had several thousand names on its rolls, 1500 of whom were Samurai of the town of Kagoshima, and nearly all of whom had seen service in the field. Several of the pupils had been sent to France to study military tactics, and more were to follow shortly.

The arsenal of Kagoshima was also, so to say, working full time. It employed 388 skilled workmen and 156 labourers in turning out bronze and iron cannon, and shot and shell of all descriptions. This establishment had, it is true, been handed over to the ministry of marine a short time before this date, but this transfer was simply nominal, since Satsuma allowed none but native officials within her limits. There were also two powder factories in the province, and a large cotton spinning and weaving factory, where large quantities of the material most worn in Japan could be produced. Finally, the practice of wearing swords, which, since the issue in 1871 of the Imperial permission to lay them aside, had been discontinued to a great extent in the other large towns of the empire, was still the rule rather than the exception in Kagoshima.

In this state of things there was much to cause disquiet to the Tôkiô government, and this feeling was no doubt the chief reason for their decision relative to Korea. The grounds upon which it was justified in the eyes of foreigners were of a similar nature to those which have been mentioned above as having been publicly urged by the war party in the cabinet of 1873. Since then no improvement had taken place in the relations of the two countries. The Korean government still refused, on one pretext or another, to receive the Mikado's envoy, one of their pretexts being the European fashioned uniform, which it would be the envoy's duty to wear at his official interview with the ministers, and which the Koreans declared it impossible to tolerate. More bad blood had also been caused lately by the firing of some shots from a Korean fort near the island of Kokwa, on the boats of a Japanese man-of-war, which had been surveying the coast and had entered the river leading to the capital.

This incident brought matters to a crisis, and in January 1876, the Mikado's envoys departed on their mission. They were supported by a mixed squadron of seven men-of-war and transports, and with this imposing force, the strength of which they greatly exaggerated in the eyes of the Koreans by painting port-holes on the transports, and by other similar stratagems, they so overawed the government of Séoul, that, without having recourse to force, they speedily succeeded in obtaining the signature and ratification of a treaty, by which permanent diplomatic relations were at once established between the two countries, and three Korean ports were to be opened at a given date to Japanese commerce. The expedition returned in March, and the result, which was certainly satisfactory, was heralded abroad by the government as a marked success. It was, nevertheless, far from being regarded in that light either by the Samurai in general, or by the Satsuma people. They argued that it was worse than folly to enter into amicable relations with Korea. The subjection of that country by Japan, they said, began in the second and third centuries A.D, and for generations afterwards Korea never omitted to send envoys and presents to the Mikados. In the middle ages, when Japan was torn by civil wars, Korea took advantage of the intestine disorder, and ceased paying tribute, until Taikô Sama recovered Japan's ancient rights by force of arms: "Consequently, "to make a treaty with Korea on equal terms "in the present reign was to brave the anger "of the august spirits of previous generations "of sovereigns." "Besides," they added, "the Koreans still send envoys with presents "to China, and observe the etiquette of sub-"jects in their relations with that country. "Thus Japan actually appears to consent to "take lower rank than China, and this is an "infinite stain on our national character."

Thus, though the Korean expedition had diverted the attention of the Samurai and of the Satsuma people for a few months from their supposed grievances by exciting warlike aspirations and hopes of military distinction in their ranks, its peaceable termination disappointed them and augmented their discontent.

These feelings were further excited by the enforcement at this time, March 1876, of a measure which the government had been contemplating for some time, and which was precipitated by Shimadzu's late attempt to upset the cabinet, as well as by the successful issue of the Korean mission, which, in the opinion of the government, had increased their popularity with the masses of the people. This measure was the prohibition of the practice of wearing swords, and the limitation of the right of bearing arms to the regular forces. We have seen that the decree of September 1871, making this custom optional, had had some effect as early as 1873. Since then, the more general adoption of European costume, with which the heavy Japanese sword cannot be conveniently worn, the increased number of the police force for keeping order, and the spread of European ideas, had contributed to render the custom less prevalent, and it had now almost entirely disappeared from the large cities of the empire. The older generation of Samurai, however, still clung to the practice of constantly wearing their two swords—the brightest emblems of honour in their eyes—as one of their most valuable privileges, and to them the interdict was most distasteful. To Shimadzu Saburô it appeared like the *coup de grâce*—the knell of all his hopes and dreams of a return to the old order of things in Japan.—He left Tôkiô at once (April 5, 1876), for his home at Kagoshima, and the spectacle of the few followers, who accompanied him, carrying their swords in cotton bags is said to have convinced him at last that his part in politics was completely played out.

This measure, for which the government had the support of the agricultural and mercantile classes and of the mass of the people, again brought home politics to the foreground. The position of parties was becoming more sharply defined, and was well described in the following article which appeared in a Japanese newspaper about this time:—

"There appear to be two great distinct "parties in this country, one of which may "be termed the party of the government, the "other the Satsuma party. What must be the "result of such a division? When two parties "like these are in constant conflict, both "cannot continue to exist for any great space "of time; should the government party be "worsted in the struggle, the Satsuma men "would take the reins, and this is clear to "every one.

"When Saigô resigned, the people thought "in this wise: Saigô's views differ from "those of his colleagues, and he has resigned "because it would be incompatible with his "sense of honour to remain with them. "This act does not spring from any want of "interest in political affairs, for if the other "Sangi (councillors of state) had said that "they would adopt his views he would "probably have remained in office. But as "the government again and again had to "induce him to return to Tôkiô, the people "argued that Saigô was not desirous of work-"ing with the present cabinet. . . . It is "clear, therefore, that the Satsuma party has "its own designs, and is averse to the present "government.

"There are minor parties in the country, "such as those which contend for a return "to the feudal system, but their only chance "of obtaining their wishes and aims is to "unite with the Satsuma party. Thus we "may expect that all the disaffected will be "found in Kagoshima.

"What is going on in Kagoshima? and "what is Saigô doing? are the principal "questions asked by the people. If the "government wishes to preserve peace in "the country, what policy should it adopt? "As we said before, both parties cannot long "exist."

The conviction expressed in the last phrase of this article was no doubt gaining ground in the minds of all thoughtful men, and not without reason. Satsuma, though quiet for the moment, was evidently preparing. The "private school" system had received wide development since December 1875. At Kagoshima alone it counted 7000 pupils, and branch schools of 1000, 500, or 300 members, had been established in other towns and villages of the province. Before being admitted to these schools, from the members of which all the local officials of the principality of Satsuma were selected, the candidates were required to take a solemn oath that they would be faithful to their party and to each other even to death; and each novice then subscribed a copy of the rules with his own blood. In order to maintain uniform discipline amongst them all, the country schools sent up monthly a certain number of their students to the head school. No candidates from other provinces were admitted; and members above fifteen years of age were not allowed to travel to any place more than sixty miles distant without permission.

Educational questions were not much discussed in these schools; Chinese literature was studied daily from 9 to 10 A.M., and drill and the discussion of politics generally occupied the rest of the day. Athletic exercises were much practised, and marches were made every week into the country. The pupils were taught that the object of their training was to protect the Mikado's power and the rights of the people (especially those of the Satsuma people), which were threatened by the Tôkiô government; the members of which, they were told, merely sought their own advancement and enrichment in all they undertook, and had no care for the welfare of the country.

Whilst Satsuma was thus developing her military resources, the Tôkiô government was consolidating its position and augmenting both its army and navy. The former now numbered 30,000 men in round numbers, and the latter nine men-of-war, bearing from four to ten guns each, and eight steam transports.

The struggle was, however, not yet to commence, and during the summer months of 1876 peace reigned throughout Japan.

CHAPTER VIII.

The Pension Commutation Act—Discontent of the Samurai—Rising in Higo, and massacre of part of the garrison of Kumamoto—Mayebara's insurrection in Chôshiu—Quiescent attitude of Satsuma—Conciliatory treatment of Satsuma pensioners—Shimadzu's and Saigô's views of the national policy.

THE state of tranquillity recorded at the close of the last chapter probably encouraged the government to carry out another measure, which had been for some time under consideration, and for the enforcement of which they had only awaited a favourable opportunity. I refer to the compulsory commutation of all the hereditary pensions and allowances of the ex-Daimiô and Samurai, the enactment of which was proclaimed by Imperial Decree in August 1876. This decree ordained that all these pensions and allowances were to be at once commuted into capital sums, the payment of which would commence within five, and terminate within thirty years. The rate of commutation varied from five years' purchase for the largest, to fourteen years' purchase for the smallest pensions, and until the payment of the commuted capital sums all the pensioners were to receive government bonds of the proper amount bearing from five to seven per cent. interest.

The total number of pensioners was at this time 318,428, of which only 586—almost all nobles—had pensions of above 1000 yen.* These were the men most affected by the edict. For instance, a pensioner of the first class, instead of a hereditary annual income of 70,000 yen, was now entitled to a capital sum

* 1 yen = 4*s*. The yen is divided into 100 sen or cents.

of 350,000 yen, payable at the convenience of the government, in the course of thirty years; and would meanwhile receive interest at five per cent. on that amount, i.e. only 17,500, or one quarter of his former income. The smaller pensioners were treated less harshly. Those who had enjoyed pensions above 100 yen and below 1000, of whom there were 15,484, were to retain two-thirds of their former income; and though the 302,358 pensioners of the lowest class, i.e. having pensions under 100 yen, were to suffer still less loss, still all were to be mulcted to a considerable extent.

This radical measure was not a surprise either to the nation or to the persons most affected by it. Since the promulgation of what we have termed the voluntary commutation scheme of 1873, the agricultural and trading classes had been advocating its conversion into a compulsory statute, and the government had seen that such conversion was the only means of lightening the burdens of the 15,000,000 cultivators of the soil, whom it was of course their interest to conciliate by means of a reduction of the land-tax. The Samurai above all had been for some time aware that the adoption of this compulsory measure was only a question of time. But when the blow fell it did not find them prepared either to resign themselves to the change it must necessarily cause in their position, or to resist it as a class. The ties of clanship were stronger than class interests, and the opportunity for a rising of the whole body of discontented Samurai throughout the length and breadth of the empire passed, never to return. Had such a rising taken place, the malcontents, all accustomed to the use of the sword at least, would have vastly outnumbered the Samurai adherents of the government, and it seems more than probable that they would have been more than a match for all the forces, both trained soldiers and two-sworded men, which the government could have ranged against them. It is idle to speculate on what would have been the results of their success; but, if it be allowed to draw inferences from the antecedents of these men, we may conclude that these results would have been injurious not only to foreign intercourse with Japan, but also to the real interests of the Japanese nation.

But, though the Samurai did not unite in resisting a decree which diminished their pecuniary resources, undermined the administrative and governing supremacy which they had monopolised for centuries, and reduced them to the level of the despised Heimin—a decree which the great majority of them could regard in no other light than as an act of spoliation—partial discontent was not long in manifesting itself. In the month of October a night-attack was made by about 170 Samurai on the government barracks at Kumamoto, the chief town of the province of Higo in the island of Kiushiu. The insurgents were specimens of the most prejudiced men in their class; men who clung with fanatical tenacity to their old traditions. "Honour the Emperor and expel the foreigner" were their watchwords, and the manifesto which they issued bore ample traces of the ultra-conservative nature of their sentiments. "Our country," they stated in this document, "differs from all other lands, in that "it is the country of the gods, and for this "reason it should not even for a moment be "held to rank below any foreign land. But "diabolical spirits now prevailing are bent "on abolishing customs which have been "cherished and observed from the time of "the gods, and on making our people imitate "foreigners. These facts cause us the deepest "sorrow. Some time ago we were deprived of "our swords, and now we are ordered to cut "off our topknots,* a fashion which has come "down to us from the divine era, and to wear "our hair in foreign style. Therefore the "only good thing we can now do is to use "our swords in the houses of officials † who "imitate foreigners. This alone is worthy "of men of our class."

Dressed in the style of the old Japanese warrior, in helmet and chain armour, and armed with swords and halberds, this band of reckless men surprised the garrison of Kumamoto in the dead of night and butchered or

---

* In September 1871, when permission was granted to the Samurai to leave off wearing their swords, a notice was simultaneously issued allowing all classes to wear their hair in European fashion. No compulsory order of the nature mentioned in the text was ever issued by the central government. It is possible, however, that an over zealous official may have published such an order in the province of Higo.

† This phrase refers to the Imperial troops which wear European cut uniforms.

wounded 300 of the Imperial troops in their beds. In the eyes of such men this was a chivalrous exploit, and their subsequent conduct was not less chivalrous, according to Japanese ideas; for after performing this cold-blooded massacre, they retired to the hills, and, finding there was no probability of a general rising in the province, eighty-four of them manifested the sincerity of their intentions by committing *hara-kiri*, whilst only twenty-nine surrendered to the Imperial troops which soon dispersed or killed the rest of the band.

Disturbances also occurred at the same time in the northern parts of Kiushiu, chiefly at Akidzuki, but these were easily suppressed. A more serious revolt shortly followed in Chôshiu. Here the movement was headed by Mayebara, a man who had distinguished himself in the war of the Restoration and been appointed vice-minister of war soon afterwards. He is said to have been found wanting in the administrative capacity requisite for the fulfilment of his duties in this post, and had been honourably dismissed and rewarded with a pension eight years previously. Retiring to his home he had there brooded over his imaginary wrongs, and now, thinking that the discontent of the Samurai might be used to his own interest, raised the standard of revolt. The manifesto which he issued in November, contained many of the same phrases as are to be found in almost all those which have preluded civil war in Japan. The Mikado, it stated, was a prisoner in the hands of evil councillors. His gaolers were men who laid heavy burdens on the people in order to gratify their own lusts. They were heedless of the continued drain of Japanese treasure into the hands of foreign barbarians, and bent alone on securing their own personal interests. "It is in His Sacred "Majesty's behalf," Mayebara concluded, "that I take up arms. Follow me. Destroy "the wicked officials of the capital and re-"lease the Emperor from confinement. Delay "not. The laws and the Emperor are oui "guide and strength, and by them our con-"duct shall be judged."

There was no mention in this document of the special grievance of the Samurai, the law for the commutation of pensions, and it soon became evident that there was no community of feeling or aim between Mayebara and that class, and that he had failed to attract their sympathy. Only five or six hundred of them joined him. Some fighting took place at Hagi, the chief town of Chôshiu, but the government, warned of the critical state of things in that province, speedily* collected a considerable force of regular troops and armed police. The insurgents were outnumbered and defeated, and the insurrection was crushed in a fortnight. Mayebara fled with some of his chief partisans, but was soon captured; and he and ten of the leaders of the Kumamoto and Akidzuki risings were beheaded, whilst about 250 of their followers were sentenced to various terms of imprisonment and hard labour.

These three insurrections had been of short duration, and had been suppressed with comparative ease by the government. But they caused a good deal of anxiety in Tôkiô. It was there well known that the country was in

* On this occasion the telegraph no doubt stood the government in good stead.

that state in which these outbreaks might be expected to spread, and whilst they lasted much anxiety existed as to the attitude of Saigô in regard to them. As one of these risings was suppressed after the other and no signs of Satsuma's open participation in them were perceived, the attitude of the clan became the subject of much discussion, and was generally attributed to the same motives as those which actuated its conduct during the Hizen revolt of 1874. It was said, on the one hand, that Saigô foresaw the futility of these attempts to upset the government and the certainty of their failure, and that his own preparations were not yet completed; on the other, that he had incited these movements in order to weaken the possible resistance of Higo and Chôshiu to his future projects.

It is impossible to say which of these theories is the correct one. The fact remains that Satsuma did not move on this occasion, and the peace of the empire was undisturbed during the rest of the year 1876, except by some Agrarian riots which arose from the unwillingness of the farmers in some districts to comply with the conditions of a new law, issued about this time, ordering the land-tax to be henceforth paid in money instead of in kind. In these riots the Samurai sided with the government, and they were easily suppressed.

The government were nevertheless apprehensive of further disturbances breaking out in consequence of the discontent caused by the pension commutation law, and their fears were increased by the discovery of a plot to assassinate Ôkubo, the minister of the interior. It is not publicly known whether the conspirators had any connection with the Chôshiu, Akidzuki, or Kumamoto insurgents, but there is no doubt that the plot was of a very serious nature; and though the ringleaders were arrested before they could execute their project, the lives of all the ministers were considered to be in danger. Their houses were therefore constantly guarded by large bodies of police, and escorts of cavalry accompanied them whenever they drove out.

Ôkubo's life was especially aimed at, because he was the most resolute and determined spirit in the government, and because his name was most closely associated with all the recent enactments, and more particularly with that regarding the pensions. Against this measure the Satsuma Samurai protested more vehemently than any of the others, stating that they were in an exceptional position, inasmuch as the mass of them still held possession of the land from which their pensions were derived, whereas this was not the case with the pensioners in the rest of the empire. This difference was considered by the government, and it was decided that on this account the state bonds issued to the Satsuma Samurai for the commuted capital of their pensions, should bear 10 instead of 5 or 7 per cent. interest as in the other provinces.

This promised concession had no effect on coming events, but it shows that the government still desired to conciliate Satsuma, and to continue their temporising policy, in the hope that time and the chapter of accidents might prevent an open rupture. At the same time they endeavoured to strengthen their own position, and to gain popularity with the agricultural class by reducing the land-tax from 3 to 2½ per cent. on the value of the land, thus diminishing the tax by £1,600,000 per annum, a measure which would have more certainly gained its object if it had not been accompanied by stringent orders to collect the whole of this tax * in money.

From the foregoing pages it will, I think, appear evident that in using all their resources to bring about the Restoration of the Mikado, the Satsuma leaders aimed, firstly, at the destruction of the Tokugawa Shôguns, and secondly, at a transfer of a large share of their power and authority to themselves.

After 1869, when Ôkubo, Terashima, and other less notable Satsuma men, threw in their lot once for all with the central government, Shimadzu Saburô and Saigô remained all powerful over a united clan.

The former was a conservative of the purest

* Like many recent legislative measures in Japan, this one regarding money payments was premature; and a year's experience of its workings proved that it was unjust to the farmers. It was accordingly modified in 1877, and since then the farmers have been allowed to pay half their land-tax in kind on giving a month's notice of their intention to do so.

water and most stubborn sort. Having satisfied his hereditary feelings of hatred and jealousy of the Tokugawa family, he aimed at holding a paramount position in the new government, which, according to his views, ought to be composed of a species of central board of representatives of three or four of the greatest south-western clans, in which Satsuma was of course to have a preponderating voice; and he, further, desired the retention of the feudal system; the maintenance of the Samurai in the enjoyment of their old position and privileges; the restriction of foreigners to the very narrowest limits around the open ports; and as little change as possible in the institutions, customs, and manners of his country.

This was his programme, and from it he seems never to have departed. He was not a practical statesman, and was equally incapable of measuring the forces and obstacles opposed to him, and of divising means for overcoming them. For eight years after the Restoration he held unwaveringly to his opinions, and it was not till the beginning of the year of 1876, when the practice of wearing swords was finally abolished, that he seems to have become alive to the great changes which had occurred in Japan ; it was not till then that he came to acknowledge the impossibility of realising his dream ; having at last arrived at this conviction, he retired from the political arena.

Saigô's views appear to have differed in some respects from those of Shimadzu, but not sufficiently to prevent his acting in concert with him on most political questions, and the first point in both their programmes was the supremacy of Satsuma in the national councils. Saigô, however, knew that the attainment of this object was surrounded with difficulties. He was well acquainted with the views of the other clans and parties in the state, and knew that their opposition to his schemes could only be finally overcome by force. Hence his never-ceasing efforts to keep the population of his province fully armed and drilled, and hence his desire to wait for what he should consider the most favourable opportunity for active measures.

He did not desire the retention of the feudal system in its entirety, and it will be remembered that he was a member of the government which abolished the clans in 1871, and that he incurred Shimadzu's displeasure for the part which he took in this measure. Subsequent events lead to the inference that he acquiesced in, and possibly suggested its execution, because he was well aware that the Chôshiu, Tosa, and Hizen clans were strong enough to enforce it in face of his opposition, and because he felt assured that his acquiescence in or suggestion of the measure would entitle him to stipulate that the leaders of his clan should be free to fix the date and manner of its application to his own province, which, as above stated, remained almost exempt from its effects up to the beginning of 1877.

There was probably another reason for his action in this matter, a reason closely connected with what seems to have been the second principal point in Saigô's programme. That point, as will appear from the sequel of this story, was that whilst Satsuma governed Japan, Saigô was to lead Satsuma. Now Saigô was not a Daimiô, and as long as the clans existed, he must necessarily remain subordinate to the Satsuma chieftain. When the feudal system should be swept away, no hierarchical title of nobility would stand between him and the evident object of his desires and aims, the supreme direction of the nation's policy.

His appointment to the post of commander-in-chief of the Mikado's land forces probably appeared to him to be a step onwards to the goal of his ambition, and this explains his retention of that title, when he resigned office in 1873, on account of the Korean and conscription questions. Saigô was not a man of words, and the only record of his political ideas which has been published in English is the document already given in the foregoing pages. But all the acts of his public life seem to point to the conclusion that, in his opinion, a military despotism, of which he should be the head under the Mikado, was the best government for Japan.

He of course desired to retain the privileges of the military class, and he was of opinion that all the civil officials, and all the rank and file, as well as the officers, of the army and navy should be taken from its ranks. But it is probable that he was more liberal than Shimadzu in his views regarding the treatment of foreigners and the adoption of some of their inventions. Little, however, is known positively of his recent opinions on these subjects, except that he was decidedly opposed to the pace with which the the Tôkiô government introduced Western civilisation in Japan.

PART IV.

THE REBELLION.

CHAPTER IX.

Relative position and resources of the Imperial government, and of Satsuma—The cabinet—Army and navy—Post and telegraphs—Saigô's character and prestige—His lieutenants—Military strength and other material resources of Satsuma.

In the preceding parts of this work I have attempted to trace the causes of the Satsuma Rebellion, down to the end of the year 1876, as far as they can be ascertained from the most authentic sources of information now available. The position and moral and material resources of the central government and of the Satsuma party at that date next require notice, and I shall then proceed to describe the outbreak and course of the Rebellion.

The central government was the government of the Mikado, whose right to the absolute and submissive obedience of his people, based on his acknowledged and direct descent from the gods, has never yet been impugned and is universally inculcated by the priests of Shintôism and Japanese Buddhism. The extent of this moral force may be inferred from the fact that not one of the many insurrections in Japan has been openly directed against the Mikado's authority. His Majesty's government was composed at this time of the following members: Sanjô and Iwakura, prime and vice-prime ministers; Kugé or nobles of the Mikado's court; Ôkubo, minister of the interior; Kawamura Sumiyoshi, vice-minister of marine; Terashima, minister for foreign affairs; and Kuroda, minister of the colonial department, all Satsuma Samurai; the men referred to in Shimadzu Saburô's memorial to the Mikado, of 1875, as "clan retainers, who set their lords at nought." Two other Satsuma men, General Saigô and General Kawaji, also held important posts, the first being commander of the Imperial guard, and the second prefect of the Tôkiô police. The other ministers were Itô Hirobumi, minister of public works; Yamagata Ariaki, minister of war (both from

Chôshiu); Ôkuma Shigenobu, minister of finance; and Ôgi Takato, minister of justice (from Hizen). The Satsuma men thus held a very large proportion of the most important portfolios, and as they had for long been considered as traitors in their native province, their preponderating influence in the cabinet was calculated to envenom the struggle* which was about to commence with the Satsuma clan. For them, even if not for the existence of a centralised government of any sort, the combat was mortal.

All the above-mentioned members of the government had been some years in office, many of them indeed ever since the Restoration. They were well versed in all the details of the administration, and were aided by a large number of employés in the capital, all

* A Japanese statesman thus epitomised the causes of the struggle:

"The conflict," he said, "might be looked upon as a struggle between the Satsuma men in the government aided by those of Chôshiu on the one side and the Satsuma Shizoku in general on the other. The latter consider that the men who went forth from the province a few years ago to take a share in the administration of the country, in a certain sense as representatives of the clan, have acted in a manner completely at variance with their mandate."

bound to them more or less by ties of gratitude for the posts which they held, and which they would in all probability lose if the existing order of things were reversed.

The government had too appointed nearly all the provincial authorities in the thirty-five ken or prefectures into which the empire was then divided, and could count on the fidelity of most of them. They had the support of an army,* drilled and instructed under the direction of European officers, which was composed of men recruited from all ranks of the people and in great measure from the Heimin class, and which now numbered 31,000 men in time of peace, and 46,000 when on a war footing. These figures do not include the Imperial guard, a fine body of 3961 officers and men, who are chiefly Samurai, selected from the regiments of the

* By the Japanese conscription law every male is liable to military service from the age of seventeen to that of forty. The service is as follows: three years with the colours, two in the 1st Reserve, two in the 2nd Reserve and the rest in a sort of landwehr. It is calculated that 6,762,030 men are liable to military service, and from this number recruits are taken by lot to fill up the vacancies caused in the Regular Army by the annual drafts of men into the Reserve.

line. The navy consisted of nine steamers bearing more than fifty guns, and crews of 1250 men, and though it was officered to a great extent by Satsuma men, the government felt sure of its loyalty. To these forces must be added 18,000 well-drilled and efficient policemen.

The government had further, in their hands, the postal and telegraph services, both of which had been widely developed since their institution in 1871. It was in that year that the first government mail route, between Tôkiô and Ôzaka, was opened, but, in the six years which had since elapsed, mail routes of the length of 33,000 English miles had been brought into active service and 700 post offices, supplemented by 1700 stamp agencies and letter-boxes, had been established, whilst telegraph lines had been laid down to most of the capitals of the thirty-five prefectures. The government had also the use of the fleet of thirty-eight merchant steamers, belonging to the Mitsu Bishi Company, which receives a large subsidy from the treasury on condition of placing its vessels at the disposal of the state when required to do so. They had thus complete command of the sea. They had also considerable reserves in rice, and in corn and bullion, and possessed in their efficient paper-money factory the means of temporarily increasing their pecuniary resources to an almost unlimited extent.

Besides all the above, the government had the advantages of having the law on its side and being in possession of the supreme power; and finally there must be added the numerous other resources which governments, good or bad, must in the natural course of things acquire by a continuous tenure of office.

On the side of Satsuma was Saigô, a man who had acquired a popularity and prestige greater than that of any other individual in the empire. His public life, as sketched above, had long since rendered his name familiar to all Japanese, by the mass of whom he was considered the greatest military genius of the age. His fame no doubt rested on the services he had rendered as a General and a public man and on the prestige attaching to his position of chief councillor of the most powerful of the clans; but his popularity was due in a great measure to his personal character and qualities. Physically he was extraordinarily tall for a Japanese, being a full head above all his fellows: he was proportionately broad, had massive limbs, and would have been considered a well-built powerful man in any country. His head was well formed, and spite of his dark bushy eyebrows his face generally wore an expression of frank simplicity as well as of manliness. He was a good swordsman, and passionately fond of field sports, such as shooting and fishing, in which he passed much of his time after his retirement from office; but by temperament and disposition he was averse to continuous study of any sort, and whilst in office, is said to have found the routine duties of his department most irksome and distasteful. Morally he had the reputation of being surpassingly intrepid and courageous; he was calm, resolute, and generous at the same time, as well as sincere and true in his friendships. Wealth had apparently no attractions for him, and the money he had he spent with a liberal hand. His house near Kagoshima was like that of a well-to-do farmer, and he appears to have been frugal and sober in his habits. His retirement from office, and the unostentatious manner of his country life led people to believe that he had no ambition for himself, and he was thus endowed in the imagination of his admirers with all the self-denial of a true patriot. In all these qualities his character contrasted most favourably, in the opinion of large numbers of the Samurai and people, with those of the Satsuma and, indeed, most other clansmen who had risen to high places in the government, and who were considered in many parts of the country, and especially in the south, as mere place-hunters. Saigô's manner, too, captivated the minds of all who came in contact with him, and this combination of prepossessing qualities endeared his name amongst the people, and made him appear as the beau ideal of a Samurai to all the military class, who considered him the representative of their best interests.

His influence in the principality of Satsuma had for some time completely superseded that of the Shimadzu family. The young ex-prince, Shimadzu Saburô's eldest son, had never taken any interest in politics, and his father was now getting old and feeble. His political opinions had become more reactionary with advancing years, and what he desired was nothing less than a return to the feudal system, and to the state of things which existed before the Restoration, the Mikado being substituted for the Shôgun, and the Satsuma clan being entrusted with the direction of the national affairs. But, as we have seen, he appears to have given up all hopes of realising this dream in 1876, when the practice of wearing swords was abolished, and the Satsuma Samurai, though blindly ignorant of the great changes that had taken place outside their province, were nevertheless sufficiently well informed to perceive the impracticability of his ideas. They had therefore attached themselves to Saigô, the main points of whose programme, as far as it was known to the public, were the acquisition for Satsuma of a preponderating voice in the national councils, and the exclusion of all but Samurai from the governing body. The army and navy were to be recruited from the ranks of the Samurai alone, and they were also to fill all posts in the civil administration. To his own partisans Saigô probably promised the restitution of all their old privileges, such as the wearing of swords, and it was taken for granted that he would repeal the pension commutation act. These were objects which might be attained, and which completely satisfied the aspirations of the Samurai, who necessarily formed the strength of the separatist party in Satsuma. Thus it was that Shimadzu Saburô continued to live in retirement near Kagoshima, or on the island of Sakurajima, during the whole of the civil war, and took no open part in it, though it is possible that he may have been forced to give secret and pecuniary assistance to his clansmen.

Saigô's most active supporters were Shinowara Kunimori, Kirino Toshiaki, and Ôyama Tsunayoshi, all Satsuma Samurai of modest birth. Shinowara had greatly distinguished himself in the war of the Restoration, and was specially known in the army for his dauntless bravery, which had won for him the post of commander of the Imperial guard. He is said to have been one of the very few men who enjoyed Saigô's intimate confidence, and the latter sought his advice before that of all others in critical moments. Kirino was also a distinguished soldier in the war of the

Restoration, during which he commanded the 1st battalion of the Satsuma contingent, and had risen to the rank of major-general. Both of them had sent in their resignations, when Saigô left the government and Tôkiô, and had since then been employed in organising the "private schools." Ôyama had been rewarded with a pension for his services in 1868. He was a trusted friend of Saigô and entirely devoted to his interests. When the latter resigned his post of chief administrator of the affairs of Satsuma, in order to accept that of councillor of state in the central government, in 1871, it was of great importance to him to leave behind him a thoroughly confidential agent at the head of affairs at Kagoshima. His choice fell upon Ôyama, and he not only procured for him the title of vice-governor, but was also able to retain him in that capacity at Kagoshima, after the abolition of the feudal system, when all the other clans were obliged to accept Imperial governors of indiscriminate origin. During his tenure of this office Ôyama had always administered the province in accordance with the views and policy of his patron.

As to the material resources of the prin cipality, i.e. the three provinces of Satsuma, Ôsumi, and Hiuga, the census states their population to be 1,182,783, and that of the whole island of Kiushiu at 4,800,000 souls. The total population of Japan being nearly 34 millions, the principality contained little more than one twenty-eighth of the nation, and the Satsuma party would only have had one-seventh of it on their side, even if the whole of Kiushiu had joined in the Rebellion. This was not, however, the case, though Satsuma undoubtedly received considerable assistance, both in men and money, from the provinces of Higo and Bungo.

This disproportion in the numbers of the population about to be ranged against each other was not of much importance, as the masses of the nation were completely indifferent to the results of this, and all other civil wars in Japan. Even the richest class of merchants and farmers, though not entirely ignorant of the use of arms and allowed under the old regime to wear and use one sword for their protection against brigands and robbers, had no political rights, and were certain to remain passive spectators of the coming struggle for power; whilst the masses below them were, as regards all political questions, pretty much in the position of the Russian serfs, though more favoured than the latter in other respects. They were sure, therefore, to take no part in the conflict, except in Satsuma, where the peasants resented the imposition of the new land-tax, and the tradespeople disliked the new taxes on their business transactions, where, too, Saigô was personally so well known and so much admired, that the whole population applauded and aided his enterprise against the Tôkiô government.

This disproportion was further very much diminished as regards the number of fighting men who could be arrayed on the side of Satsuma. For in that province the proportion of the Samurai to the Heimin class was very much larger than elsewhere. Of its gross population of 812,327 souls, no less than 204,143 belonged to the Samurai class, all the adults of which were enrolled, and the members of the "private schools" alone numbered 20,000 at this time. The Satsuma leaders were, moreover, certain to have the active support of the men of Hiuga and Ôsumi, and no doubt hoped to be joined by many Samurai from other provinces of Kiushiu, and by the discontented spirits on the mainland. Thus they might count on being able to place between thirty and forty thousand men in the field, if necessary, and the Imperial forces did not exceed fifty thousand men.

As to arms and munitions of war, they appear to have had a small park of artillery, and a very considerable supply of Snider and Enfield rifles, and of powder and ball; and amongst the foreign merchants in Japan, there were not wanting some who were ready to supplement any deficiencies in these respects. It was in their swords, however, that the Satsuma men placed the greatest reliance, feeling confident that that weapon in the hands of Samurai, would be more than a match for the rifle in those of Heimin, who formed the chief part of the rank and file of the Imperial army. Their pride and exclusiveness had prevented their seeing the great progress in discipline and efficiency, which had been made by this army during the last three years, i.e. since Saigô quitted the capital. These same feelings also made them blind to the fact that the Heimin, who had entered the army and been quartered in the capital and other large towns, were fast beginning to see that they and their class were most interested in the abolition of the privileges and pensions of the Samurai, and that this was an object worth fighting for.

Pride and ignorance of the actual state of the rest of the country contributed, indeed, in no slight degree to the outbreak of the Rebellion. They pervaded the minds of all classes in Satsuma; of the leaders as well as of the men. The former, for instance, entertained strong hopes that defection would at once show itself in the navy, which was chiefly manned and commanded by Satsuma men, ignoring completely the fact that all these men had thrown in their lot with the central government, and had far better prospects of advancement and distinction in its service, than by joining a movement, the success of which seemed impossible to many, and doubtful to all.

The calculation to be subsequently mentioned, which the Satsuma leaders entertained, that they and their troops would be unopposed by the Imperial forces, in their march from Kagoshima to the capital, was based on such monstrous ignorance of the state of things in the rest of the empire, that it is almost impossible to believe that they counted on its realisation. In short, Saigô and his chief advisers would appear to have thought that the country had stood still since his secession from the government in 1873.

The pecuniary resources of the Satsuma party were inconsiderable, consisting only of the private fortunes of its members and about £100,000 in the local treasury of Kagoshima. But they could draw supplies of food, almost gratis, from the neighbouring province of Higo, which is famous for its rice crop, and as long as their forces were in Kiushiu, could maintain them at slight expense, as the population was generally favourable to the expedition. Satsuma had also the advantage of having made all its preparations before the central government were aware of its intentions, and until the latter had had time to bring down its troops from the northern provinces and concentrate them in Kiushiu, it could count with certainty on being superior in the field. Such was the state of the two parties in December 1876.

CHAPTER X.

The students of the "private schools" oppose the removal of ammunition from Kagoshima—Admiral Kawamura sent to pacify them—Failure of his mission—Story of the plot to assassinate Saigô—Civil war proclaimed.

THE year 1876, as above stated, closed peacefully in Japan, and there was then nothing on the surface of public affairs to indicate the imminence of any internal disturbances of a more serious nature than those which had occurred from time to time since the Restoration. The government were, it is true, disquieted and anxious, but the foregoing pages have shown that there was nothing exceptional in this state of feeling. Having easily suppressed the isolated and ill-advised revolts in the north of Kiushiu and in Chôshiu, they may have justly considered that they had diminished the number of seats of discontent, and might well hope to deal as successfully with those that still existed. Satsuma they of course knew to be the chief of the latter, though they had little reliable information as to the real state of that province, and as to the immediate intentions of its chief clansmen. They knew enough, however, to show them the advisability of taking some precautionary measures against any aggressive projects which might be entertained by the clan. Accordingly, early in January 1877, they commenced bringing away from Kagoshima as many of the arms and munitions stored in the arsenal of that place as they could quietly remove.

This proceeding soon came to the ears of the Samurai of that town, and they at once determined to oppose it. On the 29th of January a body of the pupils of the "private schools," fully armed, broke into the arsenal and carried off as many rifles and as much powder as they could remove. On the 30th and following night they repeated these acts, and on the 2nd of February they forcibly stopped the lading of a large government transport, sent down from Tôkiô to embark and bring away all the powder * in the magazines. The vessel got away with difficulty, and her captain steamed as fast as he could to Kôbe to report what had happened to the central

* The powder was said to have been recently purchased by the government from the Ex-Prince of Satsuma, but the pupils affirmed that the purchase-money had not been paid.

government, arriving there early on the morning of the 4th February.

Now the 5th of that month had been fixed for the official opening, by the Mikado in person, of the railway recently constructed between Ôzaka and Kiôto, and connecting the latter, the ancient and sacred capital of the empire, with the Eastern Sea. Great preparations had been made for this event. The Mikado and all his court had gone down from Tôkiô some days previously; most of the cabinet ministers had followed, and the representatives of the foreign powers had received and accepted invitations to witness the inauguration of a work which was of great importance to the welfare of the country, as well as a further proof of the progress of Japan in Western civilisation. All were assembled in the picturesque old city, which had put on its most festive garb for the occasion. The Mikado was no doubt pleased to revisit the scenes of his youth, and the foreigners and their hosts looked forward to the fêtes which had been prepared for them. It was under these circumstances that, in the evening of the 4th of February, news was brought of the occurrence just mentioned at

Kagoshima; an occurrence which contrasted sadly with the peaceable opening of a railway, and, in its consequences, was to prove that, spite of the rapid introduction and adoption of many of the appliances and usages of European society, old Japan is not yet extinct.

The news was certainly considered grave, but the ministers decided that it should not be divulged until after the ceremony of the next day, which accordingly took place as originally arranged. A cabinet council was then held, and resulted in the despatch of Admiral Kawamura, the vice-minister of marine and a Satsuma man, to Kagoshima. He started from Kôbe on the morning of the 6th, in the fastest steamer in the navy, then used as the Mikado's yacht, and arrived at his destination on the 9th. He then found that the town was filled with armed men, that two small government steamers had been seized by them, and that it would be imprudent for him to land at once. He therefore sent two of his officers ashore to arrange a meeting with Saigô. During their absence the vice-governor of the town, Ôyama, came on board his ship, and informed him that the military class of the clan had risen in arms, in consequence of their belief that the government were about to attack Satsuma, and had sent emissaries to assassinate Saigô; that these emissaries had been arrested, and had made a full confession of the plot; that both Saigô and Shimadzu had nevertheless tried to restrain their followers, and failing in this, had retired to their country houses.

Admiral Kawamura assured Ôyama that there were no grounds for this belief, that if the charges in question could be proved, he, as a Satsuma man, and a relation by marriage of his old friend and comrade Saigô, would be the first to make common cause with the latter's retainers, and that he had been sent by the Mikado to ascertain the causes of discontent, and to reassure the clan. For this purpose he must have an interview with Saigô.

Ôyama then left the ship, saying that he would make arrangements for this interview, and for the admiral's visit to the town; but, soon after his departure, five boats filled with armed men were seen approaching the ship, evidently with hostile intentions; and, to avoid a conflict which would inevitably have put an end to all possibility of a peaceful arrangement, the admiral slipped his cable and stood across the bay. There he was again visited by Ôyama, who came to tell him that an interview with Saigô was out of the question, that some of his troops had already marched northwards; in short, that the time for negotiation had now passed. On hearing this message, and learning at the same time that the two officers he had sent on shore had been arrested, the admiral reluctantly came to the same conclusion, and steamed away on the evening of the 9th to the nearest telegraph station on the main island to announce to the government the failure of his mission and the outbreak of civil war.

The leaders of the Satsuma clan had decided that the moment for action was come, Saigô's name was still the most popular and powerful, not only in Satsuma, but also throughout the empire. The military class of the province was now thoroughly imbued with the conviction that the Mikado was merely a puppet in the hands of a clique of iniquitous men who governed, or rather misgoverned the country, solely in their own interest. The enactment of the compulsory pension law, an act, in their eyes, of the most unjustifiable spoliation, had convinced them that the government were intent on consummating their ruin. They were now fully equipped and armed, and if they allowed their arms and munitions to be carried away, their leaders foresaw that the favourable opportunity for reasserting the supremacy of Satsuma would pass, never to return. A spark alone was necessary to cause the mine, which had been so patiently and carefully laid, to explode. To ensure an explosion, a torch was applied to the mine, and this torch was the story of a plot to assassinate Saigô, which, it was stated, had been conceived by the government, and was about to be executed by its agents.

On what evidence does the existence of this plot rest? On the confessions of a corporal of the Tôkiô police, named Nakahara Hisao* and twenty-one privates of that force, who were on furlough at this time in their native province, and on that of a man who is stated to have been a Kagoshima Samurai.

* Vide Appendix.

The gist of these confessions was to the effect that in the previous month of January, Kawaji, the prefect of the police at Tôkiô, had given the policemen leave of absence, in order that they might proceed to Kagoshima, for the purpose of bringing about a division amongst the members of the "private schools." They were to effect this by gaining over some of the pupils, by argument, to the government side. This done, the two parties were to be incited to acts of violence, and the conspirators were to take advantage of the disturbances thus caused, to assassinate Saigô. When this deed was accomplished, they were to telegraph to Tôkiô, and in the event of a rising of the clan, the government would be prepared with naval and military forces to attack and annihilate the pupils of the "private schools" to a man. The confession of the Kagoshima Samurai differed from the others in one respect, inasmuch as its author stated that he had received his instructions from Ôkubo, the minister of the interior and not from the prefect of police.

Now there is no evidence to show that these men had made any attempts to cause dissensions and bring about disturbances amongst the pupils. It appears also that the leading man amongst them, Nakahara Hisao, was not arrested until the 3rd of February, i.e. more than four full days after the first forcible entrance of the pupils into the arsenal and their first seizure of the arms and powder there stored. It is also almost certain that all the confessions in question were made under torture. Torture is still allowed by the Japanese laws, though its practice is limited to exceptional cases, and can only be enforced by the express permission of the minister of justice; it is not repulsive to the Japanese mind, and, under the circumstances above described, when it was all-important to the Satsuma leaders to afford the Satsuma people convincing proofs of the existence of the plot to assassinate Saigô, its application was both probable and in keeping with the rest of their proceedings. But beyond this probability, we have the evidence of both the tortured and the torturers. For, anticipating future events, we may here state, that on the entrance of the Imperial troops into Kagoshima in April, the authors of the confessions were found there still in prison, and that, on the termination of the war, they were tried at Tôkiô by a special court under the presidency of His Imperial Highness Arisugawa-no-Miya, and acquitted of the charge of plotting against the life of Saigô; whilst several of the Satsuma Samurai and policemen, who were tried by the same court, were proved to have extorted the confessions by means of torture, and were therefore condemned to various periods of penal servitude. This trial was not, it is true, a public one, but amongst the judges was one of the highest and most respected men in the country, whose presidency of the court is a guarantee, of no slight value, of the justice of its verdict.

Again, it does not appear that the Tôkiô government were at all prepared to sweep down on their supposed victims with naval and military forces and kill them off to a man. They had not concentrated any force on the frontiers of Satsuma, or even at Ôzaka or Kiôto. No extraordinary movements of troops or men-of-war had been ordered. The army and navy were in their normal state, and in their usual positions. The only circumstance which, to an impartial observer, could give the slightest colour to the charge brought against the government of Tôkiô was the presence of so many policemen in and about Kagoshima. But if the normal condition of the province of Satsuma, as described above, be taken into consideration, it will be evident that the government had for long had great difficulty in learning the real state of things there. It seems, therefore, a justifiable assumption that these men, or some of them, were sent down to spy out the land and report on its condition. Between an admission of this sort, and insinuations such as were made at the time by at least one, and that the most influential, of the English newspapers published at Yokohama, to the effect that men in high position in the Mikado's government had sent emissaries down to assassinate Saigô, there is a vast gulf, and it is much to be regretted that this paper did not use more discreet and impartial language regarding the Rebellion generally, and this point in particular.* For there is now no doubt that the statements made to Admiral Kawamura, by the

* *Vide* Appendix.

vice-governor of Kagoshima, were false. That functionary was arrested some time subsequently, and was tried on the termination of the war. In the confession* which he made previous to his execution, he states that in reply to the questions put to him by the admiral relative to the state of things at Kagoshima, "he said nothing about his connection "with Saigô, but made answers which he "thought suitable to the occasion;" that he reported Kawamura's proposal for an interview to Saigô, and that the latter consented to it, but that the pupils prevented the proposal being carried out. He also states that Saigô, whom he saw on the 7th of February, said to him, "If I had been on the spot I "would, in all probability, have prevented the "pupils from acting so recklessly as to take "possession of the government powder by "force, but as this has been done, things must "take their course. There is no mistake as to "Nakahara and others having been sent by "Kawaji, at the instance of Ôkubo, to carry "out some plot, and I am determined to march

* *Vide* Appendix.

" to Tôkiô at the head of my former troops
" and demand an explanation from Ôkubo."

It has been inferred from the above quoted statements of this confession that Saigô was the dupe of Shinowara, Kirino, Ôyama, and other influential men in the clan; that his avowal that he would have prevented the violent proceedings of the pupils if he had been on the spot, is a proof that he was opposed to an outbreak of hostilities at this moment; and that Ôyama and his confederates prevented an interview between Saigô and Kawamura, because they had good grounds for thinking that it would result in creating doubts in the former's mind as to the existence of the plot against his life, and thus pave the way for an amicable and peaceable settlement of the grievances of the clan.

This inference is certainly neither far-fetched nor unreasonable, and it is supported by another consideration of the nature of circumstantial evidence, the fact, namely, that the apparent head of a Japanese clan has not for many years been its real leader. The Daimiô, we have seen, had for long before their abolition been mere puppets in the hands of their Karô, or councillors, and we should now add that the authority of the latter was not supreme in the clan, since they were obliged to listen to the advice of the most energetic and influential of the clansmen in all matters of importance. Shimadzu Saburô had, by his absurdly conservative opinions, been relegated to the position of the Daimiô, and it is quite possible that Saigô, though recognised outside the limits of Satsuma as the leader of the clan, had drifted, within its limits, into the position of a Karô, and that Shinowara and Kirino were the real directors of affairs. They, there is no doubt, had decided on active measures; but they could not make the clan move unless Saigô placed himself at its head, and the surest means of obtaining his leadership at this time was by securing his unhesitating belief in the plot to assassinate him.

It may, on the other hand, be objected against this inference, that its basis, Ôyama's confession, was also extorted by torture, and is therefore valueless. We have no means of proving whether this was or was not the case, but it was the government which published Ôyama's confession, and its tendency was to extenuate the guilt of Saigô, by showing that his only motive for placing himself at the head of his clansmen and marching towards Tôkiô, was to demand satisfaction from the supposed authors of the plot against his life. Now, if torture was applied to Ôyama by order of the government, it is only natural to suppose that the object aimed at was to inculpate and not to exculpate Saigô.

Whether any plot against Saigô's life really existed, or whether the one in question was imagined by Shinowara and Kirino or others, and subsequently supported by evidence extracted by torture, will probably never be positively known, since implicit reliance cannot be placed in any of the confessions relating to it. What seems certain is that Saigô really believed in the genuineness of the confessions of the Tôkiô policemen, which were, it is stated, placed before him by Shinowara and Kirino. It is equally certain that every precaution was taken to give these confessions the widest publicity, for copies of them were at once printed and scattered broadcast throughout the principality of Satsuma and the adjacent provinces.

The die was cast: on the one hand the refusal of the Satsuma leaders to treat with Admiral Kawamura could not be considered by the Mikado's government in any other light than as an act of defiance; on the other, the Satsuma clan had gone too far to retreat. The sword alone could now decide between the two parties.

On the 9th of February, Saigô, Shinowara, and Kirino addressed the following letter to the vice-governor of Kagoshima:—

"Some time back, having taken our leave,*
"we returned to this prefecture on half-pay,
"but now, having some inquiries to address
"to the government, we shall shortly start
"from this place, in consequence where-
"of we beg to give you notice for your
"information.

"Further, as a large number of the former
"troops will start with us, we beg you to take
"measures to prevent the people from being
"perturbed."

On the 12th the vice-governor affixed notices on all the notice boards embodying the above letter, and stating that he approved the proceedings of Saigô and his lieutenants. He at the same time forwarded a circular letter to all the prefects and military commanders of the districts through which the

* i.e. when Saigô resigned in 1873.

expedition intended to march. This letter, to which were appended copies of the confessions of Nakahara and the other policemen implicated in the supposed Assassination Plot, is subjoined in full, as it shows that Ôyama's intention and object was to prevent the possibility of any opposition from the Imperial authorities to Saigô's march, by leading them to believe that his proceedings were of a legitimate nature, and had the sanction of the Emperor:

"The following matters I beg to report "to you by special messenger. Nakahara "Hisao, formerly appointed to the post of "sergeant in the police department, and "others, all natives of this ken, whose "names are stated in the enclosure, relying "on the pretext of having returned to their "province on retirement from government "service, returned to this ken, when it was "discovered that they were secretly harbour"ing a wicked design, by which they would "violate the constitution of the country.

"Therefore, in accordance with the regula"tions, orders were given to the proper "authorities and these men were arrested, "and upon examination they made the en-

"closed unexpected confession. The facts "presumably reached the ears of Saigô "Takamori, Kirino Toshiaki, and Shino-"wara Kunimori, for these three have sent "in a letter to the effect, that having a ques-"tion to ask of the government they intend "to leave this place shortly, and they beg, "therefore, to acquaint me with this for my "information. They add that as a numerous "force of former government soldiers will "accompany them they beg that the occur-"rence of any disturbance on the part of the "people in the jurisdiction of this ken may "be prevented.

"The request contained in this letter has "been acceded to by the government of this "ken. *And the fact has been reported to the "Emperor.* I beg to acquaint you with the "above for your information."

On the 20th of February the Tôkiô government published the following notification:

"As the insurgents of Satsuma have forced "their way into the Kumamoto ken, unlaw-"fully bearing arms against the Imperial au-"thority, His Majesty the Mikado has ordered "an expedition to be sent to chastise them, of "which His Imperial Highness Prince Arisu-

"gawa-no-Miya has been appointed Com-
"mander-in-chief. The above having been
"telegraphed from the Imperial Palace, Kiôto,
"is hereby made known. As many of the
"insurgents may make their escape to various
"parts of the empire, strict orders have been
"given to the authorities of the Fu and Ken*
"to take every precaution to have them
"arrested at once."

Civil war was thus proclaimed. And I now proceed to trace its course.

CHAPTER XI.

Saigô and his army march out of Kagoshima, invest Kumamoto and advance to Minami-no-seki—Position and movements of the Mikado's forces—Prince Arisugawa-no-Miya appointed commander-in-chief—Repulse of the rebels—Occupation and abandonment of Kagoshima by the Imperialists.

ALREADY on the 7th of February parties of men armed with rifles and carrying swords in their girdles began to come into the town of

* For administrative purposes, Japan is divided into three Fu: viz. the cities of Tôkiô, Kiôto, and Ôzaka, and thirty-five ken or prefectures.

Kagoshima, from the country districts. Communication with places beyond the Satsuma frontier was stopped, and pickets were placed on the high roads to examine all strangers travelling southwards. By the 10th, a large portion of the forces destined to accompany Saigô had assembled; and two days sufficed for their embodiment into companies and regiments—a proof that everything had been prepared beforehand. The vanguard of the rebel forces started on the 14th, and on the 15th, the anniversary, according to the old calendar, of the battle of Fushimi, where Saigô and his Satsuma men had contributed so much to the Mikado's restoration and the Shôgun's defeat, the first division of the main army, consisting of 4000 men under the command of Shinowara, left the town. Another division, also of 4000 men followed on the 16th, and after the departure of the rear guard of 2000 men, and of the artillery consisting of sixteen guns, early in the morning of the 17th, Saigô himself accompanied by his body guard of fifty picked men marched out of his native town. The total number of these troops was 14,000, of which 12,000 were infantry, divided into six regiments of 2000 men each. All of them belonged to the "private schools," and, it is said, that at this time Saigô would not allow any but the pupils of these establishments to accompany the expedition, although considerable numbers of volunteers presented themselves, and that he even disavowed the Samurai of Obi and Sadowara, towns of Hiuga, who had set themselves in march to join him.

His motive for this conduct sprang from his desire to give an air of legality to his enterprise, and thus disarm opposition to it. It was also with this view that he gave out that he was going to Tôkiô on a peaceful and legitimate errand, and would therefore avoid any acts that might have the appearance of confederating with others, not immediately concerned in the object of his march. He assumed, indeed, to act as commander-in-chief of the Mikado's land forces, a post which he still nominally retained, and in this capacity he sent orders to the general in command of the nearest Imperial garrison at Kumamoto not to move until he himself should arrive and give further instructions.

The "pupils" provided their own arms, and, far from receiving pay, each of them was required to have 10 yen=£2 in his purse on starting. They wore Japanese costumes sufficiently similar in cut and colour to give the appearance of uniformity, but Saigô, Shinowara and Kirino were dressed in the uniforms they had worn in the Imperial army.

On leaving Kagoshima, the troops marched along the two principal roads through the northern part of Satsuma. One of these leads straight to Hitoyoshi in Higo, and thence descends the river Kumagawa to Yatsushiro. The other approaches nearer the western coast line, passing through Minato, Mukôda, &c., and joining the first mentioned road at Yatsushiro, whence it goes due north to Kumamoto. Both these roads are hilly, and on the second of them there is a pass 1900 ft. high, in crossing which the guns had to be dismounted and carried by coolies.

At Yatsushiro the two bodies reunited, and Saigô calculated that by marching fifteen miles a day he would reach Kokura, a port in the extreme north of Kiushiu and on the straits of Shimonoseki, in twelve days. Thence it was his intention to cross to the mainland, and march up the great high road of the Sanyôdô to Kiôto. This calculation was of course based on the assumption that no opposition would be offered to him.

On the 20th of February, the rebel forces appeared before Kawajiri, and, defeating a battalion of the garrison of Kumamoto, which was sent to dislodge them, arrived on the 21st and 22nd before the latter town. Kumamoto is the capital of the province of Higo, the largest town in Kiushiu (except Kagoshima), and contains about 44,000 inhabitants; it is consequently a place of considerable importance. The castle, forming a part of the town, contains the barracks of the Imperial troops, and, like most Japanese castles, is strongly defended by a series of earthwork terraces faced with stone, rising one above the other, and intersected by deep moats. The latter are extensive and formidable, and a former Daimiô of the district had added a further means of defence, by constructing a net-work of canals, provided with sluices, by which a considerable portion of the adjacent country can be flooded.

The garrison consisted of between two and three thousand men, and there were twelve field-guns in the castle. Colonel Tani commanded, and amongst his troops there were some Satsuma men, on whose assistance the rebels appear to have counted to open the gates to them in case their senior officer refused to obey Saigô's orders.

Colonel Tani, who had been preparing for defence, and had already on the 19th burnt down all the houses in the immediate vicinity of the castle, did at once refuse to listen to any proposal from the rebel leader, and skirmishing began. Finding himself vastly outnumbered, Tani withdrew his men from the town, which he at first hoped to hold, into the castle, and the rebels formally invested the place. Turning its defences against itself, they flooded the precincts of the town, and thus prevented the exit of the garrison on three sides. To guard it on the fourth or eastern side they stationed a division of their army. The other divisions immediately marched northwards to Takase, driving out of that place, on the 22nd, a small body of Imperial troops on their way to reinforce the Kumamoto garrison, and compelling them to fall back upon Minami-no-seki. This town, about twenty-five miles north of Kumamoto, commands an important pass, and there, on the 25th of February, Saigô found himself confronted by two divisions of the Imperial army.

It has been stated above, as an indication that the government had no intention at this time of attacking Satsuma, that they had ordered no concentration of troops in the South. The army, it may now be added, was located in its usual quarters, i.e. in the six districts into which the empire is divided for military purposes. These districts, and the number of troops in each, were as follows :—

		All Arms.	
		Peace.	War.
Tôkiô	Line	7,140	10,370
	Imperial Guards	3,961	
Sendai		4,460	6,540
Nagoya		4,260	6,290
Ôzaka and Kiôto		6,700	9,820
Hiroshima		4,340	6,230
Kumamoto		4,784	6,940

The Kumamoto district includes the whole of the island of Kiushiu, and the two chief garrison towns in the district are Kumamoto and Fukuoka, at each of which there are generally, as at the outbreak of the war, about 2000 men. In order, therefore, to be able to stop the rebel march at Minami-no-seki as early as the 25th February, great expedition had to be used by the Imperial goverment.

As soon as the result of Kawamura's mission had become known to the ministers, who were still in Kiôto, they had at once sent orders to Tôkiô for the equipment of a field force, and between the 12th and 16th of February, 3000 troops of all arms, with twenty guns, had been despatched from Yokohama to Kôbe, whilst the garrisons of Ôzaka and Hiroshima had been forthwith despatched to Fukuoka, on the northern coast of Kiushiu.

The Mikado, who had gone into the country immediately after the opening of the railway, to celebrate a religious service at the tomb of his reputed ancestor, Jimmu Tennô, the founder of the nation, returned at once to Kiôto. Admiral Ito was sent off on the 13th, with three men-of-war to prepare an expedition against Kagoshima, and see if an exhibition of force would not bring the Satsuma people to reason, but before he could arrive there, the news of the rebel march from Kagoshima reached Kiôto. It then became evident that the admiral's mission would be fruitless.

A council of ministers was then held and resulted in the proclamation recorded at the end of the preceding chapter, and the publication of a further proclamation depriving Saigô, Kirino and Shinowara of their military rank and honours.

A notification was at the same time issued, stating that the Mikado would remain in Kiôto, instead of returning as he had intended to Tôkiô, and that a special board, composed of most of the ministers and other high functionaries of the government, was established at Ôzaka, an hour and a half by railway from Kiôto, for the direction of the operations against the insurgents. Three thousand more troops, and 1600 armed policemen were sent down from Tôkiô, and all available troops were pushed on to Fukuoka. There they were placed under the orders of His Imperial Highness Prince Arisugawa-no-Miya, to whom the following rescript was at the same time transmitted: "We have appointed you com-"mander-in-chief in the matter of the chastise-

"ment of the Kagoshima rebels, and we have "invested you with the control of all military "matters, both in regard to the army and "navy, and with authority to promote and "degrade officers from the rank of general "downwards, and to confer rewards and ad-"minister punishments. We therefore look "to you to exert yourself, and, acting in "accordance with the circumstances of the "case, to restore order as soon as possible."

The prince established his headquarters at Fukuoka, on the 19th of February. There he organised his troops into three divisions, and two of these, numbering about 10,000 men, and commanded by Generals Miyoshi and Nodzu, were at once sent southwards, and constituted the force which the insurgents found blocking their march northwards, at Minami-no-seki on the 25th of February.

On the 26th, fighting commenced between the two parties thus brought face to face, and resulted in the insurgents being driven back on Takase, and three miles farther south on the following day. This success of the Imperialist forces in their first encounter was of no little importance, and was at once made widely known, with a view to discouraging the adventurous spirits amongst the Samurai of other parts of the country, from making common cause with the insurgents.

The position of the two armies was then as follows: the bulk of the rebel forces occupied a triangle to the north of and covering Kumamoto, the apex of which was Uyeki, a strong strategic position, about five miles from the besieged town, where the high road bifurcates, one branch going due north and the other in a north-westerly direction. On the northern branch they held Yamaga, and, on the north-western, Kinoha, both of which villages were about ten miles in front of Uyeki, and about the same distance from each other. The base of the triangle was between the two above-mentioned villages, and formed the rebel line, which was strengthened by earthworks at its most exposed points.

On this line the Imperial troops were operating, their object being to drive the rebels south of Kumamoto, and thus relieve the garrison of that place, which was closely watched by one of Saigô's divisions.

After the fighting at Takase, skirmishing

went on along this line for some days, and on the 3rd of March, a serious attempt was made on Yamaga by the Imperial troops. This place is situated on the banks of the river Takase, a mile or so north of a series of narrow wooded defiles easily defensible by small bodies of men. The rebels held their ground, and the Imperial commanders then found it prudent to delay a general advance across the river, until they received reinforcements.

Meanwhile Admiral Ito had completed his preparations, and embarked on three of the most effective men-of-war in the navy, 1200 infantry, 800 marines, and 700 armed police, under the command of Kuroda Kiyotaka, the minister of the colonisation department, a Satsuma man who had been long in office, and had recently distinguished himself in negotiating the treaty with Korea. He was accompanied by an Imperial envoy, Yanagiwara, a noble of the Mikado's court, the original object of whose mission was to prevent, if possible, the outbreak of hostilities, but whose orders now were to assure himself of the loyalty of the Shimadzu family.

With a view to this end, he was commanded to deliver the following message to Shimadzu Saburô:

"The rebels of Kagoshima have forced "their way into the Kumamoto ken, unlaw- "fully opposed the Imperial forces and created "great disturbance. I have, therefore, "already given an order for an expedition "against them, of which Arisugawa-no-Miya "has been appointed commander-in-chief. "You have performed great and meritorious "service for the country and thereby gained "my thorough confidence. I accordingly "send Yanagiwara Chikamitsu, to you, as my "special envoy, to convey to you my desires. "Be therefore loyal."

The squadron left Nagasaki on the 7th of March, and arrived on the following day before Kagoshima. The envoy had satisfactory interviews with Tadayoshi, the young ex-prince of Satsuma, and with his father, Shimadzu Saburô, and on the 10th, the whole military force landed without opposition. The town was completely denuded of Samurai and there was no one left to offer resistance, a circumstance corroborative of Saigô's belief that he would meet with no resistance at Kumomoto, and that he would make good his march to Kiôto, and there compel the Mikado to accept his terms.

The governor of the town, Ôyama, was persuaded or forced by the Imperial authorities to go on board one of the men-of-war, and was then sent to Kôbe and there incarcerated; and Nakahara and the other Tôkiô policemen, on whose confessions the story of the plot to assassinate Saigô was founded, who were discovered in the prisons, were handed over to their relations, who gave bail for their appearance when wanted.

A few days afterwards the whole force, after removing all the powder that could be found, and spiking some of the guns, was re-embarked, and the squadron returned to Nagasaki, leaving the maintenance of tranquility in Kagoshima to the loyalty and care of the Shimadzu family.

This abandonment of the enemy's capital appeared at the time quite inexplicable to Europeans, and proved eventually to be a very grave mistake. It seems to have been effected firstly, because the Tôkiô government had at this time strong hopes of being able to annihilate Saigô's army by concentrating all their forces around him at Kumamoto, and secondly, because the idea that Saigô would ever voluntarily return to his native place without obtaining his object was one which could not, for the following reason, be seriously entertained by a Japanese. A Samurai, setting out on any enterprise of importance, feels that he is looking for the last time on his home, unless his efforts are crowned with success, and that he must die amongst strangers rather than come back to his friends with the dishonour of failure attached to his name. This feeling might be expected to be especially strong in the hearts of Saigô and his men, who, as they themselves and the whole nation were aware, had staked their honour and their lives on the success of their undertaking. The Imperial commanders therefore thought that they need not take the possibility of Saigô's return to Kagoshima into their consideration and calculations. According to their manner of reasoning, he could only return as a victor, and in that case any force left in the place would have to obey his orders, for Saigô's victory could end in nothing less than his appointment to the highest post in the Mikado's government. Their troops, too, were wanted to assist in crushing him at Kumamoto.

CHAPTER XII.

Siege of Kumamoto—Battle of Tawarazaka—Attitude of the Tosa clan—Relief of Kumamoto.

KUMAMOTO was closely invested, and constant attacks on it were made by the rebels, who had, early in March, placed some guns in positions from which they could fire into the castle. Considerable loss of life was caused by these batteries, and the garrison lost many men in fruitless attempts to capture them. During the first days of the siege Colonel Tani was able to send out foraging parties and procure small quantities of rice and other provisions; but this was no longer possible, and the rebel leaders attempted to derive advantage from the despondency, which they thought must prevail in the garrison in consequence of its critical position, by disseminating amongst the men copies of the following proclamation, which they attached to arrows and caused to be shot into the fortress:—

"As the government have connived at "assassination, and violated the constitution "of the country, Saigô and two other leaders "placed themselves at the head of an army, "and took the field in order to enforce "explanations. But the garrison of Kuma- "moto unreasonably closed the gates against "this army, and thereby caused much distress "to the people, besides so exciting the troops "forming this army, that they threaten "wholly to exterminate the garrison. As "we feel pity for those who have been com- "pelled to remain in the castle against their "will, we will pardon them if they will "at once throw down their arms and submit "to us. The Imperial troops at Yamaga and "Takase have been thoroughly beaten, and "risings against the government are taking "place in various provinces. Such being the "case, it is useless and dangerous for you to "defend this single castle any longer, and, "if you persist in doing so, be prepared for "your fate."

This proceeding did not at all affect the

firm determination of Colonel Tani and his troops to hold out to the last extremity, but it was evident that the castle must sooner or later yield to the rebels unless the Imperial troops came to its relief.

This object, and the simultaneous destruction of Saigô's army and consequent suppression of the Rebellion, could not, it was now clear, be attained by the forces at the disposal of the commander-in-chief in Kiushiu. The whole garrison of Tôkiô was therefore sent to the seat of war and was replaced by 6000 men of the Reserve, who were called out after having recently returned to their homes on the expiration of their three years' service with the colours. Fifteen hundred of these were also sent south early in March, and thus Prince Arisugawa's army was brought up to about 20,000 men. Yamagata Ariaki took the command of the advanced divisions of the Imperial army and Admiral Kawamura cruised off the coast of Bungo in order to prevent the passage of malcontents from the mainland.

Skirmishing had been going on along the rebel line since the 3rd of March, and there had been some hard hand-to-hand combats—principally at Tawarazaka on the Tawara Pass about twelve miles north of Kumamoto, which the rebels had fortified with five earthworks armed with field-pieces. This pass, which runs through a range of wooded hills, is the most important and strongest military position in the province of Higo. It is called the Hara-kiri Pass by the Samurai of the province, as they consider that it is useless to contend against an enemy who has succeeded in overcoming the natural difficulties of the situation, and that there is then nothing further to do than to commit suicide. Another pass, Kichi-ji, some miles in advance of Yamaga had also been fortified, and between the 8th and 14th of March those two passes were repeatedly and vainly assaulted by the Imperialists. The rebels opposed a most obstinate resistance, and, trusting to their swords, threw themselves with reckless bravery, in small bodies of forty or fifty men, on their opponents. They found their match with this weapon in the corps of armed policemen, chiefly Samurai, who formed the storming-parties under cover of the fire of the regulars in these assaults. The losses on both sides were considerable, being estimated at 3000 men on the 19th. Up to this date no general engagement took place, partly on account of the difficult nature of the country—a series of wooded eminences intersected by deep ravines—and partly, it is said, owing to the want of familiarity, on the part of the commanders of the regular troops, with foreign military tactics, which they were attempting to practise.

On the 20th, however, the government troops, who were then able to bring their artillery to bear upon the rebel positions, made an attack in force and succeeded in forcing the Tawara and Kichi-ji passes, gaining possession of Yamaga and Tawarazaka and driving the rebels south of Uyeki. In this battle, which is called the battle of Tawarazaka, the Imperialist troops engaged were about 11,000 with twelve guns and the rebels had about 9000 men. The former lost 1766 killed and 2399 wounded. The latter 1200 killed and 2100 wounded, including Shinowara, Saigô's friend and one of his most experienced lieutenants, who fell covered with wounds.

The rebels took up new positions at Kidome

and Kumafu, almost in sight of Uyeki, and entrenched themselves strongly. The scene of the contest had not therefore materially changed, and though the Imperialists had gained some ground, their commanders saw that they were not yet strong enough to make further attempts to break through the rebel army, which still stood between them and Kumamoto.

Saigô had at this time 18,000 men with him, and it is just possible that, by skilful generalship, he might have deceived the garrison of Kumamoto in his rear and, uniting all his forces, have won a decisive victory over the army which barred his way to the North; but no attempt of this sort was made, and such an opportunity did not recur; for the Imperial generals were now about to employ strategy as well as superior numbers against him.

On his return to Nagasaki from Kagoshima, Kuroda received orders to proceed at once with his troops, and some reinforcements which he found awaiting him, to Hinaku; and he accordingly landed there on the 19th of March, with 4000 men, under cover of the fire from his men-of-war. Little opposition was offered to him, and he encamped the same night at Yatsushiro. Thence he was to march northwards to Kawajiri, and thus menace the rebels on the south side of Kumamoto, whilst another force was despatched from Fukuoka to watch the passes in the hills to the east of that town. Thus, whilst Saigô was held at bay by the northern army, his communications with the southern and eastern provinces friendly to his cause and the sources of his supplies and reinforcements, were to be cut off, and his army was to be completely surrounded and compelled to surrender.

If this plan could be speedly executed, the Rebellion would be at an end, for no other clan had risen *en masse* to aid Saigô, or take advantage of the embarrassment of the government to further its own ends. Discontent existed in several parts of south-western Japan, in Hizen, in Inshiu * and Bizen, two provinces on the mainland to the west of Kiôto, and especially in the powerful Tosa

* Now called Inaba.

clan, which occupies the southern portion of the island of Shikoku adjacent to Kiushiu. But Hizen was cut off from all communication with the rebels by the Imperial armies, the Samurai of Inshiu and Bizen were divided amongst themselves, and Tosa had other aims than those entertained by Satsuma. Itagaki, the most prominent man in the clan, had, as above noticed, already refused to join Saigô in any violent measures against the Mikado's government, and he still professed a determination to obtain the objects he had in view by peaceable means. He had left the cabinet because his opinions in favour of the establishment of a representative government had not been adopted. Saigô's success, he foresaw, would certainly not bring him nearer his object, and therefore, far from contributing to it, he is said to have offered to lead his clan against Satsuma, provided the government would pledge themselves to institute a representative assembly on the termination of the war. This offer, if made, was refused, but Tosa, nevertheless, did not openly oppose the government though far from reconciled to the existing order of things. It was, however, impossible to say how long the discontented men of the province would remain quiet, or what they would do if Saigô gained any considerable success; and it was evidently all important to the interests of the government to raise, without loss of time, such a force as would crush the Rebellion at once.

The necessity of some action of this sort was rendered especially urgent towards the end of March, when bands of several hundred Samurai appeared near Nakatsu and Fukuoka, and actually made an attack on the latter place, the point in Kiushiu to which all the government reinforcements and munitions were directed, and the principal base of its operations. These bands were defeated and dispersed at once and without much bloodshed, but, in consequence of them, the Mikado's commission to Prince Arisugawa to punish Satsuma was extended to the rest of Kiushiu, and thus the whole of that island was placed in a state of siege.

The hand to hand fighting which had already taken place, had shown the Tôkiô government the advisability of obtaining the services of men accustomed to the old methods of Japanese warfare—of opposing Samurai by Samurai—and they accordingly proceeded to enrol swordsmen of different clans as police or gensdarmes. By selecting men from the clans which in former days had had feuds with Satsuma, and with whom clan hatreds were stronger than class interests, and by the offer of high pay, they soon induced considerable numbers of this class, which still contains many men who have no fixed occupation and are ever ready for fighting, to enrol themselves, and these were at once sent to the South. About the same time (April 5) a special levy of 10,000 volunteers, Samurai and Heimin between the ages of seventeen and forty, was ordered, and 8000 troops, were hastily despatched to Kiushiu from the northern provinces of the empire. The execution of all these measures fell to the lot of General Saigô, a younger brother of the rebel commander, who, in the absence of Yamagata and Ôyama, the minister and vice-minister of war, had charge of the war office. His post was not an enviable one, for, putting aside the feelings induced by such near relationship, fears of disturbances in Tôkiô were entertained by many people, and were increased by the occurrence of an unusually large number of fires, many of which were attributed to incendiarism.

Besides reinforcing the army, the government had also to make more extensive arrangements for the care of the wounded, and they now sent off most of the students in the medical college at Tôkiô to serve in the field-hospitals, which already contained 1500 wounded. An appeal was also made about this time by the prime ministers, to the nobles and higher classes urging them to imitate the example set by European nations, and particularly by women of rank during the Crimean and Franco-Prussian wars, in regard to the care of the sick and wounded. Contributions of food, bandages, and lint were requested, and the preparation of the latter became the occupation of not a few of the households in the two capitals. Ultimately the nobles were invited to form an association on the model of the Marianner corps of the Teutonic order of chivalry as established in Austria.

Meantime the advance of the Imperialists on Kumamoto was progressing slowly and was stubbornly opposed at every step. From the 23rd of March till the 4th of April there was constant and severe fighting along the northern line, especially near Kidome. Some of the Imperial regiments were decimated, and of a single company which went into action on the former date, 174 strong, there remained on the latter only twenty rank and file, one field officer, and one corporal. The result of these encounters was nevertheless favourable to the Mikado's forces, for on the following days they possessed themselves of Kidome, Kigamé, and Kumafu to the north of Kumamoto; whilst Kuroda, after marching slowly up from Yatsushiro and being reinforced by 3000 men, took Udo and appeared before Kawajiri. But though their lines were thus gradually converging on the enemy and were now only ten or twelve miles from each other, the rebels still presented a bold front on all sides, besides maintaining a rigid investment of the beleaguered garrison.

The latter was now reduced to great straits. It had lost 468 officers and men in killed and wounded. Provisions were fast failing and the scanty rations of the men were composed only of rice-gruel and boiled millet. Surrender seemed almost inevitable, but Colonel Tani decided on making a final attempt to escape this catastrophe. On the 8th of April he caused a battalion of the garrison to sally forth to the south of the town, where a sortie was least expected, and it succeeded in reaching Kuroda's force without serious loss on the same evening. Kuroda then advanced close to Kawajiri, the chief position and hospital depot of the rebels to the south of Kumamoto. He attacked this place on the 10th, and fighting commenced again on the same day along the northern line, and continued without any marked success on either side until the 13th. The Imperialist generals then found, to their great surprise, that the rebels had withdrawn their forces from the positions they had hitherto occupied and that they had abandoned the siege. Their retreat was conducted in a most masterly manner by Saigô, who, in the face of superior forces, was able to draw off all his men in good order, carrying with him his wounded, ammunition, and camp equipage.

The road to Kumamoto was thus open, and

the Mikado's troops advancing from north and south occupied the town and castle on the 14th of April, the southern division being the first to enter. The garrison, it was then seen, could not have held out more than ten days longer.

CHAPTER XIII.

Position of affairs after the relief of Kumamoto—Attempts at mediation—Plans of the rebel leaders—Importance to both parties of the possession of Kagoshima.

The relief of Kumamoto, though effected with difficulty and after a lapse of fifty-five days, was nevertheless a most satisfactory event for the government, since it raised the prestige of the Imperial arms and discouraged outbreaks in other parts of the country. On receipt of the news, the Mikado immediately despatched one of his attendants to thank Prince Arisugawa and his troops for the zeal they had displayed in his service, and to present Saké * and dried fish, the customary

* The national beverage of Japan. It is brewed from rice, and the best quality is not unlike Manzanilla in colour and flavour.

congratulatory gifts in Japan, to the commander-in-chief and leading officers of the army. The relief was, however, only a partial success, as Saigô had escaped with his army, instead of being surrounded and forced to surrender, as some members of the government expected. To effect this relief above 33,000 men and twenty-four guns had been employed, and their loss up to its date had been 3876 killed and 6748 wounded. It was therefore evident that a still larger force than the 36,000 men originally placed in the field would be necessary to annihilate the rebels, who, having recognised their mistake in attempting the formal siege of a fortified place, were not likely to repeat it and might be expected to be more active in their movements than hitherto. Their losses had been about 2600 killed and 5300 wounded, but their ranks had been refilled, and their retreat from Kumamoto showed that their army was still highly efficient. Kuroda's entry into that town left the whole country south of it open to them, and it was a country of a mountainous and difficult character, where their knowledge of the passes afforded them no little advantage over their opponents. The scene of the war was thus likely to become more extensive, and reinforcements were required to execute the plan of the campaign now adopted by the Imperialist generals, which was to drive the rebels down to the south of Kiushiu and there exterminate them.

The Imperialist army was accordingly reinforced, and by the middle of April there were again 33,000 men ready for active operations in Kiushiu. Saigô had still 18,000 men, and a body of 1500 or 2000, which had been lately raised in Satsuma, and had harassed Kuroda's rear during his march from Yatsushiro, was on its way to join him.

A rumour was published by several Japanese newspapers about this time, to the effect that some members of the Shimadzu family, thinking the relief of Kumamoto a favourable opportunity for mediation, had gone to Kiôto, and there attempted to bring about a peaceable arrangement. But it seems much more probable that the object of their journey was to explain to the Mikado's government the inability of the family to prevent assistance being sent from Satsuma to Saigô, and to disclaim all responsibility for the proceedings of the Samurai and people of their province. That family, it is natural to suppose, was anxious to stay the horrors of war before they approached nearer to their own thresholds, but unless they carried with them peaceable proposals from Saigô, any mediation on their part must have been futile, and it is extremely improbable that either Saigô and his men, or the government of Tôkiô, were prepared to make any concessions to each other at this juncture.

A very short time previously, i.e. during the siege of Kumamoto, Admiral Kawamura, a Satsuma man, connected with Saigô by marriage, and entitled by his frank sailor character to think that he still retained some influence with his clansmen, had attempted to stay the further effusion of blood by entering into correspondence with the rebel Samurai. With or without the authority of the government, he had written them a letter, which, with the answer returned to it, is printed below, as tending to throw light on the views and feelings of the two parties :—

"Saigô Takamori, at the head of a hostile
"army, has marched into Higo with evil
"intent, and has thereby incurred the dis-
"pleasure of the Mikado. His Majesty has
"sent military and naval forces to punish both
"him and his followers. After a lapse of
"several weeks, as might have been expected,
"the insurgents have been defeated by the
"Imperialists, for an unjust cause can never
"make headway against a just one. The
"insurgents can neither advance nor retreat,
"and there is nothing left for them but to die
"among the hills and on the moors. Day
"after day have the insurgents looked that
"some other clans would come to their assist-
"ance, but, as their cause is an evil one, such
"expectations must for ever go unfulfilled.

"My heart overflowed with sorrow when I
"heard that Beppu and Hemmi* were endea-
"vouring to induce men in Kagoshima to
"join them, by means of false representations,
"or by exciting their fears. As their cause
"is bad, and they have met with no suc-
"cesses, they are necessarily compelled to
"have recourse to such means.

* Two of Saigô's adherents.

"I have for some time past been intending
"to write a letter to you, but have been
"unable before to do so, on account of my
"many duties. Hearing that Yamazaki, the
"commander of the *Hô-shô-kan*,* had written
"to you on two occasions in the same spirit
"as that in which I wished to address you, I
"trusted that you might receive his argu-
"ments with favour. I now write a few
"words to explain to you the justice of my
"views.

"It is needless to say that it can never be
"justifiable for a subject to take up arms
"against his ruler, or to plunge his country
"into strife, in support of an unjust cause.
"At the present time our country has a mass
"of foreign and internal questions to deal
"with, and the present state of the country
"demands that they receive the greatest
"attention, in order that the foundations of
"progress and civilisation may be soundly
"laid. If, then, at a time when such im-
"portant questions are pending, you allow
"yourselves to be roused to anger and dis-
"turb the peace of the country, you do your-

* A Japanese man-of-war.

"selves infinite harm, inasmuch as you are "weakening the power of your own nation. "Now I am well aware that, although you "have involved yourselves in the present "Rebellion, you are not the originators of "it, and if you will confess yourselves in the "wrong, and surrender yourselves, as I ear-"nestly hope you may be induced to do, I "will petition the government to extend to "you all possible leniency. If it be your "intention to die, is it not better for you "to die in your country's cause than to die "rebels, disgraced and dishonoured? Let me "entreat you to put this question to your-"selves, and to endeavour to come to a right "decision."

The following was the answer to the above:

"We have had the honour of receiving a "communication from your Excellency, Kawa-"mura Sumiyoshi, vice-minister of marine. "Having considered your arguments, we have "come to the conclusion that they are one-"sided, and that your Excellency does not "weigh the questions fairly.

"The originators of the present troubles

"are Ôkubo and Kawaji. Saigô Takamori,
"when residing in Kagoshima, held the
"rank of general-in-chief of the army. He
"is thus a high officer of the throne. But
"Ôkubo, Kawaji, and others, in direct viola-
"tion of the laws of the nation, attempted or
"caused to be attempted his assassination.
"This is the entire cause of the present civil
"war. Yet the government take no notice of
"those who thus violated its laws. If, there-
"fore, laws are not to be binding on certain
"individuals, confusion must prevail, and bad
"men will usurp the place of good. Under
"such circumstances, it is useless to look for
"any tranquillity in the empire.

"These were the causes that induced Saigô
"Takamori to set out from Kagoshima to
"obtain redress from the government, but on
"his arrival in Higo, he was opposed by the
"Imperial troops, his rank and titles were
"taken from him, and he was proclaimed a
"traitor. This was not done by consent of
"the Emperor, but by those who wished to
"conceal their own crimes and deceive the
"Mikado.

"We are therefore much angered, and have

"determined to destroy these corrupt officials,
"and to disperse the infernal clouds which
"surround the Emperor and the Imperial
"throne.

"Those whom your Excellency in your
"letter styles Imperialists, are in our eyes
"merely rebels, used by a set of corrupt
"officials to destroy reason and justice. As
"such they must be destroyed.

"You say you will petition the government
"to extend its clemency toward us if we will
"surrender. This is ridiculous. We are
"fighting for justice, and in a just cause we
"care not what our fate may prove. Your
"Excellency further says that we may recover
"our honour. This we cannot understand.
"Surely the cause of justice is honourable.
"How then have we lost our honour?

"So greatly do we differ from the views
"expressed by your Excellency, that we think
"your Excellency must be out of your mind,
"or speaking under the influence of night-
"mare. When your Excellency has exhausted
"all your talents, you had better come to
"Kumamoto and ask our pardon. We beg
"to inform your Excellency that this is the

"last time we shall hold any communication "with you."

These letters speak for themselves, and it is scarcely necessary to point out, on the one hand, that in referring to the possibility of leniency being extended to the men, Kawamura significantly omits all mention of the leaders—or to call attention, on the other, to the contemptuous tone of the rebel answer. The feelings which dictated it still existed with undiminished force; and, besides, Saigô was still at the head of a formidable army—an army of Samurai, who hold generally that it is disgraceful to retreat before a superior force unless when utterly broken, and with many of whom, especially those of Satsuma, this doctrine has a power like that of religion.

On the other side the feelings of animosity and fear with which Saigô was regarded by several members of the government, especially the Satsuma members of it, were too intense to admit of conciliation, and the latter, flushed with the Kumamoto success, were now more hopeful than ever of ultimate and complete victory. They, at any rate, expressed no desire for a truce, but openly stated their conviction that the war was *à outrance* and that Saigô would never surrender.

As regards the rebel commander, the relief of Kumamoto and the junction of all the Imperial troops in that town, which became Prince Arisugawa's headquarters on the 16th of April, convinced him of the futility of all further attempts on his part to march northwards. It is said that this event raised serious doubts in his mind as to the eventual success of his enterprise, and that in a fit of despondency he even contemplated putting an end to what might be a hopeless war and would probably bring terrible misery and distress upon his native province, by committing *hara-kiri*. Dissuaded from this purpose by Kirino, he declared himself in favour of marching with all his forces directly to the northern borders of Satsuma and confining his action to a vigorous defence of that province. A council of war was held, but Saigô being in a minority, it was decided to make a stand in Hiuga and Bungo, a part of which latter province is separated from the Island of Shikoku by a branch of the sea only fifteen miles wide at its narrowest point. Thus a hand might be stretched to any bands from that island who might wish to join the rebels and who might succeed in escaping the vigilance of the Imperial men-of-war cruising in the straits. This movement would, it was calculated, also allow time for organising resistance in Bungo, where the rebel cause was favourably viewed. The mass of Saigô's forces accordingly took up and fortified with earthworks the strong positions of Koyama, Mifune, Ôtsu, &c., some ten or twenty miles east and south-east of Kumamoto; whilst orders were sent to the commanders of the force which had been hanging on the rear of Kuroda's troops to oppose any southward movement of the Imperialists in the direction of Yatsushiro. At the same time great efforts were made to obtain recruits for the rebel forces from the south, and a strong body of their men was despatched to Kagoshima.

After the evacuation of that town by the Imperialists on the 13th March it had remained quiet, but had never ceased to aid the rebel cause. The Shimadzu family had neither the influence nor the material force requisite to prevent this assistance being given, and the municipal authority had been seized by Katsura Yémon, an ardent supporter of Saigô. Alleging that he was acting under official orders, he obtained large quantities of ammunition from the arsenal, and these, together with much rice which he easily procured from the people of Satsuma and Ôsumi, were sent up to Saigô, whilst bodies of men from the adjacent country were as constantly joining him. The magnitude of the error of evacuating Kagoshima now became apparent to the Imperialist commanders, who were assembled in the castle of Kumamoto for the purpose of drawing up the future plans of the campaign, and its re-occupation was at once decided upon. A force consisting of 7000 infantry and police, a detachment of artillery with eight field-pieces, and a body of engineers under the command of Admiral Kawamura and Generals Takashima and Ôyama was consequently despatched southwards by sea on the 23rd of April, and landed at Kagoshima on the 27th without resistance, Admiral Kawamura being furnished with full powers relative to the government of the town.

The Imperialists found Kagoshima almost deserted. The inhabitants had heard of their coming, and, under the impression that they would burn it, hurriedly left the town for the neighbouring islands. The wealthy took their portable valuables with them, and the poor whatever they could carry off in small boats. The rabble of the town had waited till the last moment and looted many of the *godowns** in which the owners had deposited their property. Almost every house of importance had been sacked, and the place was a scene of devastation and desolation.

The importance of the possession of the town of Kagoshima was also fully recognised by the rebels, and they had as above stated sent a corps to occupy it. This corps arrived too late, and before describing its operations it is necessary to trace the course of the Rebellion in the more northerly provinces.

---

* Fire-proof store-houses. The word *godown* is said to be of Indian origin. It is used by all European residents in China and Japan.

CHAPTER XIV.

Course of the civil war in the north—Division of the rebel army into three corps—Annesty proclamations—The Imperialists take Hitoyoshi, and enter Satsuma — Merciless character of the war.

It would appear that the Imperial commanders on entering Kumamoto were uncertain of the direction in which Saigô had retreated from that place.

The following order of the day, issued by the adviser to the commander-in-chief immediately after the relief of Kumamoto, bears evidence of this uncertainty: "After fighting "both night and day for the past fifty days, "we have succeeded in reaching Kumamoto "castle. But the insurgents after retreating "have, it is said, posted themselves at Koyama, "Yabe, and Ôtsu, where they have con- "structed batteries and are defending them- "selves persistently. We must therefore con- "tinue zealous and press onwards in support "of our cause."

Bodies of armed police were therefore despatched to reconnoitre the enemy's position and a body of 600 of these men, having attacked Mifune, were repulsed with considerable loss by the rebels.

It then became evident that the latter were still in great force and that considerable preparations would be necessary before attacking them. These being completed, Generals Yamada, Kawaji, and Takashima made a combined attack on the 20th April on Koyama, Ôtsu and Mifune. Severe fighting took place on that and the following day, which resulted in the retreat of the rebels from their positions. The most obstinate resistance was made at Mifune, where the rebels lost 500 men killed.

Being thus obliged to abandon their positions, the rebel army was divided into three corps. The main body retired upon Hitoyoshi, a castle town of considerable strength in the province of Higo, containing about 4000 inhabitants, and distant about 40 miles from Yatsushiro, with which it is connected by the river Kumagawa and a road running along the banks of the stream. On the 5th of May this town was occupied by 5000 men under Saigô and Murata, whilst 7000 or 8000 more were échelonned along the river and at and around Ôguchi.

The second corps was despatched in all haste towards Kagoshima and appeared on this same day at Kajiki, at the head of the Gulf of Kagoshima, and at other places to the north of the town.

A third body of insurgents retired to Nobeoka, a strong castle town of about 8000 inhabitants in the north-east corner of Hiuga, and not far from the frontiers of Bungo, into which province detached bands were sent in different directions and as far north as Takeda.

The Imperialists followed the rebels to the line of the Kumagawa, which they found occupied by them from a little south of Yatsushiro to above Hitoyoshi, and into the province of Bungo, and towards Nobeoka, whilst Kawamura and his corps defended Kagoshima, where they had erected batteries at all important points and covered the north side of the town with a line of rifle-pits, capable of containing about fifty men each, and protected by stockades and sand-bags.

This was the state of affairs in the early days of May, but before these operations could be completed, Prince Arisugawa issued the following proclamation:

" On examining the rebel captives, it has
" been found that many of them followed
" Saigô, the leader of the Rebellion, thinking
" that they were forwarding the interests of
" their country, and not knowing that they
" had turned traitors by opposing the Imperial
" authority; and again, it has been discovered
" that many of them think that they would
" not be forgiven, even though they should
" surrender themselves to the Imperial army,
" and for this reason have resolved to oppose
" us to the death. But such a supposition is
" entirely false. Were any among them to
" repent their opposition to the Imperial au-
" thority and submit themselves to the same,
" they would be pardoned. So all such had
" better surrender themselves without losing
" a moment and free themselves from the
" odium of Rebellion."

About the same time the newly installed Imperial prefect of Kagoshima, Iwamura Michitoshi, addressed the following letter to Saigô:

" Since you took up arms, you have re-
" peatedly offered resistance in Higo to the
" armies of the sovereign, and though you

have displayed great valour, you have in the end been defeated and it is evident that you cannot recover your lost ground. How can you have the heart to turn your spear in another direction, to stir up the Samurai and people and to trifle with war. I, Michitoshi, unworthy as I am, have accepted the office of prefect of Kagoshima. I am now in the prefecture and devote myself to contriving the happiness and safety of the inhabitants. How can you, who have lived and grown up in this place, take pleasure in what is pain and poison to them. But if you speedily come forth on behalf of your adherents and atone for your crimes, thus saving the Samurai and people from being cut off by death before their time, you will be 'sacrificing your 'life to preserve your virtue complete.' Thus you will perhaps be able to atone to a slight extent for having failed to distinguish between loyalty and treason. I, Michitoshi, am invested with the functions of a shepherd of the people and I cannot endure the pain I feel. On this account I am moved to address this letter

" to you and to offer this counsel. May you
" be influenced by it."

Neither of these appeals had any material effect. Saigô was still confident of being able to raise the Samurai of other provinces against the government, and declared to his friends that he could continue the war for two years; and the mass of the Satsuma people believed his words. So the prefect's letter remained unanswered and only about 300 Samurai of Higo availed themselves of the amnesty offered in the prince's proclamation. They had never been very ardent in Saigô's cause, and the latter's followers accused them of treachery in allowing Kuroda and his corps to land at Hinaku and march on Kumamoto.

In the three districts which had now become the scene of active operations, a great deal of fighting went on with varied success for several days. The advance of the corps from Kumamoto on Hitoyoshi and Ôguchi was obstinately disputed and the Imperialists met with several reverses in this quarter. On the 22nd of May, however, they succeeded in taking Sashiki and many of the rebel stockades on the Kumagawa, and towards the end of the month they crossed the lower part of the river, having taken Yatsushiro by a flank movement. Thus they kept gradually advancing southwards, driving the rebels before them on to the strongest point of the Kumagawa line, Hitoyoshi. On the 30th a desperate conflict took place at Nakagano, a village about five miles from the town, in which the rebels were beaten with great loss, and on the 1st of June they were driven out of Hitoyoshi.

The Imperialists lost no time in pushing forward their troops and on the 4th entered the province of Satsuma, and after several successsful engagements took Kakuto, Ôguchi, and various other strong positions within its northern borders. Thus the province of Higo was entirely restored to the Mikado's authority, and the mass of the rebel forces retreated into Hiuga and entrenched themselves at Takaoka, Miyako-no-jô, and Takajô. Sadowara nearer the coast became for a few days the headquarters of Saigô, but he subsequently removed them farther south to Miyazaki and there threw up earthworks and stockades and prepared for a determined stand.

These successes of the Imperialist arms were not gained without very considerable losses, and as the rebels still held all Hiuga and Ôsumi and the greater part of Satsuma, whilst numerous bands of them overran Bungo in several directions, there was no prospect of a speedy termination of the war.

Reinforcements were still demanded by the Imperial generals, and more troops and policemen were constantly sent down from Tôkiô to the scene of the struggle. Ten thousand men were drafted into the regular army, and the large proportion of youths and old men in their ranks showed the strain that was being put on the government resources. As the war lasted it became each day more destructive and more bloody; towns and villages were burnt by both sides, and quarter was neither asked nor given by either. Driven back to their homes, the rebels fought with increased determination, and an address which Prince Arisugawa issued to the army about this time affords evidence of the feelings which animated the troops on both sides. He reminded his men of their successes before Kumamoto, but pointed out "that the rebels "were now hard pressed and were driven to "desperation, so that additional watchfulness "and valour were called for in order that the "soldiers of the Imperial army should not be "taken unawares and defeated. The honour of "the army was concerned in carefully guard-"ing against any negligence which might "give the enemy an undue advantage."

Meantime the war in Bungo was carried on with varied success. The rebels took the towns of Saeki and Usuki on the sea coast, and held them for some time. But being inferior in numbers to their opponents in this quarter, and probably the least efficient in arms, &c., of their corps, they were gradually forced towards the southern frontier of the province, and about the 24th of June entirely driven out of it, and obliged to retire to the neighbourhood of Nobeoka.

CHAPTER XV.

Course of the war in the south—Failure of the rebels to retake Kagoshima—They retire to the province of Hiuga, and are pursued by overwhelming forces—Miyako-no-jô taken by the Imperialists—Japanese war stratagems—Effects of the fall of Miyako-no-jô.

THE chief point of interest, however, during the months of May and June, was Kagoshima. It has been stated above that after the relief of Kumamoto both parties had become alive to the importance of that town, and had sent troops to occupy it. Those of the rebels, numbering above 10,000 men, arrived too late, and, though they found the Imperialists already in possession of and prepared to defend it, their commander, Kirino, the most adventurous of Saigô's lieutenants, who could count with certainty on the active support of the neighbouring population, determined to attack it. Its outskirts had been burnt by the Imperialists, who expected an attack, but many fire-proof buildings and stone walls still remained standing, and under cover of these and of the trees and bushes, the rebels were able to approach close to the Imperialist outposts. On the 6th of May they made a general attack, which was driven off with great loss by Kawamura's artillery and riflemen, and, nothing daunted by this repulse, repeated their assaults more than once during the following fortnight. At the same time they threw a line of earthworks round the northern side of the town, and thus held Kawamura and 10,000 men at bay, though the latter had the entire command of the sea.

This state of things, varied by partial encounters, lasted till the 5th of June, when the fall of Hitoyoshi and Ôguchi enabled the Imperialist commander-in-chief to send the army which had cleared the line of the Kumagawa river, farther south. It marched in three divisions, and was constantly harassed by flying bands of rebels, as well as by the natural difficulties of the country. Thus it was not till the 23rd of June that one of the divisions under General Kawaji was able to enter Kagoshima from the south, after making a wide détour to the west.

Admiral Kawamura, thus reinforced, made a general attack on the rebels, and succeeded in driving them from some of their positions and capturing some of their guns. The two other Imperial divisions arrived in the vicinity on the 1st of July, and Kirino then saw that he was vastly outnumbered, and that further attempts to take the town would be useless. He therefore retreated at once, and succeeded in repeating the able strategy practised by Saigô before Kumamoto, and in withdrawing all his forces in good order. He directed his march northwards, towards Miyako-no-jô, thus threatening the Imperialist communications with Kumamoto.

The power of the rebels was, however, now broken. They had put forth their utmost resources to retake Kagoshima and had failed, and the occupation of that place, and of all the province of Satsuma by the Imperialists, prevented them from refilling their losses in men and munitions. All their money had been expended during the siege of Kumamoto; they had subsequently paid for their commissariat supplies in promissory notes bearing the stamp of the Satsuma commander-in-chief, but though these were for some time readily accepted by the farmers, they were now no longer considered as guarantees of future payment. The rebels were consequently now obliged to seize provisions wherever they found them, with or without the consent of the owners. In order to make projectiles for their small arms, they laid hands on the metal utensils of the peasants and merchants, leaving only those necessary for the boiling of rice, and they even took away the weights from the fishermen's nets for the same purpose.

Their strength now lay chiefly in their exact knowledge of the country, which enabled them to pass rapidly from one point to another, through the hills and valleys, menacing the Imperialists on all sides, and disappearing, if not in sufficient force to attack them. Habited in the light costume and straw sandals of the country, which allow perfect freedom to the limbs and feet; inured to the heat of their southern clime, and unembarrassed by large commissariat trains, they were more than a match in marching capabilities for their opponents. Most of the latter wore European uniforms for the first time in actual warfare; numbers of them came from the northern and cooler provinces; and very many were so distressed and footsore, from the use of the regulation leathern boot, that it was often found necessary to discard it and allow the men to resume the sandal which is worn by every Japanese of the lower class.

No Satsuma Samurai had, however, as yet thought of surrender, and Saigô and Murata, and the other leaders of the clan, were organising an obstinate resistance in the province of Hiuga, the only one which now remained completely in their possession. The population was there favourable to their cause, and they had there several castle towns of strength, such as Takanabe, Nobeoka, and Sadowara. In these towns they had also the means of making ammunition, as well as at Miyaka-no-jô, which is in the centre of the richest rice district of the province. This town is of considerable size, containing about 7500 inhabitants, and is situated in a fertile plain, surrounded at a distance of seven or eight miles, by rugged hills. It now became the headquarters of the rebels in southern Hiuga, and Nobeoka was strongly occupied by them in the north, whilst Saigô himself held a central position at Miyazaki.

Against these places the Imperial forces

were now directed, and their plan was to penetrate into Hiuga between them so as to divide the rebel corps in two and prevent them from supporting each other. To effect this object five colümns were sent against Miyaka-no-jô. One under General Takashima was despatched from Kagoshima by sea, and landed at Shifushi, to the south of Miyaka-no-jô. Two others under Generals Soga and Ôyama marched from the Gulf of Kagoshima, or south-west, and two other columns commanded by Generals Miyoshi and Miura were to approach Miyaka-no-jô from the north-west. At the same time Nobeoka was to be assailed by two other columns, one consisting of most of the garrison of Kumamoto and other troops which had swept Bungo free of the rebels advancing from the north, under General Tani, and the other from the west. All these columns were strongly reinforced in July, 10,000 men having been sent down to Kiushiu about the middle of the month under Prince Higashi Fushimi. The fleet was to co-operate with the land forces. Thus it was hoped that the Rebellion would be crushed in Hiuga, against which 26,000 men were to be concentrated.

It was not without difficulty that the Mikado's government met all the calls on its resources at this time, but it was as determined as ever to suppress the Rebellion by force, and at the same time maintain tranquillity in the rest of the empire. It had 40,000 men in Kiushiu, where, besides the field forces, garrisons were required in the provinces recovered from the rebels, and it was now obliged to augment the number of its troops in Tosa and disarm the inhabitants of that province; for, though Itagaki remained true to his plan of reforming the government of the country by lawful means, a considerable number of the Tosa Samurai were of a different opinion, and strong grounds existed for believing that they intended to cause a diversion in Saigô's favour.*

The march of these converging divisions of

* Proofs of the existence of this plot, as well as of another for the murder of some of the ministers, were obtained by the government in July 1878, and the originators of it, twenty-one in number, were condemned to degradation from their Samurai rank, and to terms of imprisonment varying from ten years to one hundred days.

the Imperial army was impeded at every step by guerilla bands, which were kept well-informed of the movements of their enemies by the peasantry, and resisted their advance at every mountain pass. Thus by the 16th of July the divisions under Soga and Ôyama had only reached Kirishima-yama, about forty-five miles from Kagoshima. Many days were spent by the division coming from Hitoyoshi and Kakuto in reducing the strongly entrenched rebel positions on the north-eastern side of Miyako-no-jô, and the Bungo column was retarded by a fresh irruption of the rebels into that province.

It was thus not till the 24th of July that a general attack was made on Miyako-no-jô. The three divisions of the Imperial army under the command of Generals Takashima, Soga, and Ôyama, and a battalion of armed police then assaulted the place and a desperate engagement ensued which lasted the whole day. The town, it is said, was finally taken by stratagem. Two young officers, desirous of distinction, organised a forlorn hope of about eighty men, and making a wide détour during the night, approached it from the side opposite to that from which the general attack was being made. Challenged by the outposts, the officers feigned to be leading a rebel reinforcement, and, addressing their men in a loud voice, shouted to them: "Here is a town of the Imperialists, let us "make a desperate attack on it and endeavour "to take it, so that we may be rewarded by "our Commander Kirino." This ruse succeeded; the adventurous band was allowed to approach, and at once fell upon the surprised garrison, by whom its members were killed almost to a man; but during the diversion thus created, the general assault was continued with renewed vigour and the Mikado's flag soon floated above the walls of Miyako-no-jô.

Stratagems of all sorts are said to have been employed in the almost daily encounters which took place during the war. The accounts of some of them given by the Japanese newspapers are probably not always reliable—but the mere fact of their publication shows that there was a good deal of fighting of a primitive character during the campaign. Thus both the rebels and

Imperialists are stated to have frequently resorted to the device of planting pointed bamboos and sharp nails in the ground, and covering them with loose earth, in front of their positions, for the purpose of retarding and harassing each other's advance. On other occasions the rebels are said to have been in the habit of rolling barrels down the hill-sides towards the enemy's lines. Each barrel contained a man fully armed, who, on disengaging himself from his envelope, attracted the attention of the outposts, who at once rushed to cut him down. Whilst thus engaged, volley upon volley was poured upon them by the rebels at the top of the hill. This stratagem was sometimes varied by filling the barrels with powder or other combustible matter intended to explode in the Imperialist lines.

In the early period of the war, too, there was a band amongst the rebels who, in an engagement, fell to the ground and feigned death, in order to rise and take their enemies in the rear: whilst the garrison of Kumamoto lured the rebels on to attack by throwing open the castle gates—before which they had laid mines. This stratagem succeeded once or twice, and the rebels lost many men from the explosions and the grape-shot poured into them.

The combat before Miyako-no-jô was severe. The Imperialists lost above 300 men, and the rebels many more, as they were almost surrounded. They succeeded, however, in making good their retreat, but the fall of the town was felt by both parties to be a certain indication of the final result of the civil war. Saigô himself seems to have concluded that its end was approaching, and the letter which he addressed to his followers about this time was doubtless intended to communicate this opinion to them:

"Through your determination and bravery," he said, "we have fought for the last half-" year. At first there was every prospect " of our success, but our strength having " gradually failed, we are now in a state of " great distress, having hardly any position " where to make a stand. Our troops have " been as effective as those of our opponents, " but we have been outnumbered, and hence " the present crisis. The enemy will not let

"this present opportunity slip, but will un-
"doubtedly advance against us to try and
"crush us. Therefore make up your minds
"for still further zeal in our cause, die in
"advancing and not in retreating, so that
"no taint of disgrace may be attached to
"our names hereafter. This is my earnest
"advice."

The Imperialists likewise foresaw in this event the end of their labours. It placed the south of Hiuga completely in their power; they were so strong in Higo that they could leave the defence of that province to subordinate commanders; they were masters of Satsuma and Ôsumi; and the capture of Miyako-no-jô reduced the area occupied by the insurgents to the northern half of Hiuga. The struggle was no longer considered by the government sufficiently serious to require the Mikado's presence at Kiôto, and, by their advice, his Majesty returned to Tôkiô with the Empress on the 31st of July, having left Kiôto on the 28th.

CHAPTER XVI.

Battle of Nobeoka—Desperate position of the rebels—Saigô's irruption through the Imperialist lines—Panic at Tôkiô—Saigô enters Kagoshima—Retires to Shiroyama—Is surrounded by the Imperialists—Assault of Shiroyama—Death and burial of Saigô and his Samurai.

FROM Miyako-no-jô the rebel army retreated in small bodies to Takaoka, Miyazaki and Sadowara and was hotly pursued.

These towns were taken on the 31st of July, and their garrisons, after vainly attempting to hold the castle town of Takanabé, were obliged to retire farther northwards on the 2nd of August, and to evacuate Hososhima, another strong position only twelve miles south of Nobeoka, a few days later.

There now remained only one stronghold in Saigô's hands, viz. the castle town of Nobeoka, in the north-eastern corner of Hiuga, and hither the remnants of his army directed their march. Again they were followed on all sides by the Imperial troops, who gradually closed in upon them, and succeeded in cutting them off from Nobeoka and taking possession of it on the 14th of August. Thus the district held by the rebels was reduced to a space of four or five square miles, and within these narrow bounds some bloody engagements took place between the 15th and 18th. Saigô and Kirino directed the rebel forces, and the five Imperialist divisions, numbering 25,600 men and thirty-two guns, were commanded by Generals Tani, Nodzu, Takashima, Ôyama, and Myoshi. The rebels, whose numbers were reduced to less than 10,000 men, had expended almost all their ammunition and had only a few rounds of powder, of such inferior quality that their bullets fell almost harmlessly in their enemy's ranks; they nevertheless manfully contested every inch of ground, but were finally driven to an eminence near the centre of their position and there completely hemmed in.

A council of war was held on the 18th, in the rebel camp, under the presidency of Saigô. The desperate condition of their affairs was fully recognised by all the members of the council, and it was unanimously decided that a continuation of the war was hopeless, that, consequently, the mass of the army must lay down its arms, whilst Saigô and those who were most compromised, or who preferred death to surrender, should fight on till they were killed. Orders to the above effect were accordingly issued, but the men refused obedience to them, stating that they would defend Saigô to the last, and die fighting for him. Thereupon the leaders of the clan, convinced that as long as they remained with their men, it would be impossible to alter their resolution, and animated by a desire to prevent further and useless effusion of blood, determined to leave the army secretly and make their way back to Kagoshima.

The execution of this decision was at once commenced, and was favoured by a thick fog. Saigô, accompanied by Kirino, Murata, Beppu, Hemmi, and about two hundred of the Satsuma Samurai, who were determined to follow their leader to the death, made a sudden and unexpected onslaught on the positions held by Generals Miyoshi and Nodzu, threw their troops into disorder, gained possession of their camps, where they seized supplies of ammunition and food, and having thus broken through the Imperial lines, disappeared amongst the mist-covered hills.

Several thousand rebels then laid down their arms; amongst them being Katsura Yemon, who surrendered to General Nodzu, with 8000 men, 3000 of whom were wounded; and a day or two afterwards their example was followed by other small bodies of men, who still held out in the hills of southern Hiuga or Satsuma.

The news of these surrenders was telegraphed to Tôkiô, and the government at once ordered most of the Samurai, enrolled as policemen and gensdarmes, to be disbanded. The ministers as well as the public considered that the war was at an end, and for more than a week this opinion was confidently entertained by both of them.

The former were therefore as dismayed as the latter were surprised when, on the 3rd of September, telegrams arrived in the capital from Nagasaki, announcing a rebel victory close to Kagoshima, and the re-occupation of a part of that town by Saigô and his forces. The sensation caused at Tôkiô, and throughout the country, was great; 1700 of the Tôkiô police were at once despatched to Kagoshima and were followed by 800 troops. Fears were also entertained of an attack on Nagasaki, and a division of troops was sent there, whilst the governor was instructed to construct earthworks round the town. This panic was not, however, astonishing, for even to the Imperial commanders at the seat of war, Saigô's irruption through their lines was a surprise.

At first they thought that Saigô had marched on Kumamoto, which had been left with a very small garrison, and a large number of troops was at once sent to that place to ensure its safety. When, after the lapse of several days, no news of him was received from this quarter, Prince Arisugawa appears still to have had no reliable information as to the rebel movements, though he took the precaution of despatching General Miyoshi with a considerable force to Kagoshima by sea. The following order of the day, issued by the commander-in-chief on the 2nd September, leads us indeed to the inference that it was not till that, or the previous day, when Saigô was already in Kagoshima, that absolute certainty as to his whereabouts was acquired at headquarters :—

" Half a year has now been passed in the
" work of suppressing the western rebels.
" Now, strong as the rebels were, they have
" been beaten in battle after battle, and their
" strongholds have been overthrown. All this
" is owing to the valour and zeal of the officers
" and the men of the Imperial army; but the
" rebel leader has made his escape from us, and
" once more appears in the front. He has
" again entered his old den, and is there
" committing acts of violence. We must
" not treat him and his forces with con-
" tempt, but endeavour to become still
" further zealous and careful, so that in
" the end we shall gain the day and make
" known to the Emperor that we have been
" completely victorious."

Meanwhile Saigô and his followers, after breaking through the Imperial lines, had disappeared in the hills towards Mitai, on the Higo frontier. They seem then to have avoided the high roads, and to have completely outwitted their opponents, of whose movements they were kept well informed by the peasantry.

Clinging to the hills, and marching along bridle-paths and over unfrequented passes, they moved swiftly and without molestation towards the south, and on the 28th appeared at a place called Kobayashi, not far from Kajiki. General Miyoshi had already landed at the latter place, and was making his way to Kagoshima, when on the last-mentioned date his rear-guard was surprised and defeated by Saigô and his two hundred men. Miyoshi marched on towards Kagoshima, and made a stand at the village of Yoshino, with the purpose of preventing the rebels from entering the town. Saigô, however, avoided another combat with him, and making a détour entered the city on the 1st of September from another side. Nearly the whole of its garrison had been sent northwards some time previously to co-operate with the rest of the army in Hiuga, and the defence of the place had been left to about 1000 raw recruits and some armed policemen. These were speedily driven into the lower part of the town near the harbour. The civil authorities fled on board a man-of-war, and, by their advice, many of the people departed to the country. Thereupon

Saigô notified his return in the following proclamation:—

"We entered Kagoshima to-day. The "officials of the ken have fled; the garrison "and the police forces are on the verge of "being overcome, and we have so far gained "a thorough victory. Such being the case, "whenever any policemen are seen in the "district they should be arrested and brought "to our headquarters here.

"This letter must be circulated in haste "through all parts of the province."

Messengers were accordingly at once despatched to the neighbouring villages to raise men, and 400 Samurai joined Saigô in the next two days.

He had got possession of some of the batteries and almost the whole of the town, but his efforts to capture the Imperialist troops were vain. They had entrenched themselves in the quarter abutting on the harbour, where they could not be surrounded, and there they stubbornly held their ground during the 1st and 2nd of September. On the 3rd, Admiral Kawamura, who had been watching the coast of Hiuga, arrived with the fleet, but finding that he could not land in the town itself without exposing his men to much loss, he steamed to a harbour some five miles to the north. He there disembarked, and being joined by General Miyoshi's forces, marched towards Kagoshima with the intention of taking the rebels in the rear. Saigô then withdrew, with large supplies of rice, small arms and ammunition, as well as some guns, which he had been able to seize, to the summit of a hill, called Shiroyama, in the rear of and commanding a large portion of the town, overlooking, too, the cradle of the Rebellion, the buildings, namely, of the "private schools." There he entrenched himself, with about five hundred followers, all of them Samurai of the Samurai; all probably personal friends of their chief; all determined to sell their lives dearly, and all equally determined to die rather than surrender—five hundred lions driven back, after a weary long chase, to their lair—no longer able to spring, but still capable of grappling with jaw and claw all that came within their reach.

The hunters knew full well the nature of their foes, and warily they approached what Prince Arisugawa had aptly termed their den.

Such it was—a depression in the rocky summit of a hill, where the elements have scooped out some holes scarce worthy the name of caves. In these a few of the rebel leaders found shelter, whilst their men made huts with brushwood torn from the hillsides, and fenced the steep slopes around their position with wattled stockades.

On their side, the Imperialists lost no time in surrounding the base of the hill with similar and stronger lines. They dug trenches and raised earthworks at all the exposed points, and summoning troops from all quarters, they placed a force of 15,000 men in such positions that the sorties attempted on one or two occasions by the rebels at the commencement of their imprisonment resulted in the destruction of all the men composing them. A few days sufficed for the completion of these lines, and on their expiration the rebels were helplessly confined in their eyrie prison.

A violent death, starvation, or capitulation on any conditions that might be determined by the victors, were the only alternatives before them. In any terms of surrender that might be proposed, life alone was probably all that could be offered to so great a rebel as Saigô, and this, after a career like his, he would undoubtedly spurn. On the other hand, his mere existence, even as a prisoner, would be a constant source of anxiety to the government, as well as of unrest to the country. It is therefore most probable that no endeavours to induce him to surrender were ever made by the Mikado's commanders, and that the government had decided to annihilate the Satsuma leader and his immediate adherents, who had so long been a thorn in their sides. To carry out this purpose, great deliberation was used, and everything was done to prevent a recurrence of Saigô's daring exploit at Nobeoka.

The Imperialists had completed their lines about the 10th of September, and they then proceeded to erect mortar-batteries, to arm their earthworks with fifty-pound guns from the ships, and to shell the rebel position from them and from their men-of-war. The bombardment was carried on day and night, causing a loss of about 200 men in the rebel ranks, and covered approaches were at the same time constructed up the flanks of Shiroyama. Feigned attacks were also made from time to time, and the rebels, who could only reply feebly to the Imperialist fire, were thus kept constantly harassed.

This state of things continued until the 23rd of September, when two emissaries from Shiroyama arrived in Kagoshima and demanded an interview with Admiral Kawamura. On being received by him, they commenced their parley by asking: Why they were treated as rebels? What wrong had they done? The admiral then interrupted them by saying that it was useless to ask questions of this nature, and by enquiring if they had any message for him from Saigô. They replied in the negative, but added that they had come to ask whether Saigô's life would be spared if the rebels surrendered. To this Kawamura answered that the Mikado alone could grant pardon, and that he was not in a position to entertain any other proposal than that of an unconditional surrender; that he would await a further communication from the rebel camp till 5 P.M. that day, and that, if none arrived before that hour, he would give orders for an assault on their position. The men departed and never returned; and it is highly improbable that Saigô had any knowledge of their mission.

Admiral Kawamura, whose preparations were all made, and who had reason to believe that Saigô's provisions and ammunition were nearly exhausted, kept his word. Before dawn on the 24th of September a tremendous shower of shells was poured on the summit of the hill, and under its cover and in the darkness the assaulting parties quickly scaled its slopes. They reached its brow almost without loss and thence fired volley upon volley with deadly effect into the rebel camp. Deceived by the previous feints, the rebels had been taken unawares and unprepared for a serious attack. Their batteries were seized and their gunners cut down at the first onslaught. Their guns were turned upon themselves. They resisted, as far as men could resist, with their small arms, but the contest was too unequal to last. Saigô was amongst the first to fall, wounded by a bullet in the thigh. Thereupon Hemmi Jiurôda, one of his lieutenants, performed what Samurai consider a friendly office. With one blow of his keen heavy sword he severed his chief's head from his shoulders, in order to spare him the disgrace of falling alive into his enemy's hands. This done, Hemmi handed the head to one of Saigô's servants for concealment and committed suicide. Saigô's head was buried, but so hurriedly that some of the hair remained exposed, and it was subsequently discovered by a coolie. Around Saigô fell Kirino, Murata, Beppu, Ikegami Shiro, and one hundred of the principal Samurai of the Satsuma clan, who had sought to protect their chief to the last, and refused to survive him. The rest of the rebels, 210 in number, many of whom were severely wounded, were overpowered and disarmed, and this bloody tragedy, which had commenced in the misty dawn of a fair September morning, was terminated before the sun had sped one hour and a half of his course. The Imperialist losses were only thirty men, and as a considerable quantity of ammunition and provisions for ten days were found in the camp, it is evident that the rebels did not think that their last hour was come.

On the day succeeding the combat, the dead were brought down from the battle field into the town for identification and burial. In the cemetery of the small temple of Jôkô-ji a broad trench had been dug, and near it the corpses of the fallen were laid out side by side. It was then that the bodies of Kirino, Beppu, Hemmi, Murata, and the other leaders were recognised. All bore traces of the deadliness of the fight, and many were literally covered with wounds. Close to the body of Kirino lay the headless trunk of a tall well-formed powerful man, with a bullet wound in the thigh and a stab in the stomach. Whilst the officers of the Imperial army were discussing as to whether the body was that of Saigô or not, a head was brought in by some soldiers. It fitted the trunk and was recognised as Saigô's head. It was disfigured and ghastly, clotted with blood and earth. Admiral Kawamura, the senior officer present, reverently washed the head with his own hands, as a mark of respect for his former friend and companion in arms during the war of the Restoration.

The bodies of Saigô and the leaders mentioned above by name were placed in coffins. The other corpses were wrapped in blankets. Saigô lies in the centre of the large grave where all are interred, and the rest are placed in rows on either side of him. Over the grave stands a large wooden tablet on which are inscribed the names of the dead, and the date on which they fell.

Thousands of the people of Satsuma have since visited this grave and there offered up their prayers; and, in the popular belief, the spirit of their once great general has taken up its abode in the planet Mars and his figure may there be seen, when this star is in the ascendant. The spirits of his followers have not, according to this same popular belief, soared so high; for the people say that a new race of frogs has appeared in Kiushiu; that the spirits of the dead rebels have animated this race, and so imbued it with their own courageous nature, that the frogs attack man whenever they see him and never desist from their attacks until they are killed.

CHAPTER XVII.

Termination of the Rebellion—State of public feeling in regard to Saigô—Rewards for the services of the army and navy—Festival in honour of the fallen—Punishment of the rebel prisoners.

" It is hereby made known that on the
" 24th inst. Akihito, Imperial Prince of the
" second rank (commonly called Arisugawa-
" no-Miya), and commander-in-chief of the
" army of chastisement, reported to his Im-
" perial Majesty by telegraph that the rebels
" of Kiushiu have been reduced to quiet."

This notification, signed by the prime minister of Japan, was posted on all the notice-boards of Tôkiô on the morning of the 25th of September, and it was by means of this laconic placard that the inhabitants first learnt that the Rebellion was completely stamped out, and that peace was again established throughout the Mikado's realms.

The news was received in the capital and throughout the country without enthusiasm and yet without indifference. There were no manifestations of joy, no signs of triumphal rejoicing. The predominant sentiment appeared to be one of relief, largely mingled with feelings of admiration and regret. Ever since the battle of Nobeoka, on the 17th of August, it had been evident to all that the power of Satsuma was utterly broken, and the public mind had then been relieved from much of the anxious speculation as to the consequences of the struggle which had occupied it for more than a year. The feeling of relief had therefore been, so to say, discounted to a considerable extent in the interval of five weeks which elapsed between Saigô's irruption through the Imperial lines and his death on the summit of Shiroyama, and the popular mind had now leisure to dwell on the daring nature of his last exploit and the tragic character of his death.

If, as was rumoured at the time, Saigô's intention in returning to Kagoshima had been to gain possession of a man-of-war or a merchant steamer, and seek safety in some foreign land, and if he had carried out this intention, the mention of his name would soon have failed to excite emotion in the popular mind. But there were no longer any grounds for believing that he ever entertained such an intention, and the general impression was that, refusing to survive the loss of the cause for which he had fought, and for which he had sacrificed the lives of so many of his clansmen, he had deliberately decided not only on losing his life, but also on losing it at Kagoshima.

All Japanese have a high appreciation of heroism, and whatever might have been Saigô's motives in making war upon the established government of his sovereign, this deliberate choice of the manner and place of his death tended to enlarge the heroic halo which had always surrounded his name in the eyes of the mass of the nation. The educated classes, too, were, to a considerable extent, now inclined to take a lenient view of Saigô's career. They did not of course pretend that his action in taking up arms was justifiable, but they showed a tendency to minimise the criminality of this action, and of his general conduct as a public man, by attributing to him motives, based on abstract principles. "Rule by force" was, they said, the maxim upon which he acted, and it was this which brought him to ruin. Soon after the Restoration he arrived at the conviction that the government had entered on a wrong path and that some terrible catastrophe, either internal or from abroad, must sooner or later happen to it. Hence the necessity, according to his view, of maintaining the military strength and spirit of his clan. For, when this crisis should arrive, it was his ambition to appear on the scene at the head of the Satsuma men as the Saviour of Society. In this ambition, it was argued, there was nothing discreditable; and, consequently, Saigô's great error lay in his implicit trust in the efficacy of his maxim, which made him forget that social quiet and "Rule by force" are incompatible. To use the words of this class of reasoners, it "was a source of deep regret that exclusive "reliance on military force caused Saigô to "stumble at the close of his career, and the "world to sigh over the loss of a great hero "of the East."

The members of the government no doubt participated more or less in these feelings and wisely took them into account. They therefore decided that there should be no general public rejoicings on the occasion of the termination of the Rebellion, and that the manifestations of joy in the capital should be limited to ceremonies in recognition of the services of the army and navy, and in honour and memory of those who had fallen on the Imperial side.

Accordingly, on their return from the seat of the war, there was no triumphal entry of the troops into Tôkiô, no display of pageantry, no decoration of the streets. Each regiment was marched quietly off to its barracks, and the return of the superior officers alone was greeted with military honours.

Prince Arisugawa-no-Miya, the generals commanding under him, and the admirals engaged in active service during the Rebellion, were received at Yokohama with salutes befitting their respective ranks, and afterwards conducted to the Imperial Palace by escorts of cavalry. They, the ministers and the principal civil employés, to the number of 100, were subsequently entertained at a banquet by the Mikado, and received decorations and gratuities. On Prince Arisugawa was conferred the highest order in the Emperor's gift, and the words which were addressed to him by His Imperial Majesty at the ceremony of investment, on the 2nd of November, are worth reproduction, as the mention there made of the Emperor's ancient lineage of 10,000 years' descent, in close juxtaposition with that of an Order established only the other day, and the most recent imitation of European customs, is typical of the transitional state of the country.

"I, who, by the will of Heaven, am Emperor "of Japan, descending in one unbroken line "for 10,000 years, confer on you, Prince "Arisugawa, a man of the highest merit, "commander-in-chief of the army, and "president of the senate, this decoration of "the highest class of the Order of the "Chrysanthemum, and you are herewith in- "vested with all the dignities and privileges "appertaining to the said Order."

The prince was at the same time raised to the rank of commander-in-chief of the Mikadô's land forces, or field-marshal, a title never previously granted to any one but his late opponent Saigô. The grand cordon of the Order of the Rising Sun was simultaneously bestowed on the ministers, and the second class of the same Order on all the generals and admirals who had been engaged in the war; whilst the subordinate officers of both branches of the service were named to lower grades of this Order, and the men received gratuities in money.

The ceremony, or rather festival, in memory and honour of those who had fallen during the Rebellion, was celebrated in Tôkiô on the 14th of November and two following days, after the return of the Imperial guards and the troops belonging to the garrison of the capital from the seat of the war. The place of celebration was a large open space on an eminence, commanding a fine view of a considerable portion of the city, which had been set apart, on the removal of the Imperial court from Kiôto to Tôkiô, for the purpose of holding annual festivals in memory of those who had been killed in battle during the war of the Restoration. At one end of this space a large temple had been built, to which the appropriate name of Shokonsha, or shrine for welcoming spirits, had been given. It was in pure Shintô style, i.e. of plain uncoloured and unvarnished wood, and contained neither images nor ornaments, but only a mirror, which is regarded in Japan as an emblem of the purity of the soul, and in Shintô shrines

takes the place of the cross in Christian churches. The rest of the space had been laid out, with the admirable taste of Japanese landscape gardeners, into ample pleasure-grounds, containing a race course, wrestling arena, and other places of amusement.

This year the annual festival was celebrated with more than usual solemnity. Early in the morning of the 14th of November, the Mikado, attended by all his ministers and a numerous suite, proceeded in state to the temple, and, after paying his vows at its entrance, ascended a throne erected in the inside. The troops then marched past the throne, each company halting in turn before the temple door to salute the sovereign and offer the customary prayers for the dead. The Mikado then returned to his palace, and the grounds were thrown open to the public. Horse races, wrestling, theatrical entertainments, military music, and fireworks were provided by the government on a great scale for three days, which were kept as public holidays; and this festival—such a strange mixture to the European mind of the religious and the profane—attracted enormous crowds of spectators, being attended not only by the lovers of sight-seeing (What Japanese is not?), but also by the relations of the dead, for whom a special place was set apart.

Having thus rewarded the services of the military and naval forces, the Mikado's government had next to turn its attention to the punishment of the rebels.

Some time previous to the termination of the Rebellion, a special court-martial, composed of some of the highest judicial authorities in the empire and under the supervision of Prince Arisugawa-no-Miya, had been appointed to try the prisoners, and had proceeded to Nagasaki as the most convenient place for the purpose. There it had held its sittings during the months of September and October, and its labours were brought to a close at the end of November. The number of persons accused before it, of complicity in the Rebellion, was 42,740. Of these, 246 were declared innocent of the charges brought against them, and 39,632 were pardoned and discharged. Of the remainder, 2718 were sentenced to terms of imprisonment, with hard labour, varying from five years to thirty days, or to deprivation of rank and fines, and only 124 to imprisonment for periods of from five to ten years. Twenty persons were condemned to decapitation, and the leniency of these sentences shows that both the members of the court-martial and of the government fully appreciated the desire, universally expressed by the native press and the public, that justice should be largely tempered with clemency in its treatment of the offenders. The government, it may be said, could well afford to be merciful, since nearly all the leaders of the Rebellion had been cut off during its course or had fallen with Saigô. But their conduct on this occasion will doubtless receive its due meed of praise if the duration and nature of the Rebellion be borne in mind, and if due regard be had to the fact, so often forgotten by critics of Japanese affairs, that Japan is not in Europe, but in Asia, where vengeance is more common than mercy.

Amongst the accused there was one whose punishment was held to be well merited by almost all parties. It was Ôyama Tsunayoshi, vice-governor of Kagoshima at the outbreak of the Rebellion. His sentence ran as follows:

"Ôyama Tsunayoshi, a Samurai of the "Kagoshima prefecture. During the time

" you acted as governor of the Kagoshima
" prefecture, you, in violation of the laws of
" the empire, assisted Saigô Takamori and
" others in their treason. You received the
" confessions of police sergeant Nakahara
" Hisao and others, which were merely con-
" cocted by the 'private school' party, you
" had them printed and you circulated
" throughout the Kagoshima prefecture, a
" notification to the effect that a plot to
" assassinate Saigô and others had been dis-
" covered, and that Saigô was in consequence
" about to proceed to Tôkiô at the head of
" his troops. In order to excite the sympathy
" of the people of the country, you despatched
" emissaries to other prefectures and cities.
" You further employed the officials of your
" prefecture in the service of the rebels and
" handed over 150,000 yen (£30,000) belong-
" ing to the government to Saigô. Further-
" more, you established a commissariat depart-
" ment within the grounds of the government
" house, in order to furnish the rebels with
" supplies. For these crimes you are de-
" prived of the rank of Shizoku and sentenced
" to undergo decapitation."

The sentence was carried out at once, and, as above remarked, there were few who sympathised with Ôyama's fate. By the Imperialist party he was considered a greater traitor than even Saigô. For, in their eyes, he was as much a government official as the governor of any other prefecture, and had betrayed the trust imposed in him in the most flagrant manner. By those who had all along sympathised with the Satsuma cause, and by all those who, from romantic and sentimental feelings, now deplored the death of Saigô, Ôyama could not now be regarded with favour. For, by his own confession, he had prevented Kawamura and Saigô from meeting at Kagoshima before the actual outbreak of hostilities, when, as many people now thought, an amicable settlement of the Satsuma grievances might have been arranged. Now that the Satsuma cause was lost for ever, and that its great leader was in his grave, there was little commiseration amongst either of these classes for the man whose conduct had so greatly contributed to these results, and who, it was now argued, might possibly have prevented them.

About the same time another trial of persons who had played an important part in the outbreak of this Rebellion was brought to a conclusion. Nakahara Hisao, and the other policemen, on whose confession the story of the plot to assassinate Saigô was founded, and the Kagoshima officials, who had received these confessions, were brought up and confronted before a tribunal presided over by Prince Arisugawa-no-Miya. Nakahara and his comrades were acquitted of the crime of plotting assassination, with which they were charged, and set at liberty. The chief of the Kagoshima officials, Nakayama Takamori by name, and a Satsuma Samurai, was convicted of having, "by order of the superintendent of "the Kagoshima police station, cruelly put "Nakahara Hisao and others to torture and "forced them against their will to append "their seals to the confessions drawn up by "the said superintendent." For this crime he was sentenced to deprivation of rank and to imprisonment with hard labour for ten years. Several other Satsuma Samurai were at the same time sentenced to minor terms of imprisonment for complicity in this affair.

CHAPTER XVIII.

CONCLUSION.

Cost of the Rebellion, in men, property, and money—Japanese finance—The national debt—Land-tax—Pension commutation Act—Effect of the Rebellion on the financial position of the country.

THE history of the Satsuma Rebellion would be incomplete without some account of its cost to the country. It will therefore be necessary to burden this chapter with some statistics which may appear dry to the general reader, but will, it is hoped, be of use in computing the resources of Japan.

The total number of troops actually employed by the Imperial government in the Island of Kiushiu in the suppression of the Rebellion was as follows:—

	Men.
Infantry, 58 battalions . . .	56,318
Engineers, 2 do.	1,512
Military train, ½ do . . .	310
Police	7,000
Total . . .	65,140

Artillery, 4 battalions, 48 guns.

The total number of rebels under arms,

from the date of their march from Kagoshima to that of the last combat on Shiroyama, is computed by the best authorities at 40,000, 23,000 of them being natives of Satsuma and Ôsumi. There were thus, during the seven and a half months' duration of the Rebellion, more than 100,000 fighting men in the field. The whole of this large force was never, however, present in Kiushiu at one and the same time. The Imperial army there never numbered more than about 40,000 men, and the utmost strength of the rebels at any one time did not exceed 20,000 or 22,000 men.

Besides this large number of combatants, there was a vast multitude of coolies in the service of the Imperial armies. The exact number is not known; but the authorities of the war office stated that they had paid for no less than 12,856,700 coolies' days' work. If these figures be divided by the number of days' duration of the Rebellion, it would appear that the Imperial armies employed no less than 50,000 coolies, in round numbers, per diem.

The naval forces of the empire, comprising 17 men-of-war and transports, and bearing

58 guns, and crews numbering about 1500 men, which were constantly employed in watching the coasts and bombarding the enemy's positions, must also be taken into account, as well as many of the steamers of the Mitsu Bishi Company which were frequently chartered for the conveyance of troops, ammunition, and provisions.

The losses of the Imperial army were,

	Killed.	Wounded.
Soldiers	6,220	10,000
Coolies	147	528
Missing	32	
Total	6,399	Total 10,523

The losses of the rebels were,

Killed.	Wounded.
7,000	11,000

Thus in men the Rebellion cost the country 13,399 killed and 21,523 wounded, and a large number of the latter subsequently died of their wounds.

It is difficult to compute the loss of property. The town of Kagoshima was almost entirely destroyed and a great part of Kumamoto laid in ashes. Other towns, such as Miyaka-no-jô, and a great number of villages, suffered severely, and the calculation made by the Japanese authorities, that 50,000 houses were destroyed during the Rebellion, does not consequently appear exaggerated.

Japanese houses are almost always built of wood, and this material is exceedingly cheap. They contain little furniture and their average value is said to be not more than £7. The loss caused in this item of houses would therefore be £350,000. But this sum only represents a small portion of the sacrifices entailed on the inhabitants of that part of Kiushiu where the war was carried on, because, for the greater part of its duration, the rebel forces were unable to pay for their supplies and lived entirely at the expense of the population.

These expenses, and the losses consequent on the depression of trade, induced by the long duration of the Rebellion were, nevertheless, light in comparison with the expenditure which was incurred by the Imperial government, and which had naturally to be borne by the country. The transport to the Island of Kiushiu of 50,000 soldiers, many of whom came from remote provinces of the empire; the arming and equipment of new levies; the enrolment of large bodies of police for service in the field, and in those provinces, such as Tosa, where disaffection was known to be rife; and the maintenance and hire of 50,000 coolies during a seven months' campaign, strained to their utmost the resources of the ministry of finance; and, when the accounts of the war department were finally made up, it was found that the suppression of the Rebellion had cost the state 42,000,000 yen or £8,400,000. This additional outlay is a very large sum for a small and poor country, and its effect on the financial position of the empire can hardly be explained or appreciated without some remarks on its financial system.

Amongst all the reforms which have been enacted and put in practice in Japan since the Restoration, there is perhaps none more striking than that of its financial system.* Up to the year 1868, or, more correctly

* For further information on this subject, *vide* reports by the author in "Reports by Her Majesty's Secretaries of Embassy and Legation, on the manufactures, commerce, &c., of the countries in which they reside, presented to both Houses of Parliament, by command of Her Majesty," in 1877, 1878, and 1879.

speaking, up to 1871, when the clans were finally abolished, the empire, as is well known, was divided into a large number of petty feudal states. Each of these states administered its own finances, and possessed the right of issuing paper money; a right of which many of them availed themselves to a great extent.

The central government assumed the task of unifying the financial system of the whole empire in 1871, and already in 1873 it had made such progress in elucidating the chaotic confusion of the system in practice under the feudal régime that it was able to publish estimates of the national expenditure and revenue for that year. These estimates were, it is now admitted, as incorrect in substance as they were faulty in form, but each succeeding year has brought with it improvements in both these respects, and since the year 1875 the annual statements of the estimated expenditure and revenue of the country, published by the minister of finance, have wanted little to make them as clear and explicit in form as the documents of a similar nature issued in some European states. They are, however, only estimates, and there is at present no means of verifying the correctness of the figures which they contain. Balance-sheets of the actual revenue and expenditure of the year 1875–76 have, however, been prepared, and though not yet published by the minister of finance, they will, according to the latest information, show that the errors of the estimates in question were on the right side, and that there will be a small balance from that year in favour of the treasury.

It would be out of place to enter here into a detailed explanation of these estimates and those which have since been published, but there are one or two points in them which are closely connected with some of the government measures mentioned in that part of this work which treats of the causes of the Rebellion.

The most important of these measures were the compulsory pension commutation Act, promulgated in August 1876, and the Act of February 4, 1877, reducing the land-tax from 3 to 2½ per cent. on the value of the land.

Now, according to the minister of finance's statement for the fiscal year, July 1, 1875—June 30, 1876, the public revenue and expenditure of Japan were, in round numbers,

£13,700,000; whereas, in the statement for the year 1877–78, both are reduced to about £10,250,000. Thus in two years the revenue had fallen off to the extent of above three millions, and the expenditure had to be reduced by the same amount. There had been a change equally remarkable in the state of the national debt.

The contraction of debt appears to be one of the necessary and primary results of the adoption of Western civilisation by Asiatic states, and Japan has been no exception to this rule. As long as it lived in seclusion the greater part of the taxes and of the government expenditure was paid in kind. Rice, the great staple agricultural produce of the country, was the medium for almost all payments. The measure of a man's wealth and income was calculated in rice, and it formed the standard of value in most of the transactions of daily life. But when Japan was brought into contact with the West, money became necessary, and the country was accordingly speedily endowed with the privilege, enjoyed by all European states, of borrowing money. In 1875–76 its national debt was about

£9,000,000, some £3,000,000 of which had been raised in London; whilst the amount of government paper money in circulation was about £19,000,000. Thus, the total debt of Japan at this time was in round numbers about £28,000,000. In 1877 it had risen to nearly £70,000,000.

The causes of this increase, as well as the causes of the simultaneous decrease in the revenue and expenditure of the country, are all intimately connected with each other and with the internal policy of the government.

The reduction of the land-tax caused the decrease in the revenue, and necessitated a diminution of the expenditure; this, it was thought, could only be attained by the pension commutation Act, and the latter measure induced an increase in the national debt. Each of these measures requires some further explanation.

As regards the land-tax, it may be remarked that from the most ancient times the Japanese appear to have been an essentially agricultural people. The geographical position of their country primarily, and in later times the state of complete isolation from the rest of the world in which they were for centuries kept by their government, debarred them from all trade and commerce with foreigners, and hence a careful cultivation of the soil must have been absolutely necessary, at a very remote date, for the maintenance of a population which, when we first hear of Japan, more than three centuries ago, seems to have been more dense than that of any European country at that date.

Kaempfer, who visited the country in 1690, says: "The Japanese are as good husbandmen "as, perhaps, any people in the world. Not "only the fields and flat country, which are "seldom or never turned into meadows* or

* The domestic animals of the Japanese were originally only the horse, the ox, the buffalo, the dog and the cat; sheep and goats were introduced by the Portuguese, and pigs by the Chinese; but none of these quadrupeds were used for food. The smallness of their number, perhaps, originated a distaste for animal food, and this was, no doubt, confirmed by the doctrine of the transmigration of souls, one of the most important tenets of the Buddhist religion, which is professed by a large majority of the Japanese people. Fish, which abounds in their seas and rivers, seems to have been always largely consumed, and an exception in its favour as an article of food appears to have been made by the Buddhist priests, when their religion was established in Japan. The Shintô religion does not appear to contain any disciplinary regulations regarding the diet of its votaries, and the use of animal food is now becoming common in the large towns.

"pasture grounds, but likewise the hills and "mountains afford corn, rice, peas, pulse and "numberless edible plants. Every inch of "ground is improved to the best advantage, "and hills and mountains, many inaccessible "to cattle, which would be wholly neglected "in other countries, are cultivated up to their "tops." Subsequent travellers speak in the same strain, and at the present day there is nothing more striking for a European disembarking at one of the treaty ports than the garden-like culture of every available patch of ground.

According to Japanese authorities, the whole soil of the country was, previous to the latter part of the twelfth century, actually the property of the Mikado, and they give the following as one of the systems of land tenure then in force: The land, they say, was divided into squares, each of which was subdivided into nine equal portions. Eight of these were leased to as many farmers, on condition that they should collectively cultivate the ninth portion, always the central one, for the Mikado. Whether or not this or similar arrangements were general, or how long they lasted, it is impossible to say, but it is certain that the feudal system, introduced by the Shôguns in the thirteenth century, completely put an end to them.

During this and the following centuries, the country was constantly a prey to civil strife; the Shôguns and the Daimiô, who had acquired possession of their respective provinces and distributed the land amongst their retainers, being ever at war with one another. It was from the land that they drew the means of carrying on their wars and maintaining their state and clansmen, and hence it was that the land became burdened with taxation. At the time of Taikô Sama (1585–98), four-tenths of the produce of the soil were exacted by his government, six-tenths being left to the cultivator, and this proportion seems to have been retained in the territories of the Shôguns until their extinction in 1868. In the other provinces the tax levied by the Daimiô seems to have varied considerably, and is said to have been everywhere greater than in the Shôgun's lands. In some parts of the country it was six-tenths, and Kaempfer says that in his time, the Satsumese were taxed at two-thirds of their produce by their lord.

The theory that the Mikado was lord paramount of the soil, seems, however, not to have been forgotten or lost sight of during the six or seven centuries of his forced seclusion at Kiôto; and the Daimiô, who were most instrumental in bringing about the Restoration, reaffirmed it in the most distinct terms in their petitions for permission to restore their fiefs to the crown. The Daimiô of Satsuma, Chôshiu, Tosa, Hizen, and Kaga stated in their memorial: "By the conferring "of lands and property the Emperor governs "his people; they are his to give and his to "take away; of our own selves we cannot "hold a foot of land." And again: "The "place where we live is the Emperor's land, "and the food which we eat is grown by the "Emperor's men. How can we make it our "own?"

The petitions were granted, and in 1871 the Mikado's government became the recipient of the land-tax. It was at that time paid in kind; its amount varied in different provinces of the empire; and there were all sorts of anomalies and inequalities in its collection. No general survey of the cultivated lands had been made for more than two centuries, and during this long interval the relative value of many of them had undergone great change. In some places floods had carried off part of a field; in others, irrigating streams had altered their courses. Farmers selling portions of their farms had agreed to pay the entire tax on the portion they retained, and thus brought untaxed lands into existence; whilst new lands, brought under cultivation subsequently to the last survey, had remained free of all burdens.

A reform was urgently necessary, and the first step towards it was made in 1872, when an Imperial decree was issued ordering a new assessment of the tax. The old method of calculating it according to the amount of produce was abandoned, and the saleable value of the land was adopted as the basis of the assessment. To ascertain this value a new survey was commenced, and in making it the surveyors were ordered to take into consideration the capabilities of the soil, the expense of cultivation, the means of irrigation, the proximity to or distance from markets, &c., of each property. A valuation was then struck, and on this valuation a tax of three per cent. payable in money* was levied. Title deeds were at the same time prepared and handed to the occupiers as soon as the new assessment of their respective holdings was completed. They thus became tenants in perpetuity, and their position will perhaps be more easily understood if the term land-rent be substituted for that of land-tax. All the minerals found below the surface were reserved to the crown, and the Mikado is therefore the lord of the manor of the whole of Japan.

This three per cent. land-rent was not, however, to be final, for the decree went on to state that it would be reduced gradually to one per cent. as soon as the customs duties became sufficiently remunerative to allow of this being done.

These duties had not increased to the desired extent when the land-rent was reduced to 2½ per cent. in January 1877, and there is no doubt that this reduction was made at the time in question in order to conciliate the landholders, and to prevent manifestations of discontent on their part at a

* Vide note, p. 99.

moment when the government had to deal with the disaffection caused amongst the Samurai by the pension commutation Act.

The Samurai, as was noticed in the first chapter of this work, were the military retainers of the Daimiô. Their ancestors had received grants of land under the feudal system and originally cultivated these lands themselves. But as the authority of the Mikado became circumscribed by the increasing influence of the Daimiô, and as the latter gradually added to their privileges and attained to a state of semi-independence, permanent bodies of military retainers became more and more necessary for the maintenance and service of each petty baron. The cultivation of the land was therefore handed over to an agricultural class, and the Samurai were constituted into a distinct and separate caste, to the members of which hereditary pensions were accorded. These pensions were paid in the form of allowances of rice, and in return for them the Samurai devoted themselves entirely to a military life. In course of time, and especially when the country was in a state of tranquillity, they applied themselves to letters and literature, and finally, by their monopoly of the pursuits of arms and learning, they became the de facto rulers of the country.

The central government assumed the responsibility of the payment of these pensions nominally in 1868, and actually in 1871. It soon found that the services of the Samurai were not only not required, but that the existence of bodies of armed men of their character and numbers, animated as they were by a strong feeling of clannish attachment to their chiefs, was an encumbrance to the treasury and might become a danger to the state.

The government, therefore, decided on their suppression, and the nature of the measure finally adopted by it for this purpose, in August 1876, has been already indicated. In this place we have to deal chiefly with the financial results of that measure.

In the years 1875 and 1876 the average charge on the state for the pensions of the nobles and Samurai, after deducting the income tax on the same, was in round numbers, £3,100,000. This charge was abolished by the commutation Act, and in lieu of it there appeared in the estimates of the year 1877 an addition of £35,000,000 to the principal of the national debt and a charge of £2,300,000 for interest on the same.

By the commutation Act, therefore, the state got rid of a perpetual charge of £3,100,000, and assumed a temporary charge of £2,300,000, plus the obligation to raise and pay off a capital sum of £35,000,000 within thirty years, the term fixed for the total amortisation of the bonds issued to the pensioners. The operation was, financially, simply the removal of the heaviest charge on the treasury, viz. the item "Pensions," from the estimates of the years 1875 and 1876, and its insertion in a modified form under the heading of "Interest on the Domestic Debt" in the estimates of 1877; and this circumstance is worthy of the consideration of those who take an interest in Japanese finance, as well as of those who represent the commutation of the pensions as an act of unnecessary harshness and wanton spoliation. Before condemning this measure in such sweeping terms, it would seem to be incumbent on the latter class of persons to demonstrate that Japan could continue to follow the path of Western civilisation without it, and to show that the financial position of the country would have been more satisfactory than it now is, if it had not been carried out.

The financial effects of this Act and of the reduction of the land-rent had naturally to be taken into consideration by the government in treating the cost of the Satsuma Rebellion, which, as above stated, amounted to £8,400,000. This large sum could not, it was evident, be raised by increased taxation. For the total annual revenue of the country was not more than £10,250,000, eight-tenths of which accrued from the recently reduced land-rent. Its addition to the national debt, so lately swollen by the effect of the commutation Act, would have thrown fresh burdens on the people, and seemed likely to shake the credit of the government. It was therefore considered advisable to adopt a middle course. £3,000,000 was borrowed at 5 per cent. interest from a native bank, and a new issue of paper money was made, to the amount of £5,400,000.

Thus the Satsuma Rebellion, besides the other losses and extra expenditure which it entailed on the nation, has contributed to the √ inflation and depreciation of the paper currency, from which Japan appears to be now suffering, and the extent of which may be gauged by the fact that the government paper money is now at a discount of 12 or 14 per cent. as compared with gold.

CHAPTER XIX.

Political effects of the Rebellion, as regards the province of Satsuma and the agitation for constitutional changes in Japan —Memorial of the Tosa reformers—Assassination of Ôkubo—Institution of local and elective assemblies.

THE political effects of the Satsuma Rebellion remain to be considered. This Rebellion was, it may be said, the natural outcome of the state of things which existed in the country during the later centuries of its seclusion from the rest of the world; for it could not reasonably be expected that the destruction of a political system as old and as deeply rooted as that of the feudal system of Japan would be accomplished without some violent reactionary struggles.

Hatred of the Tokugawa family and the

conviction that the existence of a dualistic form of government was incompatible with that union of all the forces of the empire which seemed the only means of maintaining the dignity and authority of the country against the fancied invasive projects of the "Western Barbarians," were the chief causes of the fall of the Shôgunate, and of the Restoration of the Mikado. But the objects and motives of the principal actors in these events were not homogeneous. Some of them aimed at the establishment of a new order of things, in which the whole political and administrative power should be centralised in the persons of the Mikado and his ministers. But it is probable that only the most enlightened of these—the small number of men who had some acquaintance with the constitutional forms of government in America and Europe—foresaw from the first the impossibility of founding a central government on a feudal substratum. It is doubtful whether even these fully realised at the time the radical nature of the changes in the political system of the country which would be necessary for the attainment of their object, and it would seem that it was only by degrees that they came to understand the necessity of thoroughly uprooting all feudal institutions.

There were others amongst the chief authors of the Restoration who neither desired nor intended that their action in overthrowing the Shôgunate should lead to the destruction of all the old institutions of their country. The enthusiasm engendered throughout the country by the Mikado's return to power induced them to surrender their fiefs to the crown, and to consent to the abolition of the clans. But they seem to have considered that in their case at least this latter measure was merely to be a nominal change, and they were most decidedly hostile to any curtailment of the power and privileges of the Samurai class, the great bulwark of feudalism. The chief representative of the men who held these opinions was the Satsuma chieftain, and he was supported in them by the mass of his clan. The Rebellion may therefore be looked upon as one of the throes—it is to be hoped the last—of expiring feudalism; and the most direct and important consequence of its suppression was the extinction of the last of the semi-independent states of Japan and the extension of the direct rule of the Mikado's government over the whole empire.

Satsuma, the last of the provinces to retain the separatist ideas of clanship, was finally reduced to the level of the other parts of the country, and rendered obedient to the general laws of the country. The "private school" system, which did not survive the death of its founder, was superseded by the location of a garrison of Imperial troops at Kagoshima. The civil administration was transferred to the hands of Imperial officials, selected without regard to their place of birth, and the taxation was placed on the same footing as elsewhere. The inhabitants of the principality are now learning that they are first of all Japanese, and that the interests of their province are secondary to those of the empire.

These changes were carried out without any disturbance of the peace. The leaders of the Rebellion had failed in their object, and the results of their failure were accepted without remonstrance.

There were, however, other questions, besides the position of Satsuma, which were affected by the suppression of the Rebellion, and which shortly after that event became the subjects of public attention and excited a considerable amount of agitation. The principal of these questions related to the present and future form of government in Japan.

If will be remembered that Itagaki Taisuke, the chief man of the Tosa clan, has been mentioned in the preceding pages as the head of a body of politicians who advocated the establishment of representative institutions, as the best form of government for Japan, and that, though he and his party were averse to the continued existence of the present government, he refused to join Saigô in attempting to upset it, because he was of opinion that the attainment of his object ought not to be attempted by other than peaceable means.

The number of sympathisers in his views in his own province and elsewhere was considerable, and had been from time to time augmented by the adhesion of a good many of the younger generation of Japanese, who had been sent to the United States to be educated and had returned to their homes indoctrinated with the opinions there prevalent regarding constitutional government, self government, popular government, and the liberties and rights of the people. They brought with them the books and treatises which had been instrumental in converting them to their new ideas, and had them translated, printed and circulated; they wrote articles in the native press in favour of their opinions; and they formed societies for their discussion and propagation. In this way Itagaki's views became widely spread and the school of politicians of which he was the head gradually increased in numbers until about the year 1877 it became what would be called in England a party in the state.

The principal of these societies was under the patronage of Itagaki himself, and held its meetings in the province of Tosa; and, in the month of July 1877, it addressed a memorial to the Mikado, praying for a change in the form of government, and setting forth the reasons which, in the opinion of the members of the society, rendered such a change necessary. These reasons were nine in number and were developed at great length. Eight of them formed a direct impeachment of the present government, and the ninth was a reminder that the solemn promise given by his Majesty before the assembled court nobles and Daimiô in 1868, and subsequently repeated on more than one occasion, to the effect that, "a deliberative assembly should be formed and that "all measures should be decided by public "opinion," had never been fulfilled.

The first accusation against the government was that, "it imposed its own oppressive "measures on the country without in any way "respecting the will of the Mikado," in other words, that it prevented the fulfilment of his Majesty's promise to establish representative institutions and constitutional government; that it enforced repressive press laws, thus stifling all expression of public opinion in regard to its proceedings, and that it was an exclusive obligarchy of Satsuma Chôshiu, Tosa, and Hizen men, instead of being composed of men taken indiscriminately from all the provinces.

The second was, that "the administration "was conducted in a random and confused "manner," in exemplification of which it was stated that each member of the government had special aims in regard to his own department and was ignorant of what went on in the other public offices. Each minister acted for himself without regard to the views of his colleagues. The subordinate officials did the same and thus procrastination and confusion were produced in the conduct of public affairs.

The third evil complained of was, that "the "power of the country had been too largely "concentrated in the central government." The duties of the governors of prefectures, it was maintained, were reduced to the collection of taxes and their remittance to the treasury; and their authority was so much circumscribed that they could not even build a bridge or repair a road without reference to the ministry of the interior.

The fourth accusation stated that "the "military system would never be placed on a "proper footing until the mode of recruiting "the army was made to agree with the form "of government." It was not, however, contended by the memoralists that the conscription law was a bad one. On the contrary, they argued that the army which it had produced was far too excellent an institution to be placed under the orders of a despotic government like the present one. The form of government must therefore be made to agree with the mode of recruiting, and the only sort of government which ought to be trusted with such a powerful weapon was a representative and constitutional one, for the memorialists considered it "a mighty wrong that the people "should have to supply the means of carrying "on war, and be compelled to sacrifice their "lives on behalf of a government in which they "had neither part nor voice."

The fifth charge was the mismanagement of the finances, and under this heading the irresponsibility of the minister of finance and the secrecy of his system were strongly dwelt upon. "The government" said the memorialists, "shows us tables of expenditure, but it never "lets us see the real accounts as to how such "expenditure is conducted." The amount of taxation was likewise complained of and the tendency to spend all the proceeds in Tôkiô was exemplified by drawing attention to the wealthy appearance of the capital and the visible poverty of the country.

The sixth accusation stated that the new system of collecting the land-tax constituted an oppression too great to be borne by the people. Here again, it was not contended that the reform was in itself a bad measure. It had only become so in the hands of the government officials who had urged on its execution with unjust and oppressive haste.

The seventh evil was the "method pursued "by the government in equalising the rights "of the Samurai and the common people."

The language used in the treatment of this topic was remarkable, especially when coming from members of the Samurai class, and after their broad statement that "they were of opin-"ion that the first step toward the formation "of a limited government was taken when the "duties of the Samurai were abolished."

"The Samurai of Japan," said the memorialists, "form a class that has existed since the "middle ages; they were controlled by feudal "lords, and their spirit of patriotism, though "confined to their own provinces, was noble. "They possessed great virtues, they hated "the idea of disgrace, they were faithful to "their lords, and they interested them-"selves in the affairs of their respective clans. "The lord of a province and his chief advisers

" were restrained from acts of oppression by
" the watchfulness of the Samurai of the clan,
" who could compel their feudal lord to trans-
" fer his duties to another member of his house,
" or enforce the resignation of an official.
" Since your Majesty took the administration
" into your hands, the feudal system has been
" abolished and the Samurai are no longer re-
" quired. But the Samurai still retained their
" rank, and a certain portion of their rights, in
" consideration of their being superior to the
" common people in education and knowledge.
" Steps should therefore be taken to render the
" people, by education, the equals of the Samu-
" rai, so that they may be able to take the
" same interest in the affairs of their country
" and advance in happiness. This is the will
" of your Majesty.

" But not only are the people prevented
" from taking any part in the government,
" but efforts are made to bring down the
" Samurai to the same slavish level as the lower
" classes. No matter how cruel or despotic
" the edicts of their rulers may be, they are
" expected to make no remonstrance. A great
" mistake has been made in endeavouring to

" lower the Samurai to the level of the common
" people. Encouragement should have been
" given to the latter to raise themselves to the
" level of the Samurai. Instead of this the
" government has acted in a directly contrary
" manner; great consideration should be given
" to this question. The Samurai have always
" taken part in the administration of the
" affairs of their various clans, since the com-
" mencement of the feudal times; their minds
" have thus been familiarised with political
" matters, and they are not content to be
" deprived of all their prerogatives. Although
" their services may be no longer required,
" their minds remain unchanged. It is owing
" to this that nearly all the insurrections that
" have taken place since the Restoration have
" been caused by the Samurai. To raise a
" Rebellion is undoubtedly wrong, but that
" the Samurai should be driven to do so is
" certainly due to some mismanagement on
" the part of the government.

" This is the present condition of Japan.
" Public opinion is in no way consulted.
" Efforts are made to hold both the Samurai
" and the Heimin in absolute slavery. They

"are granted no political rights. They have
"no control over their own welfare. What
"does your Majesty suppose is the cause of all
"this misery?"

The eighth accusation related to the foreign policy of the government, which the memorialists declared to be "incomprehensible" and calculated to "cause foreigners to regard Japan with contempt." It was incomprehensible, because neither the people nor foreigners could understand why the government had refused to listen to the voice of the nation, which demanded that the notorious insolence of the Korean government should be chastised in 1873, and yet had two years later sent an expedition against that country merely because a shot had beed fired by a subordinate Korean officer, possibly without any authority to do so, on a Japanese boat.

In support of the charge that the foreign policy of the government was calculated to cause the country to be regarded with contempt, the cession of the whole of the Island of Sagalin to the Russians in 1875* in exchange for some of the Kurile Islands which the

* The treaty is dated May 7, 1875.

memorialists and most Japanese considered to have been always a part of their empire, was adduced, as well as the despatch of Iwakura's imposing mission to Europe in 1871 for the purpose of revising the treaties with foreign nations and his return without having done anything towards that end.

Such were the principal grounds on which the memorialists founded their petition for a change in the form of government. "Nothing," they concluded, "could more tend to the well-"being of the country, than for your Majesty "to put an end to all despotic and oppressive "measures, and to consult public opinion in "the conduct of the government. To this end "a representative assembly should be estab-"lished, so that the government may become "constitutional in form. The people would "then become more interested and zealous in "looking after the affairs of the country; "public opinion would find expression and "despotism and confusion cease. The nation "would advance in civilisation; wealth "would accumulate in the country; troubles "from within, and contempt from without "would cease, and the happiness of your

"Imperial Majesty and of your Majesty's "subjects would be secured."

The immediate effect of this memorial, which was drawn up in June 1877 and found its way into the hands of the government in the following month, was to augment the feeling of distrust with which the politicians of Tosa had been for some time regarded by the ministers, and to induce the latter to take further precautions for the maintenance of order in that province. For though Itagaki and his school still affirmed that they would never have recourse to violent steps, and that they relied upon moral forces alone in order to obtain their objects, it was feared that the long continuance of the Satsuma Rebellion might encourage some of their followers to depart from this resolution and attempt to make a diversion in Saigô's favour. These fears were not unfounded; for it was about this time, when, in consequence of the memorial, stricter measures of surveillance were adopted in Tosa, that the traces of the conspiracy of some of the men of that province, mentioned in the foregoing pages, were first discovered.

What impression the memorial may have

made in other respects on the members of the government is not known. Their time was fully occupied with the suppression of the civil war; and, after the first sensation produced by the appearance of this remarkable document had subsided, public attention soon reverted to the course of the war, and little was said in public on the subject until the month of May 1878, when an event occurred which, besides being an indirect consequence of the Satsuma Rebellion, has in all probability had some influence on the policy of the government in regard to the important constitutional question raised by the Tosa memorialists.

On the morning of the 14th of that month, a bright genial May morning, Ôkubo Toshimitsu, the minister of the interior, started as usual from his house for the Mikado's palace, where the cabinet holds its councils almost every day. He drove in a brougham, drawn by a pair of horses and attended, according to the custom in Japan, by a *bettô*, or running groom. His way lay through one of the numerous solitary little valleys which intersect the undulating site of the capital, and add so much to its picturesque appearance. It was a sylvan dell, bounded on each side by grassy slopes, crested with grotesque old pine trees and studded here and there with bamboo groves: a dell where the philosopher might think undisturbed, and the painter find worthy studies for his canvas.

As the carriage entered the valley, two men, habited in the costume of the Japanese peasant, in dark blue cotton garments and kerchiefs of the same material and colour, tied negligently round their heads, were seen strolling along the road-way, with bunches of wild flowers in their hands. As soon as it drew sufficiently near for them to recognise its inmate, the men threw away their flowers, drew from under their clothes their long heavy swords, killed the coachman and hamstrung the horses. At the same moment, and almost before the flowers could fall to the ground, four other men, similarly armed and clad, sprang forth from a neighbouring bamboo thicket, and rushed to the assistance of their confederates. Ôkubo, half opened one of the carriage doors. Two men with drawn swords stood before it. He tried to descend by the other, but there was faced by two more keen blades, and then perceived that his hour was come. In attempting to get out, his hand, which he had raised to protect himself, was cut off and his head was cloven by one blow; he was then dragged from the carriage and despatched with numerous cuts and stabs; after which his assassins threw away their weapons and left the ground. The mangled remains of the murdered man were found by General Saigô, a brother of the Satsuma leader, who happened to drive through the sylvan dell shortly afterwards, and were by him conveyed to Ôkubo's house. Meantime the *bettô* had run to the palace, only a few hundred yards distant, and had given the alarm, but before any orders could be issued for the apprehension of the murderers, six men presented themselves to the Imperial guard at the great gate and surrendered themselves as the destroyers of Ôkubo.

On this same morning and about the same hour the editors of two of the principal native newspapers of the capital received by post and for publication, copies of a document signed by the six assassins and addressed to the Mikado, the original of which was subsequently found on the person of the leader of the band. It was entitled "A tale of a traitor's assassination."

This document, as may be inferred from its title, contained a long list of accusations against the ministers and an equally long explanation of the motives which had actuated the assassins. A translation of it was issued some time later by one of the English newspapers of Yokohama, but though it may thus be said to have become public property, it would be unseemly to dwell at length upon its contents, as their publication was at once prohibited by the government as being calculated to promote sedition and disturb the public peace. We shall therefore confine ourselves to a brief notice of two of the statements contained in it regarding the motives and objects of the assassins.

The first of these statements was in general terms, that Ôkubo and others of the ministers, besides being guilty of all the crimes laid to their charge by the memorialists of Tosa, had plotted the assassination of Saigô, Kirino, and Shinowara, and that, this plot being discovered before it could be carried out, they had deceived the Mikado as to the intentions of the Satsuma leaders and driven them into rebellion. Ôkubo and his colleagues were therefore declared to be traitors deserving of death.

The assassins were not Satsuma men; they came from Kaga, one of the central provinces of Japan, but they stated in their "Tale," that having attempted and failed to join Saigô and assist him in ridding the country of its oppressors, their duty as patriots obliged them to obtain this end in the manner above described and by the forfeit of their own lives.

Thus the principal motive of the assassins was to avenge the death of Saigô, and thus the assassination of Ôkubo was one of the consequences of the Satsuma Rebellion. To show the connection of these two events with the question of a change in the constitution, mention must be made of the object of the assassins, and hence the necessity of referring to the second statement in their "Tale."

This second statement was to the effect that the peace and prosperity of the empire could only be insured by the accomplishment of the Mikado's promise relative to the establishment of constitutional government.

Now, it would probably be going too far to assert that this statement had of itself any immediate effect on the government. But taken in conjunction with the representations of the Tosa memorialists and other expressions of public opinion in a similar sense, it may have shown the government that the party which desired a change in the constitution was more numerous and had wider ramifications than they had supposed, and it may therefore have contributed to induce them to take the matter into their serious consideration.

Whether this was the case, or whether the government had already arrived at the conclusion that the time was come to introduce the principle of representative institutions into the constitution, it is impossible to say. But however this may be, a notification was issued by the prime minister on the 22nd of July, 1878, stating that the Mikado had decided on establishing elective assemblies in all the provinces of the empire. A second notification of the same date contained the decisions of the council of state, regulating the election of the members of these assemblies and defining the manner and scope of their proceedings. According to these regulations the assemblies are to hold sessions of not more than one month's duration, in the month of March every year, in each of their respective electoral districts. An account of the actual receipts and expenditure of the local taxes during the previous year is to be presented to them, and, subject to the approval of the ministry of the interior, they are to discuss and settle the method of levying these taxes and of expending the produce of the same during the next year. They can also, under certain conditions, draw up petitions on other matters regarding the welfare of their districts and forward them to the central government.

The number of members in each assembly is to vary according to the size of the districts, and the members must be males of the full age of twenty-five years, who have been resident for three years in the district and pay the sum of £2 as land-tax within its limits.

Insane persons, bankrupts, government

officials, persons holding religious offices, and those who have been sentenced to one year or more of penal servitude for offences not commutable by fine, are not eligible.

The qualifications of voters for the election of members are: that they shall be males of the full age of twenty years, that their names are inscribed on the registers of their districts, and that they pay the sum of £1 as land-tax within the limits of the same.

The disqualifications for voters are the same as those for members.

Finally, the elections are to be made by ballot and the ballot is to be taken by means of balloting papers on which the voters are to inscribe their own names, residences, and ages, as well as those of the persons for whom they vote.

These provincial assemblies are to meet for the first time in the ensuing month of March, and time alone will show whether this cautious and experimental step towards the introduction of representative institutions will prove advantageous to the country, and whether it can at some future time be developed into the establishment of a national parliamentary system of government.

The Satsuma Rebellion and its suppression and the assassination of Ôkubo have no doubt given an impulse to the discussion of constitutional questions, and a large number of Japanese have been led, by these events, to pay increased attention to the consideration of the best form of government for their country. As at present constituted, their government is an oligarchy, composed of a small body of the most enlightened and enterprising men in the country, ruling under the supreme authority of the Mikado; but, if Japan is to continue to assimilate European institutions, this form of government can only be transitional, and the provincial assemblies will, in all probability, be eventually developed into National Parliaments.

The difficulties in the way of such a vast change must be self-evident to all who bear in mind the shortness of the interval which separates Japan from its first acquaintance with Europe, and the country will require the services of all its best men to surmount them. It is therefore to be hoped that the Satsuma Rebellion, which deprived Japan of two of her most prominent public men, viz. Saigô, the most conspicuous amongst those who brought about the Restoration, and Ôkubo, the most resolute of those who have laboured to remodel Japanese institutions on the lines of European civilisation and modern progress, may have proved to the members of all political schools in Japan the uselessness of precipitation and violence, and the necessity of moderation; and that thus any constitutional changes which may be considered advantageous to the country may be effected without civil war or bloodshed, and in a gradual and peaceable manner.

APPENDIX.

CONFESSION OF NAKAHARA HISAO.

"NAKAHARA Hisao, *shô-keibu*,* eldest son of Shôbei, *shizoku* of the district of Ishiu-in in the Kagoshima *ken*: †

"Arrested after search on the 3rd of February, 1877. I was appointed *shô-keibu* on the 4th of January, 1876. Towards the end of November of the same year—I forget the exact day—I went to the house of Kawaji Toshiyoshi, chief of the police, and after learning from him various matters concerning the different *ken*, he ended by telling me that there had been of late indications of disquiet in the Kagoshima *ken*, but said that as Saigô was residing in the *ken*, he did not think there would be any disloyal and riotous proceedings; he added, however, that in case a rising should break out, there was no help for it but for me to confront Saigô and kill him. I submitted to his order, and subsequently—I do not recollect the exact day—I went to the house of Ôyama Kansuke, a *shizoku* of the Kagoshima *ken*, and was told by him, that if Saigô originated any insurrectionary movement he must be killed. I kept these intentions secret, and on the 24th December

* *Shô-keibu*, police corporal. † Prefecture.

Sonoda Nagateru, Suyehiro Nawokata, *chiu-keibu*,* came to my house and informed me of their intention to apply for permission to return to their native districts, and of the many rumours in circulation respecting disturbances in the Kagoshima *ken*. Accordingly I expressed a wish to return with them, to which they consented, and left my house. On the following day, the 25th, I saw Kawaji for a moment at the police office, and told him of my intention to apply for leave to return home, and asked him to use his good offices on my behalf. He replied that that was a good thing, and urged me to show zeal in the service. In view of what had already passed, as above stated, my resolution became fixed. As I had already made a compact with Sonoda Nagateru to meet at his house, I went there at 3 P.M. and there were assembled there, Hirata Saishichi, Nomaguchi Kaneichi, Igakura Tamotsu, Ôyama Tsunasuke, Sugai Seibi, Itani Chikatsune, Suyehiro Nawokata, Yamazaki Motoaki, Takasaki Chikaakira, Anraku Kanemichi, Tsuchimochi Takashi, and others. All present exchanged their views on the subject, and it was settled that we should, on our return, urge upon the members of the *shi-gakko*† from the various districts, and upon other people generally, the impropriety on the part of loyal subjects of exciting a war on no good pretext, and that we should dissuade both those who had already joined the *shi-gakko*, and those who were thinking of so doing from their hostile view. It was arranged that we should all meet on the afternoon of the following day, at an empty house formerly the

---

* *Chiu-keibu*, police sergeant.

† *Shi-gakko*, the private schools.

residence of Kawaji, and applications for leave to return home were sent in, and at once granted. A council was then held at which all attended, and it was there resolved, as the main plan of action, that a division should be brought about amongst the members of the *shi-gakko*, that they should be won over to our side, and that the *shi-gakko* should be broken up; that in the event of the rising taking place, Saigô was to be assassinated, and the fact at once telegraphed to Tôkiô; that then a combined attack should be made by the navy and army, and the members of the *shi-gakko* killed to a man. With regard to the task of despatching the telegraphic news, Sonada and Nomaguchi, being natives of the districts on the borders of Higo, it was arranged that they were to hurry to Kumamoto garrison and that the telegram was to be sent from that place. With regard to the receipt and despatch of other information also, a cipher was agreed to be used in every case. After everything had been settled, the following day was fixed as the date of departure from Tôkiô. As it might excite the suspicion of other people if all were to leave in company, it was also settled that each should leave as soon as his preparations were made. The meeting then broke up and all returned to their own houses. On the 27th I left Tôkiô and proceeded as far as Yokohama, where I stayed the night. The following day, the 28th, I went on board of the *Genkai-maru* at 9 P.M. and left Yokohama, but the passage was very unfavourable, and the ship had to anchor at several places, and I only reached Kagoshima on the 11th of January, 1877. I remained on the spot, going nowhere, but Suyehiro, Takasaki and others came to see me. Before I had commenced any of the detective operations previously mentioned, the secret plot of assassination was discovered, and I was arrested. Now, in consequence of your examination, I have confessed that by the order of Kawaji I formed a plot to assassinate Saigô, and that I futher laid a scheme to create dissension in the minds of the people, for which acts I am truly ashamed. The above statements which I have made are correct.

(Signed) "NAKAHARA HISAO."

CONFESSION OF ÔYAMA TSUNAYOSHI.

"After leaving Tôkiô for Kagoshima *ken*, in December 1877, I reached the latter place on the 27th of that month in company with Hayashi, junior vice-minister of the home department. When Hayashi again left Kagoshima I accompanied him as far as the district of Takayama, in the province of Ôsumi, arriving there on the 18th of January, 1877. I parted from Hayashi on the 21st, and commenced my return to Kagoshima the next day, where I arrived on the 25th, and on the 26th resumed my duties at the *kencho*.* On the morning of the 30th of January I received intelligence that on the previous night about thirty disorderly persons had broken into the magazine of the army department in the village of Kusamuroto, and had seized the powder there. I at once sent police sergeant Nakajima Takehiko to investigate the matter with the officers belonging to the magazine. The same night, about 12

---

* Central office of prefecture.

o'clock, a *tai-i* (captain) named Shinnô Gunpachi came to my house and informed me that about one thousand men had again visited the magazine and carried off more powder, and begged that I would take the matter in hand and send a force to protect the magazine. Shinnô then withdrew, saying that he would further consult with Nakajima Takehiko. I then immediately went to the *kencho*, and saw on the road much powder being conveyed away by *jinrikisha* * or by pack horses. I sent the officials who were at the *Kencho* that night to summon 12 or 13 police sergeants. By this time Nakajima Takehiko arrived, called me into a room, where we were alone, and then told me that on account of the discovery of a monstrous plot, the private school party had taken up arms and were then engaged in carrying away the government powder. He said that the reason of the outbreak was that Nakahara Hisao, and twenty-one others who were in the service of the bureau of police, and who had been in Kagoshima since December, had been discovered plotting to cause dissension among the private school party, to assassinate Saigô and then call upon the Kumamoto garrison troops and utterly annihilate the members of the private school. This plot was overheard by a spy while Nakahara Hisao was relating it to an old friend of his named Taniguchi Tôda, and information was at once given to the private school party. When this came to the ears of Kirino and Shinowara they immediately went to Takayama, in Ôsumi, where Saigô was residing, and after repeated consultations they decided to proceed to Tôkiô at the head of the troops formerly under their command. Then

* Small two-wheeled vehicle.

Nakajima and the police sergeants present said that it was their duty to arrest Nakahara and the others implicated, and immediately left the *kencho*. Shortly afterwards the Kirino brothers and Shinowara came to the *kencho* and informed me of the existence of this plot. They further requested, that as they would shortly call upon Saigô to proceed to the capital at the head of the troops, they should be supplied with the necessary money and provisions. I knowing that money would be the first necessity for Saigô to collect troops for this expedition, wrote a letter with my own hand to Hirata Toyoji, a member of a company called Shôkei-sha at Nagasaki, and sent the same to him by one Hatanaka Genzayemon. The letter was to the following effect: 'A plot to assassinate General Saigô has been discovered, and consequently he will at once proceed to the capital at the head of his troops. I have therefore to request that you will forward to me at once the twenty thousand *yen* which are deposited with Kasano Kumakitchi, to cover the expenses of the expedition. At all events, send at once as much money as you can procure, and borrow thirty or forty thousand *yen* from Kumakitchi. The people of the *ken* are now as much excited as at the time of the Restoration. For further particulars I refer you to Hatanaka.'

"I told Hatanaka that the people were in a great state of excitement, as he himself could see, and that Saigô would probably start from Kagoshima about the 12th or 13th of February. I directed him to caution Hirata to be careful of the letter I had sent him, as it must be kept secret.

"On the same day Sugeno, a lieutenant of the navy, came to the *kencho* and informed me that a large number of armed men had made an attack upon the dockyard the night previous, and breaking into several of the godowns had taken possession of arms, ammunition, etc. He therefore requested the *kencho* to afford him the requisite assistance, and if this could not be done, he would apply for help to the Kumamoto garrison. I, thinking that if application were made to the Kumamoto garrison the Satsuma troops might be attacked unexpectedly, therefore informed him that I would render him ample assistance. After he had retired, I sent a letter to one Awoyama, ordering him to protect the docks. Awoyama answered that, as the remaining powder had been soaked with water by Sugeno, all was now safe. On the 2nd of February the *Saibansho** sent a letter informing the government of the seizure of the powder, and thinking that the *kencho* should do the same, I ordered Shibuya Kuniyasu and Nakamura Kaneyuki, of the *kencho*, to take a despatch to a vessel that was to leave that day, informing the home minister of the whole affair. I stated in this despatch that some men unknown had stolen government property from the godowns within the dockyards at Iso, and that I was then engaged in strictly investigating the matter with a view to arrest those implicated.

"I have been questioned about this despatch, but I was very busy at the time, and it was written for me by one Iwafuji Hiroshi of the *kencho*, and sent away immediately. The statement made therein, through press of business, was incorrect, but it was not written for the purpose of deceiving the home minister, or to prevent the government from taking prompt steps to suppress the outbreak.

* Provincial Court of Justice.

"Although the fifth of the same month (February) was a Sunday, and therefore a holiday, I ordered Minoda Nagayoshi, Kamada Masanao and others to collect together all the government moneys then in the *ken*, which were the reserve funds to meet any extraordinary expenditure, the ordinary annual allowance, and the moneys that the *kencho* was in charge of for the *mombusho* (educational department), the *okurasho* (finance department), and the local taxes which had been collected. This was at once done. I also sent Terada Moriyuki, and Hamajima Shinsuki to the branch *kencho* at Miyazaki, in Hiuga, with orders to do the same there. The result of these orders was that a total amount of one hundred and twenty or thirty thousand *yen* were collected, and adding to this sum twenty-one or twenty-two thousand *yen* that were placed in the care of the *kencho* for the magazine and dockyard, I then handed the whole sum to Saigô and his party. On the 6th a letter came from Saigô announcing that he had arrived at his home in Kagoshima, and, as he desired to see me, requested that I would meet him at the private school. On the 7th I had an interview with Saigô, who said to me, '*Had I been here I should, in all probability, have prevented the members of the private school from acting so recklessly as to take possession of the government powder by force. But now the die is cast, and matters must take their course.*' Saigô further said that he had discovered that there was no mistake as to Nakahara and others having been sent by Kawaji, at the order of Ôkubo, to carry out some plot, so that he had decided to proceed to the capital with his former troops, and demand an explanation from Ôkubo. I then told him that some trouble might arise if his intention should not be made known to all the *fu*,* *ken*, and garrisons on his route to the capital. Saigô replied by saying that he would send me a draft of the notification he intended to issue, and requested me to allow the *kencho* to undertake the distribution of the same, and also to make known to the central government the confessions of Nakahara and others. All this I consented to do. On the 11th of the same month I sent Imafuji to the private school for the draft of the notice, but Saigô did not give it, though he sent instead the confession of Nakahara and twenty-one others, with the intimation that they (Nakahara and others) would be compelled to affix their seals afterwards. On reading the confessions I perceived that they were not inconsistent with the plot related to me by Takehiko, and I became convinced of the truth of it. After correcting such parts of the confessions as were requisite, I sent them back to Saigô by Imafugi, and Saigô then forwarded certain drafts of documents, one of which was a despatch to be sent by the *kencho* to the government, stating that permission had been given Saigô and others to proceed to the capital. The other was the notification of Saigô's proceedings, which was to be issued by the *kencho* to the *fu*, *ken*, and garrisons on the way. Copies of these drafts were then immediately made out, and thirty-one messengers were appointed to distribute them, and money for their expenses given them by the *kencho*. I told them that if they should meet with any obstruction upon their way, they should immediately apply for assistance to the police authorities of whatever *ken* they then happened to be in. These messengers set out on the 14th.

---

* Cities.

This was done for the purpose of making known the state of feeling in Satsuma and to incite the sympathy of the people. For this reason messengers were sent to the Kôchi, Wakayama (Shikoku) and Yamagata (in the north) *kens*, although these places were out of the route which Saigô was to take. On the 9th the *Takao-maru* came into Kagoshima, with Kawamura, the vice-minister of the navy, and Hayashi, the junior vice-minister of home affairs, on board. They informed me by letter that they intended to land. But the private school party guarded the coast, and as their landing seemed impossible, I went on board the steamer and had an interview with them. I was there questioned about the seizure of the powder, about the arrest and trial of Nakahara and others, and also about the state of the Kagoshima *ken* since the occurrence of those events. *I told them nothing about my connection with Saigô, but made answers which I thought were suitable for the occasion.* Kawamura then said that he would like to land and have an interview with Saigô. *I then landed, and ascertained that Saigô would consent to an interview*, so I returned on board the *Takao-kan* to make this known. *Just at this moment the private school party put off in some vessels to attack* the *Takao-kan*, so I landed again without having made any further communication, and the steamer immediately left the coast. On the 12th the twenty thousand *yen* which I requested Hirata to forward were brought to me by Ishizawa Yatarô and Hashiguchi Kumajirô. I received this money, and gave the messengers five *yen* as a present. I then sent the messengers back with several letters. One was to the following effect: 'Your letter of the day before yesterday was received at 11 A.M. on the 12th, and I have also received what accompanied it.' Another was to this effect: 'What I requested you to do through Hatano you have done promptly and I am in receipt of the sum I wanted. But this money, I wish it to be understood, is that which Kasano borrowed from me. As soon as Kasano returns, tell him, please, to get money together. Under the present circumstances I shall not be able to afford much interest. As regards our condition, we are prepared to stand against the army of the whole nation. On the 14th about fifteen thousand men are to advance in two directions, towards Ôguchi and Kajiki. So far large reinforcements have arrived from various districts. I think that Shiba must have arrived by this time. Such is our condition. Whenever you hear any news about the state of Kumamoto, please inform me. Kawamura, the vice-minister of the navy, and Hayashi, the junior vice-minister of the home department, arrived here by the *Takao-maru*, and I interviewed them on two occasions, but they went away without any suspicion. I heard from them with pleasure about the state of affairs at Nagasaki. Many men have arrived from Hiuga, and we are troubled because we have only men and but few of the necessaries they require. I tell you all this in return to you for your kindness. Wait until the turn of affairs. I am now busy both night and day.' Another letter was to this effect: 'Two large guns, 1500 men, forming 24 regiments, march for Ôguchi, 7500 men, forming 135 regiments, and another body of 6500 men for Ishiuin. They are to enter Higo after resting two nights on the way. There is still a reserve force here of five or six thousand.'

"As soon as the plot of Nakahara and others was discovered, I stationed policemen on the frontier and the coast to prevent them escaping, and the news of our proceedings spreading, and for this reason the port was closed, and even officials were not allowed to pass to and fro. To all those who had to pass the barriers, passports were issued by the *kencho*. But Nakajima and almost all the sergeants and policemen joined the expedition, and there were not enough policemen left for duty in the *ken*. I think it was on the 12th of February that Kifuji Takeakira, Ise Sadamune, Tanimura Magohaci, and Kuroye Kagenori of the Kagoshima, *Saibansho* came to me and said that they desired to assist Saigô, and requested to be appointed to the police, and therefore, although I did not give them their dismissal from their posts in the *Saibansho*, I immediately granted their request. At the time Saigô departed, I asked him what should be done with Nakahara and the others, and he replied that he in tended to reach Ôzaka by the end of February or the beginning of March, and that he would let me know from there. They were kept under guard by the *kencho*, but about the 21st of February an English man-of-war came into the port, and gave information that the government was about to send some vessels to Kagoshima, so Nakahara and the others were confined in a new prison erected within the grounds of the *kencho*. A *daikióshô* (high priest) named Osu Tetsunen, with other priests who had been imprisoned by the private school party, were also confined in the same prison. Kawakami Chigata, Osakabe Kio, and Hiwatashi Goro arrived at Iso on the 13th or 14th of February in the *Teibô-kan*, but they left Iso and proceeded to the bay of Sari, in the district of Sashishiku (13 *ri* from Kagoshima). They landed there and sent letters to Kirino and

Shinowara, who were then in the Teikei district (Kawakami was formerly a soldier under Kirino and Osokabe under Shinowara). The letter was to the effect that on hearing that Saigô had inaugurated an expedition, they had returned immediately to Kagoshima and requested that they might be allowed to join Saigô. But Kirino, thinking that if they really intended to join the expedition they should have landed at Iso or appeared in person, and suspecting some plot, sent these letters to the *kencho*, just as he was about to start, with the request that the writers should be strictly examined. This examination was entrusted to Migimatsu Sukenaga, a 1st class police sergeant. After three days Migimatsu told me that the three men had arrived, and that Kirino had ordered beforehand that should they not confess by ordinary examination the reason of their return to Kagoshima, they were to be put to torture.

"The names of Kawabata, Tajiri and Tsurakimo, three men who had already joined the expedition, were discovered in some papers in the possession of Nakahara, so they were ordered to leave the expedition. They then applied through Kodama Junnosuke, for passports to proceed to Hiuga, but fearing that if they left the *ken* they might cause trouble to Saigô's party, I ordered Migimatsu to arrest and examine them. After thorough examination, police sergeant Kifuji announced that they were in no way connected with the plot. But still thinking that it would be dangerous to let them out of the *ken*, I kept them under surveillance.

"Kishima Kiyoshi, a *Samurai* of Satsuma, was one of the leaders of the private school party, but he was discharged for certain reasons. He then asked Saigô for permission to join his expedition, but this Saigô would not grant. About the 16th of February, Kishima came and begged me to request Kirino to intercede for him, so I got a letter from Kirino which I sent to Saigô. But still Saigô would not grant the required permission, saying that he would have no intercourse with Kishima. This decision I then communicated to Kishima.

"On the 3rd of March, 6th class police sergeant Tanaka Teisuke of Miyazaki, Hiuga, came with Ogura Shôhei, the younger brother of a *Samurai* of Oita, who was an official of Kagoshima *ken*, named Nagakura, and I interviewed them. Ogara said that he was trying to assist Saigô with Arima Tôda and others at both Ôzaka and Kiôto, but that, unfortunately, his plot had been discovered and Arima arrested, though he himself managed to escape and reached Kagoshima. As the Imperialist force in Bungo was weak, if the expedition should advance through Hiuga into Bungo it would probably prove an advantageous move on their part. But as Ogura was a man whom I had met for the first time and did not therefore like to trust implicitly, I made indifferent answers to his information. Ogura then said he would himself join Saigô's expedition in the event of it entering Hiuga. After this our interview ceased. When Saigô was leaving Kagoshima he said that he would limit his adherents to the members of the private school, so that I interested myself no more about military affairs. I did not set about enlisting recruits, neither did I inform Saigô of the advice which Ogura gave that it would be well for the expedition to march through Hiuga.

"When I first heard the details of the plot of Nakahara and others, I took no steps to thoroughly investigate the matter, but took the statements of Nakajima and his friends for proof, and, siding with them, ordered the arrest of Nakahara and others, and permitted Nakajima and the private school party to examine them, assisted by police sergeants Nakayama Yukitaka, Kôno Hanzô, Furukawa Gensuke, Miya-uchi Shunzô, Katayama Kiubei, Niré Kagemichi and others.

"On receiving the confessions of Nakahara and others from Saigô I believed in them, had them printed and issued within the Kagoshima *ken*. At the time these men (Nakahara and others) were taken before the board of examiners, I sent police sergeant Kifugi to Kumamoto, where Saigô was at the time, to obtain proofs against them, but none were forthcoming. Again, at the time that I accompanied the Mikado's special envoy on board his vessel, I heard that those men had been put to cruel torture while under examination by Nakajima and his assistants. Judging from all these circumstances, I now believe that those confessions were extorted by means of threats on the part of the Satsuma men, in order that they might obtain a pretext for breaking out into Rebellion.

"Furthermore, at the request of Saigô, I established a commissariat within the *kencho*, whence the Satsuma troops were furnished with supplies.

"I am now thoroughly convinced that all my actions materially assisted Saigô in his treason.

(Signed) "ÔYAMA TSUNAYOSHI."

SPECIMENS OF INDISCREET JOURNALISM.

March 18, 1877.

"Now can this confession (of Nakahara) be true? We shrink from believing it, and yet the statement seems so straightforward, so substantiated by what we know of the circumstances attending the commencement of the Revolt, that we cannot reject the story, as we would we could do, *as either improbable or devoid of foundation.*"

* * * * *

March 24, 1877.

"It is perfectly conceivable that, without actually countenancing so dastardly and infamous a scheme as the cold-blooded assassination of a man, who had given his best years and his most devoted energies in its service, and to whose undaunted courage it owes its very existence, the government should send agents into Satsuma, in order to sow dissension among the different influential members of the clan—perhaps even to foment disturbance—so that excuses might be afforded to send forces there, nominally to preserve order, but actually to impose a check upon the dangerously increasing military power of the province. It is also conceivable that * *those to whom the selection of fitting agents was entrusted*, may have imagined they were doing what would best relieve the government from the principal source of its anxieties, when, on their own authority, they instructed their creatures to take Saigô's life. *This appears to us the most probable, as well as the*

* Ôkubo and Kawaji are evidently here referred to.

most charitable explanation of this dark plot, for we are loath to believe that assassination can be considered by a government, so anxious to stand well in the eyes of the world as that of Japan, as a legitimate political argument."

March 24, 1877.

"Ôyama's only crime appears to have been the arrest and examination of the men who were undoubtedly sent by some one or other to create a disturbance in Satsuma, and *either to assassinate those leaders whose principles are too patriotic to suit the present government, or to involve them in certain schemes so as to give a fair excuse for their judicial murder.*"

April 14, 1877.

"It is melancholy to think how much the present administration has done to alienate from itself the world's sympathy, which was at one time so readily, nay, almost injudiciously, extended towards the efforts which it was imagined it intended to make for the advance of the people whom it represented. It certainly promised most fairly. A constitution; a representative assembly; revision and equalisation of taxes; development of the resources of the country, for the better employment and improvement of the condition of the people, to say nothing of pledges given to the nobles and their retainers in return for the sacrifices they consented to make. It was a programme well fitted indeed to gain the confidence of the people, and to engage the attention and good will of other nations. How have any of these pledges been fulfilled; pledges made under solemn edicts, and in the name of the Mikado? It can be little matter for wonder, that discontent which takes the form of open rebellion, should arise from repudiation and non-fulfilment of promises so liberally given, and that force of arms should be employed to change into a national government *what is now only a self interested committee of administration.*"

* * * * *

"Hungry subjects become desperate enemies, and we feel convinced that the temper of the people, patient and long-suffering though it is, will not stand the strain that must be put on it by prolongation of this cruel and useless war. We publish to-day the translation of an article in which the writer bitterly deplores the want of spirit in the people, but its very publication—only one of many expressing similar sentiments—shows that the spirit, beaten down and sorely weakened as it is by *a long course of injustice and frivolous interference and oppression*, is not dead. It will live again—God hasten the day—endowed with vigour that comes of new life, and force its rights *from a government that now treats its prayers as a crime.*"

May 12, 1877.

"It is still believed that an effort will be made, through the medium of his brother, to bring about some kind of compromise, but it is even more likely that Saigô and those who think with him, and are working to the same end, will combine, and dictate their own terms for peace. The rumours of a split in the ministry are thickening, and Saigô and others are probably only waiting *for the bundle of faggots to fall apart,** when by united action they will be able to break up *the obnoxious coalition.*"

* i. e. the government.

June 9th, 1877.

"It is quite reasonable to suppose that the government is anxious to bring about a settlement by the only course which seems likely to preserve, at least, a portion of its credit, and to save it from utter defeat, and there is little doubt that the rumour of a compromise has very good foundation. The pressure that is being brought against the government cannot long be withstood. It is coming to the end of its resources, both of men and money, while it is making no headway whatever against those who have risen up against it. The fighting in Kiushiu during the last ten days has been of the most insignificant nature, *and in most cases the insurgents have everything their own way.* They have no lack of cannon, arms, ammunition, and supplies of all kinds, and are in numbers largely superior to the Imperialists. It is only by compromise that a speedy peace can be looked for, and it would probably have to be made on such terms as Saigô and those who think and act with him might choose to dictate. He knows full well the power he now possesses, and, unless his demands are granted, he will continue the war until he enforces them."

June 16th, 1877.

"Saigô is not the man to sacrifice lives in useless conflict, when his aims can be better attained by delay that wearies and weakens his opponents far more seriously than indecisive engagements. Unfortunately every day adds to the weight of debt that is pressing so heavily on the suffering country; every day brings nearer the time of national bankruptcy. The people are powerless in the iron grasp *of a corrupt and pitiless despotism, from which they can only be liberated by the unwearied efforts of men like Saigô. As peace seems unattainable by any other means, the sooner those efforts are crowned with success, the better will it be for the nation at large.*"

The indiscretion, to say the least of it, of this sort of language, which was constantly used for several months, is all the greater, because the Japanese government appears to be debarred, by the extra territorial clauses of the treaties with foreign powers, from seeking redress for calumnies, published by the foreign newspapers of the treaty ports, in any other way than by becoming plaintiff before foreign tribunals sitting within its own territory.

It is only fair to state that all the above extracts are taken from one paper, the *Japan Weekly Mail*, that it was not at the time under the direction of its late able editor, Mr. Howell, and that it has since changed hands.

A. H. M.

LONDON: PRINTED BY WILLIAM CLOWES AND SONS, STAMFORD STREET AND CHARING CROSS.

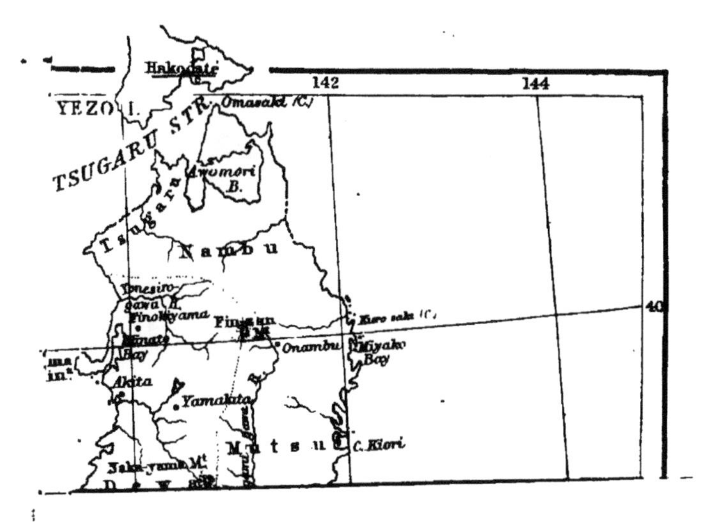
Hakodate
142
144
YEZO I.
TSUGARU STR.
Omasaki (C.)
B.
Tsugaru
Nambu
Yonesiro-
gawa R.
Onambu
Miyako
Bay
Akita
Yamakata
Mutsu
C. Kiori
40

MR. MURRAY'S

GENERAL LIST OF WORKS.

ABINGER'S (LORD Chief Baron of the Exchequer) Life. By the Hon. P. CAMPBELL SCARLETT. Portrait. 8vo. 15*s.*

ALBERT MEMORIAL. A Descriptive and Illustrated Account of the National Monument erected to the PRINCE CONSORT at Kensington. Illustrated by Engravings of its Architecture, Decorations, Sculptured Groups, Statues, Mosaics, Metalwork, &c. With Descriptive Text. By DOYNE C. BELL. With 24 Plates. Folio. 12*l.* 12*s.*

——— HANDBOOK TO, 1*s.*; or Illustrated Edition, 2*s.* 6*d.*

——— (PRINCE) SPEECHES AND ADDRESSES, with an Introduction, giving some outline of his Character. With Portrait. 8vo. 10*s.* 6*d.*; or *Popular Edition*, fcap. 8vo. 1*s.*

ALBERT DÜRER; his Life, with a History of his Art. By DR. THAUSING, Keeper of Archduke Albert's Art Collection at Vienna. Translated from the German. With Portrait and Illustrations 2 vols. 8vo. [*In the Press.*

ABBOTT (REV. J.). Memoirs of a Church of England Missionary in the North American Colonies. Post 8vo. 2*s.*

ABERCROMBIE (JOHN). Enquiries concerning the Intellectual Powers and the Investigation of Truth. Fcap. 8vo. 3*s.* 6*d.*

——— Philosophy of the Moral Feelings. Fcap. 8vo. 2*s.* 6*d.*

ACLAND (REV. CHARLES). Popular Account of the Manners and Customs of India. Post 8vo. 2*s.*

ÆSOP'S FABLES. A New Version. With Historical Preface. By Rev. THOMAS JAMES. With 100 Woodcuts, by TENNIEL and WOLF. Post 8vo. 2*s.* 6*d.*

AGRICULTURAL (ROYAL) **JOURNAL.** (*Published half-yearly.*)

AIDS TO FAITH: a Series of Theological Essays. By various Authors. 8vo. 9*s.*

Contents:—Miracles; Evidences of Christianity; Prophecy & Mosaic Record of Creation; Ideology and Subscription; The Pentateuch; Inspiration; Death of Christ; Scripture and its Interpretation.

AMBER-WITCH (THE). A most interesting Trial for Witchcraft. Translated by LADY DUFF GORDON. Post 8vo. 2*s.*

ARMY LIST (THE). *Published Monthly by Authority.*

ARTHUR'S (LITTLE) History of England. By LADY CALLCOTT. *New Edition, continued to* 1872. With 36 Woodcuts. Fcap. 8vo. 1*s.* 6*d.*

AUSTIN (JOHN). LECTURES ON GENERAL JURISPRUDENCE; or, the Philosophy of Positive Law. Edited by ROBERT CAMPBELL. 2 Vols. 8vo. 32*s.*

——— STUDENT'S EDITION, by ROBERT CAMPBELL, compiled from the above work. Post 8vo. 12*s.*

——— Analysis of. By GORDON CAMPBELL, M.A. Post 8vo. 6*s.*

ARNOLD (THOS.). Ecclesiastical and Secular Architecture of Scotland: The Abbeys, Churches, Castles, and Mansions. With Illustrations. Medium 8vo. [*In Preparation.*

ATKINSON (Dr. R.) Vie de Seint Auban. A Poem in Norman-French. Ascribed to Matthew Paris. With Concordance, Glossary and Notes. Small 4to, 10s. 6d.

ADMIRALTY PUBLICATIONS; Issued by direction of the Lords Commissioners of the Admiralty:—

A MANUAL OF SCIENTIFIC ENQUIRY, for the Use of Travellers. *Fourth Edition.* Edited by Robert Main, M.A. Woodcuts. Post 8vo. 3s. 6d.

GREENWICH ASTRONOMICAL OBSERVATIONS 1841 to 1846, and 1847 to 1871. Royal 4to. 20s. each.

MAGNETICAL AND METEOROLOGICAL OBSERVATIONS. 1840 to 1847. Royal 4to. 20s. each.

APPENDICES TO OBSERVATIONS.

1837. Logarithms of Sines and Cosines in Time. 3s.
1842. Catalogue of 1439 Stars, from Observations made in 1836 to 1841. 4s.
1845. Longitude of Valentia (Chronometrical). 3s.
1847. Description of Altazimuth. 3s.
Twelve Years' Catalogue of Stars, from Observations made in 1836 to 1847. 4s.
Description of Photographic Apparatus. 2s.
1851. Maskelyne's Ledger of Stars. 3s.
1852. I. Description of the Transit Circle. 3s.
1853. Refraction Tables. 3s.
1854. Description of the Zenith Tube. 3s.
Six Years' Catalogue of Stars, from Observations. 1848 to 1853. 4s.
1862. Seven Years' Catalogue of Stars, from Observations. 1854 to 1860. 10s.
Plan of Ground Buildings. 3s.
Longitude of Valentia (Galvanic). 2s.
1864. Moon's Semid. from Occultations. 2s.
Planetary Observations, 1831 to 1835. 2s.
1868. Corrections of Elements of Jupiter and Saturn. 2s.
Second Seven Years' Catalogue of 2760 Stars for 1861 to 1867. 4s.
Description of the Great Equatorial. 3s.
1856. Descriptive Chronograph. 3s.
1860. Reduction of Deep Thermometer Observations. 2s.
1871. History and Description of Water Telescope. 3s.

Cape of Good Hope Observations (Star Ledgers: 1856 to 1863. 2s.
——————— 1856. 5s.
——————— Astronomical Results. 1857 to 1858. 5s.
Report on Teneriffe Astronomical Experiment. 1856. 5s.
Paramatta Catalogue of 7385 Stars. 1822 to 1826. 4s.

ASTRONOMICAL RESULTS. 1847 to 1871. 4to. 3s. each.

MAGNETICAL AND METEOROLOGICAL RESULTS. 1847 to 1871. 4to. 3s. each.

REDUCTION OF THE OBSERVATIONS OF PLANETS. 1750 to 1830. Royal 4to. 20s each.

——————— LUNAR OBSERVATIONS. 1750 to 1830. 2 Vols. Royal 4to. 20s. each.

——————— 1831 to 1851. 4to. 10s. each.

BERNOULLI'S SEXCENTENARY TABLE. 1779. 4to. 5s.

BESSEL'S AUXILIARY TABLES FOR HIS METHOD OF CLEARING LUNAR DISTANCES. 8vo. 2s.

ENCKE'S BERLINER JAHRBUCH, for 830. *Berlin*, 1828. 8vo. 9s.

HANSEN'S TABLES DE LA LUNE. 4to. 20s.

LAX'S TABLES FOR FINDING THE LATITUDE AND LONGITUDE. 1821. 8vo. 10s.

LUNAR OBSERVATIONS at GREENWICH. 1783 to 1819. Compared with the Tables, 1821. 4to. 7s. 6d.

MACLEAR ON LACAILLE'S ARC OF MERIDIAN. 2 Vols. 20s. each

ADMIRALTY PUBLICATIONS—*continued.*

MAYER'S DISTANCES of the MOON'S CENTRE from the PLANETS. 1822, 3*s.*; 1823, 4*s.* 6*d.* 1824 to 1835. 8vo. 4*s.* each.

——— TABULÆ MOTUUM SOLIS ET LUNÆ. 1770. 5*s.*

——— ASTRONOMICAL OBSERVATIONS MADE AT GOTTINGEN, from 1756 to 1761. 1826. Folio. 7*s.* 6*d.*

NAUTICAL ALMANACS, from 1767 to 1877, 80*s.* 2*s.* 6*d.* each.

——— SELECTIONS FROM, up to 1812. 8vo. 5*s.* 1834-54. 5*s.*

——— SUPPLEMENTS, 1828 to 1833, 1837 and 1838. 2*s.* each.

——— TABLE requisite to be used with the N.A. 1781. 8vo. 5*s.*

SABINE'S PENDULUM EXPERIMENTS to DETERMINE THE FIGURE OF THE EARTH. 1825. 4to. 40*s.*

SHEPHERD'S TABLES for CORRECTING LUNAR DISTANCES. 1772. Royal 4to. 21*s.*

——— TABLES, GENERAL, of the MOON'S DISTANCE from the SUN, and 10 STARS. 1787. Folio. 5*s.* 6*d.*

TAYLOR'S SEXAGESIMAL TABLE. 1780. 4to. 15*s.*

——— TABLES OF LOGARITHMS. 4to. 60*s.*

TIARK'S ASTRONOMICAL OBSERVATIONS for the LONGITUDE of MADEIRA. 1822. 4to. 5*s.*

——— CHRONOMETRICAL OBSERVATIONS for DIFFERENCES of LONGITUDE between DOVER, PORTSMOUTH, and FALMOUTH. 1823. 4to. 5*s.*

VENUS and JUPITER: OBSERVATIONS of, compared with the TABLES. *London*, 1822. 4to. 2*s.*

WALES AND BAYLY'S ASTRONOMICAL OBSERVATIONS. 1777. 4to. 21*s.*

——— REDUCTION OF ASTRONOMICAL OBSERVATIONS MADE IN THE SOUTHERN HEMISPHERE. 1764—1771. 1788. 4to. 10*s.* 6*d.*

BARBAULD (MRS.). Hymns in Prose for Children. With Illustrations. Crown 8vo.

BARCLAY (JOSEPH). The Talmud: Selected Extracts, chiefly illustrating the Teaching of the Bible. With an Introduction. 8vo. 14*s.*

BARKLEY (H. C.). Five Years among the Bulgarians and Turks between the Danube and the Black Sea. Post 8vo. 10*s* 6*d.*

——— Bulgaria North of the Balkans before the War, derived from a Seven Years' Experience of European Turkey and its Inhabitants. Post 8vo. 10*s.* 6*d.*

——— My Boyhood: a Story Book for Boys. With Illustrations. Post 8vo. 6*s.*

BARROW (SIR JOHN). Autobiographical Memoir, from Early Life to Advanced Age. Portrait. 8vo. 16*s.*

——— (JOHN) Life, Exploits, and Voyages of Sir Francis Drake. Post 8vo. 2*s.*

BARRY (SIR CHARLES). Life and Works. By CANON BARRY. With Portrait and Illustrations. Medium 8vo. 15*s.*

BATES' (H. W.) Records of a Naturalist on the River Amazon during eleven years of Adventure and Travel. Illustrations. Post 8vo. 7*s.* 6*d.*

BAX (CAPT. R.N.). Russian Tartary, Eastern Siberia, China, Japan, and Formosa. A Narrative of a Cruise in the Eastern Seas. With Map and Illustrations. Crown 8vo. 12*s.*

BELCHER (LADY). Account of the Mutineers of the 'Bounty,' and their Descendants; with their Settlements in Pitcairn and Norfolk Islands. With Illustrations. Post 8vo. 12*s.*

BELL'S (Sir Chas.) Familiar Letters. Portrait. Post 8vo. 12*s*.

BELL'S (Doyne C.) Notices of the Historic Interments in the Chapel in the Tower of London, with an account of the discovery of the remains of Queen Anne Boleyn With Illustrations. Crown 8vo. 14*s*.

BELT'S (Thos.) Naturalist in Nicaragua, including a Residence at the Gold Mines of Chontales; with Journeys in the Savannahs and Forests; and Observations on Animals and Plants. Illustrations. Post 8vo. 12*s*.

BERTRAM'S (Jas. G.) Harvest of the Sea: an Account of British Food Fishes, including sketches of Fisheries and Fisher Folk. With 50 Illustrations. 8vo. 9*s*.

BIBLE COMMENTARY. Explanatory and Critical. With a Revision of the Translation. By BISHOPS and CLERGY of the ANGLICAN CHURCH. Edited by F. C. Cook, M.A., Canon of Exeter. Vols. I. to VI. (The Old Testament). Medium 8vo. 6*l*. 15*s*.

Volume	Books	Volume	Books
Vol. I. 30*s*.	Genesis. Exodus. Leviticus. Numbers. Deuteronomy.	Vol. IV. 24*s*.	Job. Psalms. Proverbs. Ecclesiastes. Song of Solomon.
Vols. II. 20*s*. and III. 16*s*.	Joshua, Judges, Ruth, Samuel, Kings, Chronicles, Ezra, Nehemiah, Esther.	Vol. V. 20*s*.	Isaiah. Jeremiah.
		Vol. VI. 25*s*.	Ezekiel. Daniel. Minor Prophets.

BIGG-WITHER (T. P.). Pioneering in S. Brazil; three years of forest and prairie life in the province of Parana. Map and Illustrations. 8vo.

BIRCH (Samuel). A History of Ancient Pottery and Porcelain: Egyptian, Assyrian, Greek, Roman, and Etruscan. With Coloured Plates and 200 Illustrations. Medium 8vo. 42*s*.

BIRD (Isabella). Hawaiian Archipelago; or Six Months among the Palm Groves, Coral Reefs, and Volcanoes of the Sandwich Islands. With Illustrations. Crown 8vo. 7*s*. 6*d*.

BISSET (General). Sport and War in South Africa from 1834 to 1867, with a Narrative of the Duke of Edinburgh's Visit. With Map and Illustrations. Crown 8vo. 14*s*.

BLACKSTONE'S COMMENTARIES; adapted to the Present State of the Law. By R. Malcolm Kerr, LL.D. *Revised Edition*, incorporating all the Recent Changes in the Law. 4 vols. 8vo. 60*s*.

BLUNT (Rev. J. J.). Undesigned Coincidences in the Writings of the Old and New Testaments, an Argument of their Veracity: containing the Books of Moses, Historical and Prophetical Scriptures, and the Gospels and Acts. Post 8vo. 6*s*.

——— History of the Church in the First Three Centuries. Post 8vo. 6*s*.

——— Parish Priest; His Duties, Acquirements and Obligations. Post 8vo. 6*s*.

——— Lectures on the Right Use of the Early Fathers. 8vo. 9*s*.

——— University Sermons. Post 8vo. 6*s*.

——— Plain Sermons. 2 vols. Post 8vo. 12*s*.

BLOMFIELD'S (Bishop) Memoir, with Selections from his Correspondence. By his Son. Portrait, post 8vo. 12*s*.

BOSWELL'S Life of Samuel Johnson, LL.D. Including the Tour to the Hebrides. Edited by Mr. CROKER. *Seventh Edition.* Portraits. 1 vol. Medium 8vo. 12*s.*

BRACE (C. L.). Manual of Ethnology; or the Races of the Old World. Post 8vo. 6*s.*

BOOK OF COMMON PRAYER. Illustrated with Coloured Borders, Initial Letters, and Woodcuts. 8vo. 18*s.*

BORROW (GEORGE). Bible in Spain; or the Journeys, Adventures, and Imprisonments of an Englishman in an Attempt to circulate the Scriptures in the Peninsula. Post 8vo. 5*s.*

——— Gypsies of Spain; their Manners, Customs, Religion, and Language. With Portrait. Post 8vo. 5*s.*

——— Lavengro; The Scholar—The Gypsy—and the Priest. Post 8vo. 5*s.*

——— Romany Rye—a Sequel to "Lavengro." Post 8vo. 5*s.*

——— WILD WALES: its People, Language, and Scenery. Post 8vo. 5*s.*

——— Romano Lavo-Lil; Word-Book of the Romany, or English Gypsy Language; with Specimens of their Poetry, and an account of certain Gypsyries. Post 8vo. 10*s.* 6*d.*

BRAY (MRS.). Life of Thomas Stothard, R.A. With Portrait and 60 Woodcuts. 4to. 21*s.*

BRITISH ASSOCIATION REPORTS. 8vo.

York and Oxford, 1831-32, 13*s.* 6*d.*
Cambridge, 1833, 12*s.*
Edinburgh, 1834, 15*s.*
Dublin, 1835, 13*s.* 6*d.*
Bristol, 1836, 12*s.*
Liverpool, 1837, 16*s.* 6*d.*
Newcastle, 1838, 15*s.*
Birmingham, 1839, 13*s.* 6*d.*
Glasgow, 1840, 15*s.*
Plymouth, 1841, 13*s.* 6*d.*
Manchester, 1842, 10*s.* 6*d.*
Cork, 1843, 12*s.*
York, 1844, 20*s.*
Cambridge, 1845, 12*s.*
Southampton, 1846, 15*s.*
Oxford, 1847, 18*s.*
Swansea, 1848, 9*s.*
Birmingham, 1849, 10*s.*
Edinburgh, 1850, 15*s.*
Ipswich, 1851, 16*s.* 6*d.*
Belfast, 1852, 15*s.*
Hull, 1853, 10*s.* 6*d.*
Liverpool, 1854, 18*s.*
Glasgow, 1855, 15*s.*
Cheltenham, 1856, 18*s.*
Dublin, 1857, 15*s.*
Leeds, 1858, 20*s.*
Aberdeen, 1859, 15*s.*
Oxford, 1860, 25*s.*
Manchester, 1861, 15*s.*
Cambridge, 1862, 20*s.*
Newcastle, 1863, 25*s.*
Bath, 1864, 18*s.*
Birmingham, 1865, 25*s.*
Nottingham, 1866, 24*s.*
Dundee, 1867, 26*s.*
Norwich, 1868, 25*s.*
Exeter, 1869, 22*s.*
Liverpool, 1870, 18*s.*
Edinburgh, 1871, 16*s.*
Brighton, 1872, 24*s.*
Bradford, 1873, 25*s.*
Belfast, 1874. 25*s.*
Bristol, 1875, 25*s.*
Glasgow, 1876, 25*s.*

BROUGHTON (LORD). A Journey through Albania, Turkey in Europe and Asia, to Constantinople. Illustrations. 2 Vols. 8vo. 30*s.*

——— Visits to Italy. 2 Vols. Post 8vo. 18*s.*

BRUGSCH (PROFESSOR). A History of Egypt, from the earliest period. Derived from Monuments and Inscriptions. *New Edition.* Translated by H. DANBY SEYMOUR. 2 vols. 8vo. [*In Preparation.*

BUCKLEY (ARABELLA B.). A Short History of Natural Science, and the Progress of Discovery from the time of the Greeks to the present day, for Schools and young Persons. Illustrations. Post 8vo. 9*s.*

BURGON (REV. J. W.). Christian Gentleman; or, Memoir of Patrick Fraser Tytler. Post 8vo. 9*s.*

——— Letters from Rome. Post 8vo. 12*s.*

BURN (Col.). Dictionary of Naval and Military Technical Terms, English and French—French and English. Crown 8vo. 15s.

BUXTON'S (Charles) Memoirs of Sir Thomas Fowell Buxton, Bart. With Selections from his Correspondence. Portrait. 8vo. 16s. *Popular Edition.* Fcap. 8vo. 5s.

——— ——. Ideas of the Day. 8vo. 5s.

BURCKHARDT'S (Dr. Jacob) Cicerone; or Art Guide to Painting in Italy. Edited by Rev. Dr. A. Von Zahn, and Translated from the German by Mrs. A. Clough. Post 8vo. 6s.

BYLES (Sir John). Foundations of Religion in the Mind and Heart of Man. Post 8vo. 6s.

BYRON'S (Lord) Life, Letters, and Journals. By Thomas Moore. *Cabinet Edition.* Plates. 6 Vols. Fcap. 8vo. 18s.; or One Volume, Portraits. Royal 8vo., 7s. 6d.

——— —— —— and Poetical Works. *Popular Edition.* Portraits. 2 vols. Royal 8vo. 15s.

—— Poetical Works. *Library Edition.* Portrait. 6 Vols. 8vo. 45s.

——— *Cabinet Edition.* Plates. 10 Vols. 12mo. 30s.

——— *Pocket Edition.* 8 Vols. 24mo. 21s. *In a case.*

——— *Popular Edition.* Plates. Royal 8vo. 7s. 6d.

——— *Pearl Edition.* Crown 8vo. 2s. 6d.

——— Childe Harold. With 80 Engravings. Crown 8vo. 12s.

——— 16mo. 2s. 6d.

——— Vignettes. 16mo. 1s.

——— Portrait. 16mo. 6d.

——— Tales and Poems. 24mo. 2s. 6d.

——— Miscellaneous. 2 Vols. 24mo. 5s.

——— Dramas and Plays. 2 Vols. 24mo. 5s.

——— Don Juan and Beppo. 2 Vols. 24mo. 5s.

——— Beauties. Poetry and Prose. Portrait. Fcap. 8vo. 3s. 6d.

BUTTMANN'S Lexilogus; a Critical Examination of the Meaning of numerous Greek Words, chiefly in Homer and Hesiod. By Rev. J. R. Fishlake. 8vo. 12s.

——— Irregular Greek Verbs. With all the Tenses extant—their Formation, Meaning, and Usage, with Notes, by Rev. J. R. Fishlake. Post 8vo. 6s.

CALLCOTT (Lady). Little Arthur's History of England. *New Edition, brought down to* 1872. With Woodcuts. Fcap. 8vo. 1s. 6d.

CARNARVON (Lord). Portugal, Gallicia, and the Basque Provinces. Post 8vo. 3s. 6d.

CARTWRIGHT (W. C.). The Jesuits: their Constitution and Teaching. An Historical Sketch. 8vo. 9s.

CASTLEREAGH DESPATCHES, from the commencement of the official career of Viscount Castlereagh to the close of his life. 12 Vols. 8vo. 14s. each.

CAMPBELL (Lord). Lord Chancellors and Keepers of the Great Seal of England. From the Earliest Times to the Death of Lord Eldon in 1838. 10 Vols. Crown 8vo. 6s. each.

——— Chief Justices of England. From the Norman Conquest to the Death of Lord Tenterden. 4 Vols. Crown 8vo. 6s. each.

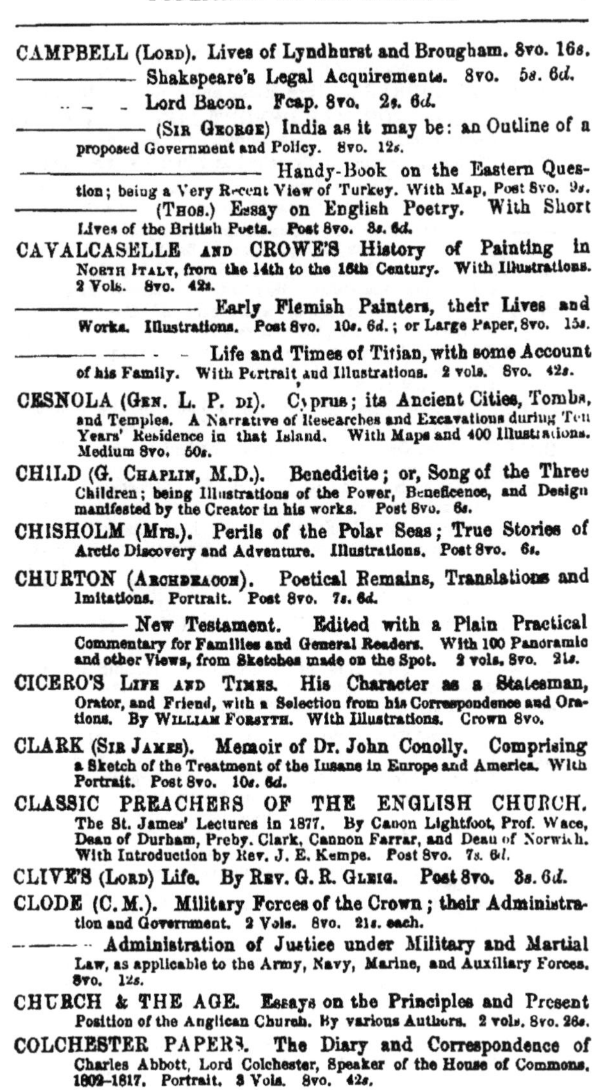

CAMPBELL (LORD). Lives of Lyndhurst and Brougham. 8vo. 16s.

———— Shakspeare's Legal Acquirements. 8vo. 5s. 6d.

———— Lord Bacon. Fcap. 8vo. 2s. 6d.

———— (SIR GEORGE) India as it may be: an Outline of a proposed Government and Policy. 8vo. 12s.

———— Handy-Book on the Eastern Question; being a Very Recent View of Turkey. With Map. Post 8vo. 9s.

———— (THOS.) Essay on English Poetry. With Short Lives of the British Poets. Post 8vo. 3s. 6d.

CAVALCASELLE AND CROWE'S History of Painting in NORTH ITALY, from the 14th to the 16th Century. With Illustrations. 2 Vols. 8vo. 42s.

———— Early Flemish Painters, their Lives and Works. Illustrations. Post 8vo. 10s. 6d.; or Large Paper, 8vo. 15s.

———— Life and Times of Titian, with some Account of his Family. With Portrait and Illustrations. 2 vols. 8vo. 42s.

CESNOLA (GEN. L. P. DI). Cyprus; its Ancient Cities, Tombs, and Temples. A Narrative of Researches and Excavations during Ten Years' Residence in that Island. With Maps and 400 Illustrations. Medium 8vo. 50s.

CHILD (G. CHAPLIN, M.D.). Benedicite; or, Song of the Three Children; being Illustrations of the Power, Beneficence, and Design manifested by the Creator in his works. Post 8vo. 6s.

CHISHOLM (Mrs.). Perils of the Polar Seas; True Stories of Arctic Discovery and Adventure. Illustrations. Post 8vo. 6s.

CHURTON (ARCHDEACON). Poetical Remains, Translations and Imitations. Portrait. Post 8vo. 7s. 6d.

———— New Testament. Edited with a Plain Practical Commentary for Families and General Readers. With 100 Panoramic and other Views, from Sketches made on the Spot. 2 vols. 8vo. 21s.

CICERO'S LIFE AND TIMES. His Character as a Statesman, Orator, and Friend, with a Selection from his Correspondence and Orations. By WILLIAM FORSYTH. With Illustrations. Crown 8vo.

CLARK (SIR JAMES). Memoir of Dr. John Conolly. Comprising a Sketch of the Treatment of the Insane in Europe and America. With Portrait. Post 8vo. 10s. 6d.

CLASSIC PREACHERS OF THE ENGLISH CHURCH. The St. James' Lectures in 1877. By Canon Lightfoot, Prof. Wace, Dean of Durham, Preby. Clark, Cannon Farrar, and Dean of Norwich. With Introduction by Rev. J. E. Kempe. Post 8vo. 7s. 6d.

CLIVE'S (LORD) Life. By REV. G. R. GLEIG. Post 8vo. 3s. 6d.

CLODE (C. M.). Military Forces of the Crown; their Administration and Government. 2 Vols. 8vo. 21s. each.

———— Administration of Justice under Military and Martial Law, as applicable to the Army, Navy, Marine, and Auxiliary Forces. 8vo. 12s.

CHURCH & THE AGE. Essays on the Principles and Present Position of the Anglican Church. By various Authors. 2 vols. 8vo. 26s.

COLCHESTER PAPERS. The Diary and Correspondence of Charles Abbott, Lord Colchester, Speaker of the House of Commons, 1802–1817. Portrait. 3 Vols. 8vo. 42s.

COLERIDGE'S (SAMUEL TAYLOR) Table-Talk. Portrait. 12mo. 3s. 6d.

COLLINGWOOD (CUTHBERT). Rambles of a Naturalist on the Shores and Waters of the China Sea. With Illustrations. 8vo. 16s.

COLONIAL LIBRARY. [See Home and Colonial Library.]

COMPANIONS FOR THE DEVOUT LIFE. The St. James' Lectures, 1875 and 1876. New Edition. Post 8vo. 6s.

COOK (Canon). Sermons Preached at Lincoln's Inn. 8vo. 9s.

COOKE (E. W.). Leaves from my Sketch-Book. A selection from sketches made during many tours. 25 Plates. Small folio. 31s. 6d.

———— Second Series. Consisting chiefly of Views in Egypt and the East. With Descriptive Text. Small folio. 31s. 6d.

COOKERY (MODERN DOMESTIC). Founded on Principles of Economy and Practical Knowledge. By a Lady. Woodcuts. Fcap. 8vo. 5s.

COOPER (T. T.). Travels of a Pioneer of Commerce on an Overland Journey from China towards India. Illustrations. 8vo. 16s.

CORNWALLIS Papers and Correspondence during the American War,—Administrations in India,—Union with Ireland, and Peace of Amiens. 3 Vols. 8vo. 63s.

COWPER'S (COUNTESS) Diary while Lady of the Bedchamber to Caroline, Princess of Wales, 1714–20. Portrait. 8vo. 10s. 6d.

CRABBE (REV. GEORGE). Life and Poetical Works. With Illustrations. Royal 8vo. 7s.

CRAWFORD & BALCARRES (Earl of). Etruscan Inscriptions. Analyzed, Translated, and Commented upon. 8vo. 12s.

CRIPPS (WILFRED). Old English Plate: Ecclesiastical, Decorative, and Domestic, its makers and marks. Illustrations. Medium 8vo [*In the Press.*

CROKER (J. W.). Progressive Geography for Children. 18mo. 1s. 6d.

———— Stories for Children, Selected from the History of England. Woodcuts. 16mo. 2s. 6d.

———— Boswell's Life of Johnson. Including the Tour to the Hebrides. *Seventh Edition.* Portraits. 8vo. 12s.

———— Early Period of the French Revolution. 8vo. 15s.

———— Historical Essay on the Guillotine. Fcap. 8vo. 1s.

CROWE AND CAVALCASELLE. Lives of the Early Flemish Painters. Woodcuts. Post 8vo, 10s. 6d.; or Large Paper, 8vo, 15s.

———— History of Painting in North Italy, from 14th to 16th Century. Derived from Researches into the Works of Art in that Country. With Illustrations. 2 Vols. 8vo. 42s.

———— Life and Times of Titian, with some Account of his Family, chiefly from new and unpublished records. With Portrait and Illustrations. 2 vols. 8vo. 42s.

CUMMING (R. GORDON). Five Years of a Hunter's Life in the Far Interior of South Africa. Woodcuts. Post 8vo. 6s.

CUNYNGHAME (SIR ARTHUR). Travels in the Eastern Caucasus, on the Caspian and Black Seas, in Daghestan and the Frontiers of Persia and Turkey. With Map and Illustrations. 8vo. 18s.

CURTIUS' (PROFESSOR) Student's Greek Grammar, for the Upper Forms. Edited by DR. WM. SMITH. Post 8vo. 6s.

———— Elucidations of the above Grammar. Translated by EVELYN ABBOT. Post 8vo. 7s. 6d.

———— Smaller Greek Grammar for the Middle and Lower Forms. Abridged from the larger work. 12mo. 3s. 6d.

CURTIUS' (PROFESSOR) Accidence of the Greek Language. Extracted from the above work. 12mo. 2s. 6d.

—— —— Principles of Greek Etymology. Translated by A. S. WILKINS, M.A., and E. B. ENGLAND, B.A. 2 vols. 8vo. 15s. each.

CURZON (HON. ROBERT). Visits to the Monasteries of the Levant. Illustrations. Post 8vo. 7s. 6d.

CUST (GENERAL). Warriors of the 17th Century—The Thirty Years' War. 2 Vols. 16s. Civil Wars of France and England. 2 Vols. 16s. Commanders of Fleets and Armies. 2 Vols. 18s.

—— Annals of the Wars—18th & 19th Century, 1700—1815. With Maps. 9 Vols. Post 8vo. 5s. each.

DAVIS (NATHAN). Ruined Cities of Numidia and Carthaginia. Illustrations. 8vo. 16s.

DAVY (SIR HUMPHRY). Consolations in Travel; or, Last Days of a Philosopher. Woodcuts. Fcap. 8vo 3s. 6d.

—— Salmonia; or, Days of Fly Fishing. Woodcuts. Fcap. 8vo. 3s. 6d.

DARWIN (CHARLES). Journal of a Naturalist during a Voyage round the World. Crown 8vo. 9s.

—— Origin of Species by Means of Natural Selection; or, the Preservation of Favoured Races in the Struggle for Life. Crown 8vo. 7s. 6d.

—— Variation of Animals and Plants under Domestication. With Illustrations. 2 Vols. Crown 8vo. 18s.

—— Descent of Man, and Selection in Relation to Sex. With Illustrations. Crown 8vo. 9s.

—— Expressions of the Emotions in Man and Animals. With Illustrations. Crown 8vo. 12s.

—— Various Contrivances by which Orchids are Fertilized by Insects. Woodcuts. Crown 8vo. 9s.

—— Movements and Habits of Climbing Plants. Woodcuts. Crown 8vo. 6s.

—— Insectivorous Plants. Woodcuts. Crown 8vo. 14s.

—— Effects of Cross and Self-Fertilization in the Vegetable Kingdom. Crown 8vo. 12s.

—— Different Forms of Flowers on Plants of the same Species. Crown 8vo. 10s. 6d.

—— Facts and Argument for Darwin. By FRITZ MULLER. Translated by W. S. DALLAS. Woodcuts. Post 8vo. 6s.

DE COSSON (E. A.). The Cradle of the Blue Nile; a Journey through Abyssinia and Soudan, and a residence at the Court of King John of Ethiopia. Map and Illustrations. 2 vols. Post 8vo. 21s.

DELEPIERRE (OCTAVE). History of Flemish Literature. 8vo. 9s.

DENNIS (GEORGE). The Cities and Cemeteries of Etruria. A new Edition, revised, recording all the latest Discoveries. With 20 Plans and 150 Illustrations. 2 vols. 8vo. 42s.

DENT (EMMA). Annals of Winchcombe and Sudeley. With 120 Portraits, Plates and Woodcuts. 4to. 42s.

DERBY (EARL OF). Iliad of Homer rendered into English Blank Verse. 10th Edition. With Portrait. 2 Vols. Post 8vo. 10s.

DERRY (BISHOP OF). Witness of the Psalms to Christ and Christianity. The Bampton Lectures for 1876. 8vo. 10s. 6d.

DEUTSCH (EMANUEL). Talmud, Islam, The Targums and other Literary Remains. 8vo. 12s.

DILKE (SIR C. W.). Papers of a Critic. Selected from the Writings of the late CHAS. WENTWORTH DILKE. With a Biographical Sketch. 2 Vols. 8vo. 24s.

DOG-BREAKING, with Odds and Ends for those who love the Dog and Gun. By GEN. HUTCHINSON. With 40 Illustrations. Crown 8vo. 7s. 6d.

DOMESTIC MODERN COOKERY. Founded on Principles of Economy and Practical Knowledge, and adapted for Private Families. Woodcuts. Fcap. 8vo. 5s.

DOUGLAS'S (SIR HOWARD) Life and Adventures. Portrait. 8vo. 15s.

——— Theory and Practice of Gunnery. Plates. 8vo. 21s.

——— — Construction of Bridges and the Passage of Rivers in Military Operations. Plates. 8vo. 21s.

——— (WM.) Horse-Shoeing; As it Is, and As it Should be. Illustrations. Post 8vo. 7s. 6d.

DRAKE'S (SIR FRANCIS) Life, Voyages, and Exploits, by Sea and Land. By JOHN BARROW. Post 8vo. 2s.

DRINKWATER (JOHN). History of the Siege of Gibraltar, 1779-1783. With a Description and Account of that Garrison from the Earliest Periods. Post 8vo. 2s.

DUCANGE'S MEDIÆVAL LATIN-ENGLISH DICTIONARY. Translated and Edited by Rev. E. A. DAYMAN and J. H. HESSELS. Small 4to. [*In preparation.*

DU CHAILLU (PAUL B.). EQUATORIAL AFRICA, with Accounts of the Gorilla, the Nest-building Ape, Chimpanzee, Crocodile, &c. Illustrations. 8vo. 21s.

——— Journey to Ashango Land; and Further Penetration into Equatorial Africa. Illustrations. 8vo. 21s.

DUFFERIN (LORD). Letters from High Latitudes; a Yacht Voyage to Iceland, Jan Mayen, and Spitzbergen. Woodcuts. Post 8vo. 7s. 6d.

DUNCAN (MAJOR). History of the Royal Artillery. Compiled from the Original Records. With Portraits. 2 Vols. 8vo. 30s.

——— The English in Spain; or, The Story of the War of Succession, 1834 and 1840. Compiled from the Letters, Journals, and Reports of the British Commissioners with Queen Isabella's Armies. With Illustrations. 8vo. 16s.

EASTLAKE (SIR CHARLES). Contributions to the Literature of the Fine Arts. With Memoir of the Author, and Selections from his Correspondence. By LADY EASTLAKE. 2 Vols. 8vo. 24s.

EDWARDS (W. H.). Voyage up the River Amazons, including a Visit to Para. Post 8vo. 2s.

EIGHT MONTHS AT ROME, during the Vatican Council, with a Daily Account of the Proceedings. By POMPONIO LETO. Translated from the Original. 8vo. 12s.

ELDON'S (LORD) Public and Private Life, with Selections from his Correspondence and Diaries. By HORACE TWISS. Portrait. 2 Vols. Post 8vo. 21s.

ELGIN (LORD). Letters and Journals. Edited by THEODORE WALROND. With Preface by Dean Stanley. 8vo. 14s.

ELLESMERE (LORD). Two Sieges of Vienna by the Turks. Translated from the German. Post 8vo. 2s.

ELLIS (W.). Madagascar Revisited. Setting forth the Persecutions and Heroic Sufferings of the Native Christians. Illustrations. 8vo. 16s.

ELLIS (W.) Memoir. By His Son. With his Character and Work. By Rev. Henry Allon, D.D. Portrait. 8vo. 10*s*. 6*d*.

——— (Robinson) Poems and Fragments of Catullus. 16mo. 5*s*.

ELPHINSTONE (Hon. Mountstuart). History of India—the Hindoo and Mahomedan Periods. Edited by Professor Cowell. Map. 8vo. 18*s*.

——— (H. W.) Patterns for Turning; Comprising Elliptical and other Figures cut on the Lathe without the use of any Ornamental Chuck. With 70 Illustrations. Small 4to. 15*s*.

ENGLAND. See Callcott, Croker, Hume, Markham, Smith, and Stanhope.

ESSAYS ON CATHEDRALS. With an Introduction. By Dean Howson. 8vo. 12*s*.

ELZE (Karl). Life of Lord Byron. With a Critical Essay on his Place in Literature. Translated from the German. With Portrait. 8vo. 16*s*.

FERGUSSON (James). History of Architecture in all Countries from the Earliest Times. With 1,600 Illustrations. 4 Vols. Medium 8vo.

Vol. I. & II. Ancient and Mediæval. 63*s*.

Vol. III. Indian and Eastern. 42*s*.

Vol. IV. Modern. 31*s*. 6*d*.

——— Rude Stone Monuments in all Countries; their Age and Uses. With 230 Illustrations. Medium 8vo. 24*s*.

——— Holy Sepulchre and the Temple at Jerusalem. Woodcuts. 8vo. 7*s*. 6*d*.

——— The Temple at Jerusalem, and the other buildings in the Haram Area, from Solomon to Saladin, with numerous Illustrations. 4to.

FLEMING (Professor). Student's Manual of Moral Philosophy. With Quotations and References. Post 8vo. 7*s*. 6*d*.

FLOWER GARDEN. By Rev. Thos. James. Fcap. 8vo. 1*s*.

FORD (Richard). Gatherings from Spain. Post 8vo. 3*s*. 6*d*.

FORSYTH (William). Life and Times of Cicero. With Selections from his Correspondence and Orations. Illustrations. Crown 8vo.

——— Hortensius; an Historical Essay on the Office and Duties of an Advocate. Illustrations. 8vo. 12*s*.

——— History of Ancient Manuscripts. Post 8vo. 2*s*. 6*d*.

——— Novels and Novelists of the 18th Century, in Illustration of the Manners and Morals of the Age. Post 8vo. 10*s*. 6*d*.

FORTUNE (Robert). Narrative of Two Visits to the Tea Countries of China, 1843-52. Woodcuts. 2 Vols. Post 8vo. 18*s*.

FORSTER (John). The Early Life of Jonathan Swift. 1667-1711. With Portrait. 8vo. 15*s*.

FOSS (Edward). Biographia Juridica, or Biographical Dictionary of the Judges of England, from the Conquest to the Present Time, 1066-1870. Medium 8vo. 21*s*.

FRANCE (History of). See Markham—Smith—Student's.

FRENCH IN ALGIERS; The Soldier of the Foreign Legion—and the Prisoners of Abd-el-Kadir. Translated by Lady Duff Gordon. Post 8vo. 2*s*.

FRERE (Sir Bartle). Indian Missions. Small 8vo. 2*s*. 6*d*.

——— Eastern Africa as a field for Missionary Labour. With Map. Crown 8vo. 5*s*.

FRERE (SIR BARTLE). Bengal Famine. How it will be Met and How to Prevent Future Famines in India. With Maps. Crown 8vo. 5s.

GALTON (FRANCIS). Art of Travel; or, Hints on the Shifts and Contrivances available in Wild Countries. Woodcuts. Post 8vo. 7s. 6d.

GEOGRAPHICAL SOCIETY'S JOURNAL. (*Published Yearly.*)

GEORGE (ERNEST). The Mosel; a Series of Twenty Etchings, with Descriptive Letterpress. Imperial 4to. 42s.

——— Loire and South of France; a Series of Twenty Etchings, with Descriptive Text. Folio. 42s.

GERMANY (HISTORY OF). See MARKHAM.

GIBBON (EDWARD). History of the Decline and Fall of the Roman Empire. Edited by MILMAN and GUIZOT. Edited, with Notes by Dr. WM. SMITH. Maps. 8 Vols. 8vo. 60s.

——— The Student's Edition; an Epitome of the above work, incorporating the Researches of Recent Commentators. By Dr. WM. SMITH. Woodcuts. Post 8vo. 7s. 6d.

GIFFARD (EDWARD). Deeds of Naval Daring; or, Anecdotes of the British Navy. Fcap. 8vo. 3s. 6d.

GLADSTONE (W. E.). Financial Statements of 1853, 1860, 63–65. 8vo. 12s.

——— Rome and the Newest Fashions in Religion. Three Tracts. 8vo. 7s. 6d.

GLEIG (G. R.). Campaigns of the British Army at Washington and New Orleans. Post 8vo. 2s.

——— Story of the Battle of Waterloo. Post 8vo. 3s. 6d.

——— Narrative of Sale's Brigade in Affghanistan. Post 8vo. 2s.

——— Life of Lord Clive. Post 8vo. 3s. 6d.

——— Sir Thomas Munro. Post 8vo. 3s. 6d.

GLYNNE (SIR STEPHEN). Notes on the Churches of Kent. With Illustrations. 8vo. 12s.

GOLDSMITH'S (OLIVER) Works. Edited with Notes by PETER CUNNINGHAM. Vignettes. 4 Vols. 8vo. 30s.

GORDON (SIR ALEX.). Sketches of German Life, and Scenes from the War of Liberation. Post 8vo. 3s. 6d.

——— (LADY DUFF) Amber-Witch: A Trial for Witchcraft. Post 8vo. 2s.

——— French in Algiers. 1. The Soldier of the Foreign Legion. 2. The Prisoners of Abd-el-Kadir. Post 8vo. 2s.

GRAMMARS. See CURTIUS; HALL; HUTTON; KING EDWARD; MATTHIÆ; MAETZNER; SMITH.

GREECE (HISTORY OF). *See* GROTE—SMITH—Student.

GREY (EARL). Parliamentary Government and Reform; with Suggestions for the Improvement of our Representative System. *Second Edition.* 8vo. 9s.

GUIZOT (M.). Meditations on Christianity. 3 Vols. Post 8vo. 30s.

GROTE (GEORGE). History of Greece. From the Earliest Times to the close of the generation contemporary with the death of Alexander the Great. *Library Edition.* Portrait, Maps, and Plans. 10 Vols. 8vo. 120s. *Cabinet Edition.* Portrait and Plans. 12 Vols. Post 8vo. 6s. each.

——— PLATO, and other Companions of Socrates. 3 Vols. 8vo. 45s.

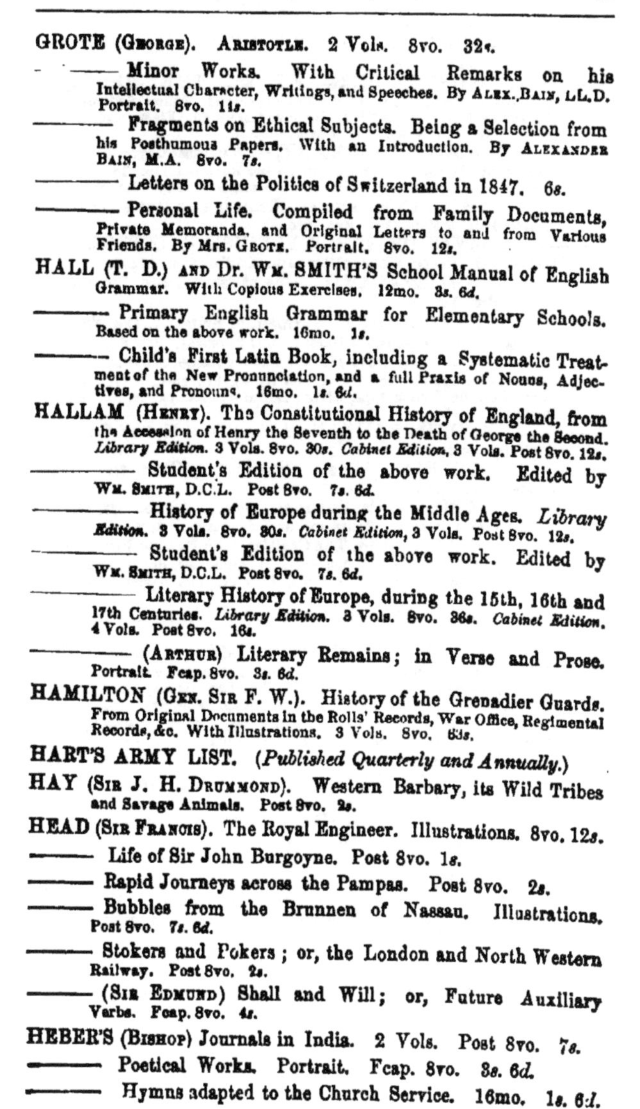

GROTE (GEORGE). ARISTOTLE. 2 Vols. 8vo. 32s.

——— Minor Works. With Critical Remarks on his Intellectual Character, Writings, and Speeches. By ALEX. BAIN, LL.D. Portrait. 8vo. 14s.

——— Fragments on Ethical Subjects. Being a Selection from his Posthumous Papers. With an Introduction. By ALEXANDER BAIN, M.A. 8vo. 7s.

——— Letters on the Politics of Switzerland in 1847. 6s.

——— Personal Life. Compiled from Family Documents, Private Memoranda, and Original Letters to and from Various Friends. By Mrs. GROTE. Portrait. 8vo. 12s.

HALL (T. D.) AND Dr. WM. SMITH'S School Manual of English Grammar. With Copious Exercises. 12mo. 3s. 6d.

——— Primary English Grammar for Elementary Schools. Based on the above work. 16mo. 1s.

——— Child's First Latin Book, including a Systematic Treatment of the New Pronunciation, and a full Praxis of Nouns, Adjectives, and Pronouns. 16mo. 1s. 6d.

HALLAM (HENRY). The Constitutional History of England, from the Accession of Henry the Seventh to the Death of George the Second. *Library Edition.* 3 Vols. 8vo. 30s. *Cabinet Edition*, 3 Vols. Post 8vo. 12s.

——— Student's Edition of the above work. Edited by WM. SMITH, D.C.L. Post 8vo. 7s. 6d.

——— History of Europe during the Middle Ages. *Library Edition.* 3 Vols. 8vo. 30s. *Cabinet Edition*, 3 Vols. Post 8vo. 12s.

——— Student's Edition of the above work. Edited by WM. SMITH, D.C.L. Post 8vo. 7s. 6d.

——— Literary History of Europe, during the 15th, 16th and 17th Centuries. *Library Edition.* 3 Vols. 8vo. 36s. *Cabinet Edition.* 4 Vols. Post 8vo. 16s.

——— (ARTHUR) Literary Remains; in Verse and Prose. Portrait. Fcap. 8vo. 3s. 6d.

HAMILTON (GEN. SIR F. W.). History of the Grenadier Guards. From Original Documents in the Rolls' Records, War Office, Regimental Records, &c. With Illustrations. 3 Vols. 8vo. 63s.

HART'S ARMY LIST. (*Published Quarterly and Annually.*)

HAY (SIR J. H. DRUMMOND). Western Barbary, its Wild Tribes and Savage Animals. Post 8vo. 2s.

HEAD (SIR FRANCIS). The Royal Engineer. Illustrations. 8vo. 12s.

——— Life of Sir John Burgoyne. Post 8vo. 1s.

——— Rapid Journeys across the Pampas. Post 8vo. 2s.

——— Bubbles from the Brunnen of Nassau. Illustrations. Post 8vo. 7s. 6d.

——— Stokers and Pokers; or, the London and North Western Railway. Post 8vo. 2s.

——— (SIR EDMUND) Shall and Will; or, Future Auxiliary Verbs. Fcap. 8vo. 4s.

HEBER'S (BISHOP) Journals in India. 2 Vols. Post 8vo. 7s.

——— Poetical Works. Portrait. Fcap. 8vo. 3s. 6d.

——— Hymns adapted to the Church Service. 16mo. 1s. 6d.

FOREIGN HANDBOOKS.

HAND-BOOK—TRAVEL-TALK. English, French, German, and Italian. 18mo. 3s. 6d.

——— HOLLAND AND BELGIUM. Map and Plans. Post 8vo. 6s.

——— NORTH GERMANY and THE RHINE,—The Black Forest, the Hartz, Thüringerwald, Saxon Switzerland, Rügen the Giant Mountains, Taunus, Odenwald, Elass, and Lothringen. Map and Plans. Post 8vo. 10s.

——— SOUTH GERMANY,—Wurtemburg, Bavaria, Austria, Styria, Salzburg, the Austrian and Bavarian Alps, Tyrol, Hungary, and the Danube, from Ulm to the Black Sea. Map. Post 8vo. 10s.

——— PAINTING. German, Flemish, and Dutch Schools. Illustrations. 2 Vols. Post 8vo. 24s.

——— LIVES OF EARLY FLEMISH PAINTERS. By Crowe and Cavalcaselle. Illustrations. Post 8vo. 10s. 6d.

——— SWITZERLAND, Alps of Savoy, and Piedmont. Maps. Post 8vo. 9s.

——— FRANCE, Part I. Normandy, Brittany, the French Alps, the Loire, the Seine, the Garonne, and Pyrenees. Post 8vo. 7s. 6d.

——— ——— Part II. Central France, Auvergne, the Cevennes, Burgundy, the Rhone and Saone, Provence, Nimes, Arles, Marseilles, the French Alps, Alsace, Lorraine, Champagne, &c. Maps. Post 8vo. 7s. 6d.

——— MEDITERRANEAN ISLANDS—Malta, Corsica, Sardinia, and Sicily. Maps. Post 8vo. [*In the Press.*

——— ALGERIA. Algiers, Constantine, Oran, the Atlas Range. Map. Post 8vo. 9s.

——— PARIS, and its Environs. Map. 16mo. 3s. 6d.

*** Murray's Plan of Paris, mounted on canvas. 3s. 6d.

——— SPAIN, Madrid, The Castiles, The Basque Provinces, Leon, The Asturias, Galicia, Estremadura, Andalusia, Ronda, Granada, Murcia, Valencia, Catalonia, Aragon, Navarre, The Balearic Islands, &c. &c. Maps. 2 Vols. Post 8vo.

——— PORTUGAL, Lisbon, Porto, Cintra, Mafra, &c. Map. Post 8vo. 12s.

——— NORTH ITALY, Turin, Milan, Cremona, the Italian Lakes, Bergamo, Brescia, Verona, Mantua, Vicenza, Padua, Ferrara, Bologna, Ravenna, Rimini, Piacenza, Genoa, the Riviera, Venice, Parma, Modena, and Romagna. Map. Post 8vo. 10s.

——— CENTRAL ITALY, Florence, Lucca, Tuscany, The Marches, Umbria, and late Patrimony of St. Peter's. Map. Post 8vo. 10s.

——— ROME and its Environs. Map. Post 8vo. 10s.

——— SOUTH ITALY, Naples, Pompeii, Herculaneum, and Vesuvius. Map. Post 8vo. 10s.

——— KNAPSACK GUIDE TO ITALY. 16mo.

——— PAINTING. The Italian Schools. Illustrations. 2 Vols. Post 8vo. 30s.

——— LIVES OF ITALIAN PAINTERS, from Cimabue to Bassano. By Mrs. Jameson. Portraits. Post 8vo. 12s.

——— NORWAY, Christiania, Bergen, Trondhjem. The Fjelds and Fjords. Map. Post 8vo. 9s.

——— SWEDEN, Stockholm, Upsala, Gothenburg, the Shores of the Baltic, &c. Post 8vo. 6s.

——— DENMARK, Sleswig, Holstein, Copenhagen, Jutland, Iceland. Map. Post 8vo. 6s.

HAND-BOOK—RUSSIA, St. Petersburg, Moscow, Poland, and Finland. Maps. Post 8vo. 18s.

———— GREECE, the Ionian Islands, Continental Greece, Athens, the Peloponnesus, the Islands of the Ægean Sea, Albania, Thessaly, and Macedonia. Maps. Post 8vo. 15s.

———— TURKEY IN ASIA—Constantinople, the Bosphorus, Dardanelles, Brousa, Plain of Troy, Crete, Cyprus, Smyrna, Ephesus, the Seven Churches, Coasts of the Black Sea, Armenia, Mesopotamia, &c. Maps. Post 8vo. 15s.

———— EGYPT, including Descriptions of the Course of the Nile through Egypt and Nubia, Alexandria, Cairo, and Thebes, the Suez Canal, the Pyramids, the Peninsula of Sinai, the Oases, the Fyoom, &c. Map. Post 8vo. 15s.

———— HOLY LAND—Syria, Palestine, Peninsula of Sinai Edom, Syrian Deserts, Petra, Damascus, and Palmyra. Maps. Post 8vo. 20s. *.* Travelling Map of Palestine. In a case. 12s.

———— INDIA — Bombay and Madras. Map. 2 Vols. Post 8vo. 12s. each.

ENGLISH HANDBOOKS.

HAND-BOOK—MODERN LONDON. Map. 16mo. 3s. 6d.

———— ENVIRONS OF LONDON within a circuit of 20 miles. 2 Vols. Crown 8vo. 21s.

———— EASTERN COUNTIES, Chelmsford, Harwich, Colchester, Maldon, Cambridge, Ely, Newmarket, Bury St. Edmunds, Ipswich, Woodbridge, Felixstowe, Lowestoft, Norwich, Yarmouth, Cromer, &c. Map and Plans. Post 8vo. 12s.

———— CATHEDRALS of Oxford, Peterborough, Norwich, Ely, and Lincoln. With 90 Illustrations. Crown 8vo. 18s.

———— KENT, Canterbury, Dover, Ramsgate, Sheerness, Rochester, Chatham, Woolwich. Map. Post 8vo. 7s. 6d.

———— SUSSEX, Brighton, Chichester, Worthing, Hastings, Lewes, Arundel, &c. Map. Post 8vo. 6s.

———— SURREY AND HANTS, Kingston, Croydon, Reigate, Guildford, Dorking, Boxhill, Winchester, Southampton, New Forest, Portsmouth, and Isle of Wight. Maps. Post 8vo. 10s.

———— BERKS, BUCKS, AND OXON, Windsor, Eton, Reading, Aylesbury, Uxbridge, Wycombe, Henley, the City and University of Oxford, Blenheim, and the Descent of the Thames. Map. Post 8vo. 7s. 6d.

———— WILTS, DORSET, AND SOMERSET, Salisbury, Chippenham, Weymouth, Sherborne, Wells, Bath, Bristol, Taunton, &c. Map. Post 8vo. 10s.

———— DEVON AND CORNWALL, Exeter, Ilfracombe, Linton, Sidmouth, Dawlish, Teignmouth, Plymouth, Devonport, Torquay, Launceston, Truro, Penzance, Falmouth, the Lizard, Land's End, &c. Maps. Post 8vo. 12s.

———— CATHEDRALS of Winchester, Salisbury, Exeter, Wells, Chichester, Rochester, Canterbury, and St. Albans. With 130 Illustrations. 2 Vols. Crown 8vo. 36s. St. Albans separately, crown 8vo. 6s.

———— GLOUCESTER, HEREFORD, and WORCESTER Cirencester, Cheltenham, Stroud, Tewkesbury, Leominster, Ross, Malvern, Kidderminster, Dudley, Bromsgrove, Evesham. Map. Post 8vo. 9s.

———— CATHEDRALS of Bristol, Gloucester, Hereford, Worcester, and Lichfield. With 50 Illustrations. Crown 8vo. 16s.

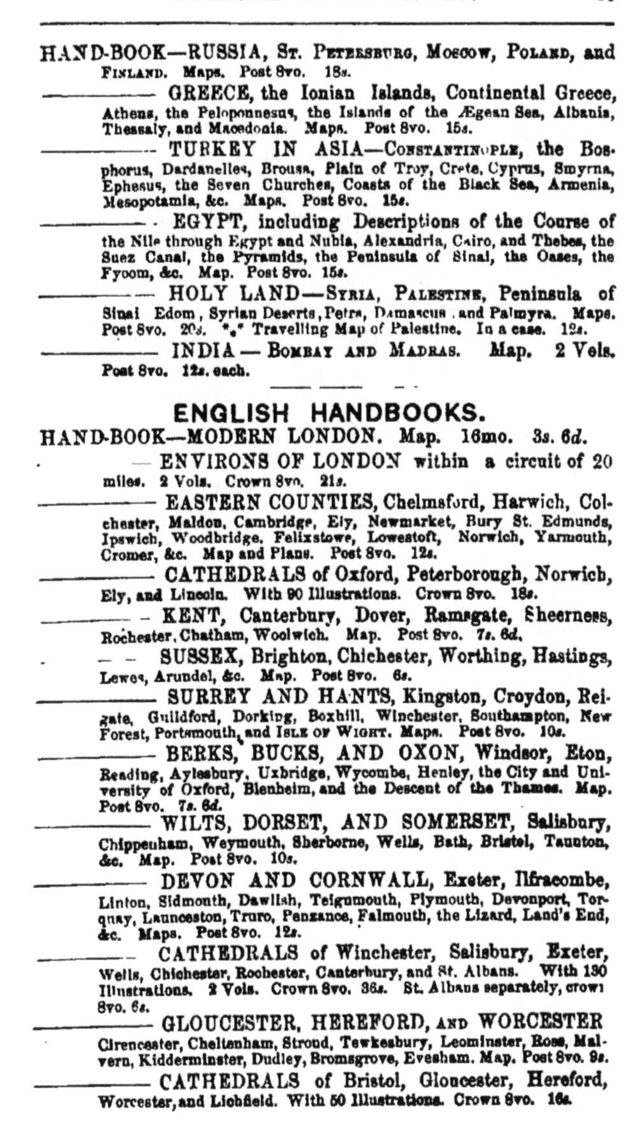

HAND-BOOK—NORTH WALES, Bangor, Carnarvon, Beaumaris, Snowdon, Llanberis, Dolgelly, Cader Idris, Conway, &c. Map. Post 8vo. 7s.

—— **SOUTH WALES,** Monmouth, Llandaff, Merthyr, Vale of Neath, Pembroke, Carmarthen, Tenby, Swansea, The Wye, &c. Map. Post 8vo. 7s.

—— **CATHEDRALS OF BANGOR, ST. ASAPH,** Llandaff, and St. David's. With Illustrations. Post 8vo. 15s.

—— **DERBY, NOTTS, LEICESTER, STAFFORD,** Matlock, Bakewell, Chatsworth, The Peak, Buxton, Hardwick, Dove Dale, Ashborne, Southwell, Mansfield, Retford, Burton, Belvoir, Melto Mowbray, Wolverhampton, Lichfield, Walsall, Tamworth. Map. Post 8vo. 9s.

—— **SHROPSHIRE, CHESHIRE AND LANCASHIRE** —Shrewsbury, Ludlow, Bridgnorth, Oswestry, Chester, Crewe, Alderley, Stockport, Birkenhead, Warrington, Bury, Manchester, Liverpool, Burnley, Clitheroe, Bolton, Blackburn, Wigan, Preston, Rochdale, Lancaster, Southport, Blackpool, &c. Map. Post 8vo. 10s.

—— **YORKSHIRE,** Doncaster, Hull, Selby, Beverley, Scarborough, Whitby, Harrogate, Ripon, Leeds, Wakefield, Bradford, Halifax, Huddersfield, Sheffield. Map and Plans. Post 8vo. 12s.

—— **CATHEDRALS** of York, Ripon, Durham, Carlisle, Chester, and Manchester. With 60 Illustrations. 2 Vols. Crown 8vo. 21s.

—— **DURHAM AND NORTHUMBERLAND,** Newcastle, Darlington, Gateshead, Bishop Auckland, Stockton, Hartlepool, Sunderland, Shields, Berwick-on-Tweed, Morpeth, Tynemouth, Coldstream, Alnwick, &c. Map. Post 8vo. 9s.

—— **WESTMORLAND AND CUMBERLAND**—Lancaster, Furness Abbey, Ambleside, Kendal, Windermere, Coniston, Keswick, Grasmere, Ulswater, Carlisle, Cockermouth, Penrith, Appleby. Map. Post 8vo. 6s.

*** MURRAY'S MAP OF THE LAKE DISTRICT, on canvas. 3s. 6d.

—— **ENGLAND AND WALES.** Alphabetically arranged and condensed into one volume. Post 8vo [*In the Press.*

—— **SCOTLAND,** Edinburgh, Melrose, Kelso, Glasgow, Dumfries, Ayr, Stirling, Arran, The Clyde, Oban, Inverary, Loch Lomond, Loch Katrine and Trossachs, Caledonian Canal, Inverness, Perth, Dundee, Aberdeen, Braemar, Skye, Caithness, Ross, Sutherland, &c. Maps and Plans. Post 8vo. 9s.

—— **IRELAND,** Dublin, Belfast, Donegal, Galway, Wexford, Cork, Limerick, Waterford, Killarney, Munster, &c. Maps. Post 8vo. 12s.

HERODOTUS. A New English Version. Edited, with Notes and Essays, historical, ethnographical, and geographical, by CANON RAWLINSON, assisted by SIR HENRY RAWLINSON and SIR J. G. WILKINSON. Maps and Woodcuts. 4 Vols. 8vo. 48s.

HERSCHEL'S (CAROLINE) Memoir and Correspondence. By MRS. JOHN HERSCHEL. With Portraits. Crown 8vo 12s.

HATHERLEY (LORD). The Continuity of Scripture, as Declared by the Testimony of our Lord and of the Evangelists and Apostles. 8vo. 6s. *Popular Edition.* Post 8vo. 2s. 6d.

HOLLWAY (J. G.). A Month in Norway. Fcap. 8vo. 2s.

HONEY BEE. By REV. THOMAS JAMES. Fcap. 8vo. 1s.

HOOK (DEAN). Church Dictionary. 8vo. 16s.

HOME AND COLONIAL LIBRARY. A Series of Works adapted for all circles and classes of Readers, having been selected for their acknowledged interest, and ability of the Authors. Post 8vo. Published at 2s. and 3s. 6d. each, and arranged under two distinctive heads as follows:—

CLASS A.

HISTORY, BIOGRAPHY, AND HISTORIC TALES.

1. SIEGE OF GIBRALTAR. By John Drinkwater. 2s.
2. THE AMBER-WITCH. By Lady Duff Gordon. 2s.
3. CROMWELL AND BUNYAN. By Robert Southey. 2s.
4. LIFE OF SIR FRANCIS DRAKE. By John Barrow. 2s.
5. CAMPAIGNS AT WASHINGTON. By Rev. G. R. Gleig. 2s.
6. THE FRENCH IN ALGIERS. By Lady Duff Gordon. 2s.
7. THE FALL OF THE JESUITS. 2s.
8. LIVONIAN TALES. 2s.
9. LIFE OF CONDÉ. By Lord Mahon. 3s. 6d.
10. SALE'S BRIGADE. By Rev. G. R. Gleig. 2s.
11. THE SIEGES OF VIENNA. By Lord Ellesmere. 2s.
12. THE WAYSIDE CROSS. By Capt. Milman. 2s.
13. SKETCHES OF GERMAN LIFE. By Sir A. Gordon. 3s. 6d.
14. THE BATTLE OF WATERLOO. By Rev. G. R. Gleig. 3s. 6d.
15. AUTOBIOGRAPHY OF STEFFENS. 2s.
16. THE BRITISH POETS. By Thomas Campbell. 3s. 6d.
17. HISTORICAL ESSAYS. By Lord Mahon. 3s. 6d.
18. LIFE OF LORD CLIVE. By Rev. G. R. Gleig. 3s. 6d.
19. NORTH - WESTERN RAILWAY. By Sir F. B. Head. 2s.
20. LIFE OF MUNRO. By Rev. G. R. Gleig. 3s. 6d.

CLASS B.

VOYAGES, TRAVELS, AND ADVENTURES.

1. BIBLE IN SPAIN. By George Borrow. 3s. 6d.
2. GYPSIES OF SPAIN. By George Borrow. 3s. 6d.
3 & 4. JOURNALS IN INDIA. By Bishop Heber. 2 Vols. 7s.
5. TRAVELS IN THE HOLY LAND. By Irby and Mangles. 2s.
6. MOROCCO AND THE MOORS. By J. Drummond Hay. 2s.
7. LETTERS FROM THE BALTIC. By a Lady.
8. NEW SOUTH WALES. By Mrs. Meredith. 2s.
9. THE WEST INDIES. By M. G. Lewis. 2s.
10. SKETCHES OF PERSIA. By Sir John Malcolm. 3s. 6d.
11. MEMOIRS OF FATHER RIPA. 2s.
12 & 13. TYPEE AND OMOO. By Hermann Melville. 2 Vols. 7s.
14. MISSIONARY LIFE IN CANADA. By Rev. J. Abbott. 2s.
15. LETTERS FROM MADRAS. By a Lady. 2s.
16. HIGHLAND SPORTS. By Charles St. John. 3s. 6d.
17. PAMPAS JOURNEYS. By Sir F. B. Head. 2s.
18. GATHERINGS FROM SPAIN. By Richard Ford. 3s. 6d.
19. THE RIVER AMAZON. By W. H. Edwards. 2s.
20. MANNERS & CUSTOMS OF INDIA. By Rev. C. Acland. 2s.
21. ADVENTURES IN MEXICO. By G. F. Ruxton. 3s. 6d.
22. PORTUGAL AND GALICIA. By Lord Carnarvon. 3s. 6d.
23. BUSH LIFE IN AUSTRALIA. By Rev. H. W. Haygarth. 2s.
24. THE LIBYAN DESERT. By Bayle St. John. 2s.
25. SIERRA LEONE. By A Lady. 3s. 6d.

*** Each work may be had separately.

HOOK'S (Theodore) Life. By J. G. Lockhart. Fcap. 8vo. 1*s.*

HOPE (T. C.). Architecture of Ahmedabad, with Historical Sketch and Architectural Notes. With Maps, Photographs, and Woodcuts. 4to. 5*l.* 5*s.*

——— (A. J. Beresford) Worship in the Church of England. 8vo. 9*s.*, or, *Popular Selections from.* 8vo. 2*s.* 6*d.*

HORACE; a New Edition of the Text. Edited by Dean Milman. With 100 Woodcuts. Crown 8vo. 7*s.* 6*d.*

——— Life of. By Dean Milman. Illustrations. 8vo. 9*s.*

HOUGHTON'S (Lord) Monographs, Personal and Social. With Portraits. Crown 8vo. 10*s.* 6*d.*

——— Poetical Works. *Collected Edition.* With Portrait. 2 Vols. Fcap. 8vo. 12*s.*

HUME (The Student's). A History of England, from the Invasion of Julius Cæsar to the Revolution of 1688. Corrected and continued to 1868 Woodcuts. Post 8vo. 7*s.* 6*d.*

HUTCHINSON (Gen.) Dog Breaking, with Odds and Ends for those who love the Dog and the Gun. With 40 Illustrations. 6th edition. 7*s.* 6*d.*

HUTTON (H. E.). Principia Græca; an Introduction to the Study of Greek. Comprehending Grammar, Delectus, and Exercise-book, with Vocabularies. *Sixth Edition.* 12mo. 3*s.* 6*d.*

IRBY AND MANGLES' Travels in Egypt, Nubia, Syria, and the Holy Land. Post 8vo. 2*s.*

JACOBSON (Bishop). Fragmentary Illustrations of the History of the Book of Common Prayer; from Manuscript Sources (Bishop Sanderson and Bishop Wren). 8vo. 5*s.*

JAMES' (Rev. Thomas) Fables of Æsop. A New Translation, with Historical Preface. With 100 Woodcuts by Tenniel and Wolf. Post 8vo. 2*s.* 6*d.*

JAMESON (Mrs.). Lives of the Early Italian Painters—and the Progress of Painting in Italy—Cimabue to Bassano. With 50 Portraits. Post 8vo. 12*s.*

JENNINGS (Louis J.). Field Paths and Green Lanes. Being Country Walks, chiefly in Surrey and Sussex. With Illustrations. Post 8vo. 10*s.* 6*d.*

JERVIS (Rev. W. H.). The Gallican Church, from the Concordat of Bologna, 1516, to the Revolution. With an Introduction. Portraits. 2 Vols. 8vo. 28*s.*

JESSE (Edward). Gleanings in Natural History. Fcp. 8vo. 3*s.* 6*d.*

JEX-BLAKE (Rev. T. W.). Life in Faith: Sermons Preached at Cheltenham and Rugby. Fcap. 8vo. 3*s.* 6*d.*

JOHNS (Rev. B. G.). Blind People; their Works and Ways. With Sketches of the Lives of some famous Blind Men. With Illustrations. Post 8vo. 7*s.* 6*d.*

JOHNSON'S (Dr. Samuel) Life. By James Boswell. Including the Tour to the Hebrides. Edited by Mr. Croker. 1 vol. Royal 8vo. 12*s* *New Edition.* Portraits. 4 Vols. 8vo. [*In Preparation.*

——— Lives of the most eminent English Poets, with Critical Observations on their Works. Edited with Notes, Corrective and Explanatory, by Peter Cunningham. 3 vols. 8vo. 22*s.* 6*d.*

JUNIUS' Handwriting Professionally investigated. By Mr. Chabot, Expert. With Preface and Collateral Evidence, by the Hon. Edward Twisleton. With Facsimiles, Woodcuts, &c. 4to. £3 3*s.*

KEN'S (BISHOP) Life. By a LAYMAN. Portrait. 2 Vols. 8vo. 18s.

———— Exposition of the Apostles' Creed. 16mo. 1s. 6d.

KERR (ROBERT). GENTLEMAN'S HOUSE; OR, HOW TO PLAN ENGLISH RESIDENCES FROM THE PARSONAGE TO THE PALACE. With Views and Plans. 8vo. 24s.

———— Small Country House. A Brief Practical Discourse on the Planning of a Residence from 2000l. to 5000l. With Supplementary Estimates to 7000l. Post 8vo. 3s.

———— Ancient Lights; a Book for Architects, Surveyors, Lawyers, and Landlords. 8vo. 5s. 6d.

———— (R. MALCOLM) Student's Blackstone. A Systematic Abridgment of the entire Commentaries, adapted to the present state of the law. Post 8vo. 7s. 6d.

KING EDWARD VIth's Latin Grammar. 12mo. 3s. 6d.

———— First Latin Book. 12mo. 2s. 6d.

KING GEORGE IIIrd's Correspondence with Lord North, 1769-82. Edited, with Notes and Introduction, by W. BODHAM DONNE. 2 vols. 8vo. 32s.

KING (R. J.). Archæology, Travel and Art; being Sketches and Studies, Historical and Descriptive. 8vo. 12s.

KIRK (J. FOSTER). History of Charles the Bold, Duke of Burgundy. Portrait. 3 Vols. 8vo. 45s.

KIRKES' Handbook of Physiology. Edited by W. MORRANT BAKER, F.R.C.S. *10th Edition*. With 400 Illustrations. Post 8vo. 14s.

KUGLER'S Handbook of Painting.—The Italian Schools. Revised and Remodelled from the most recent Researches. By LADY EASTLAKE. With 140 Illustrations. 2 Vols. Crown 8vo. 30s.

———— Handbook of Painting.—The German, Flemish, and Dutch Schools. Revised and in part re-written. By J. A. CROWE. With 60 Illustrations. 2 Vols. Crown 8vo. 24s.

LANE (E. W.). Account of the Manners and Customs of Modern Egyptians. With Illustrations. 2 Vols. Post 8vo. 12s

LAWRENCE (SIR GEO.). Reminiscences of Forty-three Years' Service in India; including Captivities in Cabul among the Affghans and among the Sikhs, and a Narrative of the Mutiny in Rajputana. Crown 8vo. 10s. 6d.

LAYARD (A. H.). Nineveh and its Remains. Being a Narrative of Researches and Discoveries amidst the Ruins of Assyria. With an Account of the Chaldean Christians of Kurdistan; the Yezedis, or Devil-worshippers; and an Enquiry into the Manners and Arts of the Ancient Assyrians. Plates and Woodcuts. 2 Vols. 8vo. 36s.

*** A POPULAR EDITION of the above work. With Illustrations. Post 8vo. 7s. 6d.

———— Nineveh and Babylon; being the Narrative of Discoveries in the Ruins, with Travels in Armenia, Kurdistan and the Desert, during a Second Expedition to Assyria. With Map and Plates. 8vo. 21s.

*** A POPULAR EDITION of the above work. With Illustrations. Post 8vo. 7s. 6d.

LEATHES' (STANLEY) Practical Hebrew Grammar. With the Hebrew Text of Genesis i.—vi., and Psalms i.—vi. Grammatical Analysis and Vocabulary. Post 8vo. 7s. 6d.

LENNEP (REV. H. J. VAN). Missionary Travels in Asia Minor. With Illustrations of Biblical History and Archæology. With Map and Woodcuts. 2 Vols. Post 8vo. 24s.

———— Modern Customs and Manners of Bible Lands in Illustration of Scripture. With Coloured Maps and 300 Illustrations. 2 Vols. 8vo. 21s.

LESLIE (C. R.). Handbook for Young Painters. With Illustrations. Post 8vo. *7s. 6d.*

——— Life and Works of Sir Joshua Reynolds. Portraits and Illustrations. 2 Vols. 8vo. *42s.*

LETO (POMPONIO). Eight Months at Rome during the Vatican Council. With a daily account of the proceedings. Translated from the original. 8vo. *12s.*

LETTERS FROM THE BALTIC. By a LADY. Post 8vo. *2s.*

——— MADRAS. By a LADY. Post 8vo. *2s.*

——— SIERRA LEONE. By a LADY. Post 8vo. *3s. 6d.*

LEVI (LEONE). History of British Commerce; and of the Economic Progress of the Nation, from 1763 to 1870. 8vo. *16s.*

LIDDELL (DEAN). Student's History of Rome, from the earliest Times to the establishment of the Empire. Woodcuts. Post 8vo. *7s. 6d.*

LLOYD (W. WATKISS). History of Sicily to the Athenian War; with Elucidations of the Sicilian Odes of Pindar. With Map. 8vo. *14s.*

LISPINGS from LOW LATITUDES; or, the Journal of the Hon. Impulsia Gushington. Edited by LORD DUFFERIN. With 24 Plates. 4to. *21s.*

LITTLE ARTHUR'S HISTORY OF ENGLAND. By LADY CALLCOTT. *New Edition, continued to* 1872. With Woodcuts. Fcap. 8vo. *1s. 6d.*

LIVINGSTONE (DR.). Popular Account of his First Expedition to Africa, 1840-56. Illustrations. Post 8vo. *7s. 6d.*

——— Popular Account of his Second Expedition to Africa, 1858-64. Map and Illustrations. Post 8vo. *7s. 6d.*

——— Last Journals in Central Africa, from 1865 to his Death. Continued by a Narrative of his last moments and sufferings. By Rev HORACE WALLER. Maps and Illustrations. 2 Vols. 8vo. *28s.*

LIVINGSTONIA. Journal of Adventures in Exploring Lake Nyassa, and Establishing a Missionary Settlement there. By E. D. YOUNG, R.N. Revised by Rev. HORACE WALLER. Maps Post 8vo. *7s. 6d.*

LIVONIAN TALES. By the Author of "Letters from the Baltic." Post 8vo. *2s.*

LOCH (H. B.). Personal Narrative of Events during Lord Elgin's Second Embassy to China. With Illustrations. Post 8vo. *s.*

LOCKHART (J. G.). Ancient Spanish Ballads. Historical and Romantic. Translated, with Notes. With Portrait and Illustrations. Crown 8vo. *5s.*

——— Life of Theodore Hook. Fcap. 8vo. *1s.*

LOUDON (MRS.) Gardening for Ladies. With Directions and Calendar of Operations for Every Month. Woodcuts. Fcap. 8vo. *3s. 6d.*

LYELL (SIR CHARLES). Principles of Geology; or, the Modern Changes of the Earth and its Inhabitants considered as illustrative of Geology. With Illustrations. 2 Vols. 8vo. *32s.*

——— Student's Elements of Geology. With Table of British Fossils and 600 Illustrations. Post 8vo. *9s.*

——— Geological Evidences of the Antiquity of Man, including an Outline of Glacial Post-Tertiary Geology, and Remarks on the Origin of Species. Illustrations. 8vo. *14s.*

——— (K. M.). Geographical Handbook of Ferns. With Tables to show their Distribution. Post 8vo. *7s. 6d.*

LYTTON (LORD). A Memoir of Julian Fane. With Portrait. Post 8vo. *5s*

McCLINTOCK (SIR L.). Narrative of the Discovery of the Fate of Sir John Franklin and his Companions in the Arctic Seas. With Illustrations. Post 8vo. *7s. 6d.*

MACDOUGALL (COL.). Modern Warfare as Influenced by Modern Artillery. With Plans. Post 8vo. *12s.*

MACGREGOR (J.). Rob Roy on the Jordan, Nile, Red Sea, Gennesareth, &c. A Canoe Cruise in Palestine and Egypt and the Waters of Damascus. With Map and 70 Illustrations. Crown 8vo. 7*s.* 6*d.*

MAETZNER'S ENGLISH GRAMMAR. A Methodical, Analytical, and Historical Treatise on the Orthography, Prosody, Inflections, and Syntax of the English Tongue. Translated from the German. By CLAIR J. GRECE, LL.D. 3 Vols. 8vo. 36*s.*

MAHON (LORD), see STANHOPE.

MAINE (SIR H. SUMNER). Ancient Law: its Connection with the Early History of Society, and its Relation to Modern Ideas. 8vo. 12*s.*

——— – Village Communities in the East and West. With additional Essays. 8vo. 12*s.*

——— Early History of Institutions. 8vo. 12*s.*

MALCOLM (SIR JOHN). Sketches of Persia. Post 8vo. 3*s.* 6*d.*

MANSEL (DEAN). Limits of Religious Thought Examined. Post 8vo. 8*s.* 6*d.*

——— Letters, Lectures, and Papers, including the Phrontisterion, or Oxford in the XIXth Century. Edited by H. W. CHANDLER, M.A. 8vo. 12*s.*

——— Gnostic Heresies of the First and Second Centuries. With a sketch of his life and character By Lord CARNARVON. Edited by Canon LIGHTFOOT. 8vo 10*s.* 6*d.*

MANUAL OF SCIENTIFIC ENQUIRY. For the Use of Travellers. Edited by REV. R. MAIN. Post 8vo. 3*s.* 6*d.* (*Published by order of the Lords of the Admiralty.*)

MARCO POLO. The Book of Ser Marco Polo, the Venetian. Concerning the Kingdoms and Marvels of the East. A new English Version. Illustrated by the light of Oriental Writers and Modern Travels. By COL. HENRY YULE. Maps and Illustrations. 2 Vols. Medium 8vo. 63*s.*

MARKHAM'S (MRS.) History of England. From the First Invasion by the Romans *to* 1867. Woodcuts. 12mo. 3*s.* 6*d.*

——— History of France. From the Conquest by the Gauls *to* 1861. Woodcuts. 12mo. 3*s.* 6*d.*

——— History of Germany. From the Invasion by Marius *to* 1867. Woodcuts. 12mo. 3*s.* 6*d.*

MARLBOROUGH'S (SARAH, DUCHESS OF) Letters. Now first published from the Original MSS. at Madresfield Court. With an Introduction. 8vo. 10*s.* 6*d.*

MARRYAT (JOSEPH). History of Modern and Mediæval Pottery and Porcelain. With a Description of the Manufacture. Plates and Woodcuts. 8vo. 42*s.*

MARSH (G. P.). Student's Manual of the English Language. [Post 8vo. 7*s.* 6*d.*

MASTERS in English Theology. The King's College Lectures, 1877. By Canon Barry, Dean of S. Paul's; Prof. Plumptre, Canon Westcott, Canon Farrar, and Prof. Cheetham. With an Historical Introduction by Canon Barry. Post 8vo. 7*s* 6*d.*

MATTHIÆ'S GREEK GRAMMAR. Abridged by BLOMFIELD, *Revised* by E. S. CROOKE. 12mo. 4*s.*

MAUREL'S Character, Actions, and Writings of Wellington. Fcap. 8vo. 1*s.* 6*d.*

MAYNE (CAPT.). Four Years in British Columbia and Vancouver Island. Illustrations. 8vo. 16*s.*

MAYO (LORD). Sport in Abyssinia; or, the Mareb and Tackazzee. With Illustrations. Crown 8vo. 12*s.*

MEADE (HON. HERBERT). Ride through the Disturbed Districts of New Zealand, with a Cruise among the South Sea Islands. With Illustrations. Medium 8vo. 12*s.*

MELVILLE (HERMANN). Marquesas and South Sea Islands. 2 Vols. Post 8vo. 7*s*.

MEREDITH (MRS. CHARLES). Notes and Sketches of New South Wales. Post 8vo. 2*s*.

MESSIAH (THE): The Life, Travels, Death, Resurrection, and Ascension of our Blessed Lord. By A Layman. Map. 8vo. 18*s*.

MICHELANGELO, Sculptor, Painter, and Architect. His Life and Works. By C. HEATH WILSON. Illustrations. Royal 8vo. 26*s*.

MILLINGTON (REV. T. S.). Signs and Wonders in the Land of Ham, or the Ten Plagues of Egypt, with Ancient and Modern Illustrations. Woodcuts. Post 8vo. 7*s*. 6*d*.

MILMAN (DEAN). History of the Jews, from the earliest Period down to Modern Times. 3 Vols. Post 8vo. 18*s*.

——— Early Christianity, from the Birth of Christ to the Abolition of Paganism in the Roman Empire. 3 Vols. Post 8vo. 18*s*.

——— Latin Christianity, including that of the Popes to the Pontificate of Nicholas V. 9 Vols. Post 8vo. 54*s*.

——— Annals of St. Paul's Cathedral, from the Romans to the funeral of Wellington. Portrait and Illustrations. 8vo. 18*s*.

——— Character and Conduct of the Apostles considered as an Evidence of Christianity. 8vo. 10*s*. 6*d*.

——— Quinti Horatii Flacci Opera. With 100 Woodcuts. Small 8vo. 7*s*. 6*d*.

——— Life of Quintus Horatius Flaccus. With Illustrations. 8vo. 9*s*.

——— Poetical Works. The Fall of Jerusalem—Martyr of Antioch—Balshazzar—Tamor—Anne Boleyn—Fazio, &c. With Portrait and Illustrations. 3 Vols. Fcap. 8vo. 18*s*.

——— Fall of Jerusalem. Fcap. 8vo. 1*s*.

——— (CAPT. E. A.) Wayside Cross. Post 8vo. 2*s*.

MIVART (ST. GEORGE). Lessons from Nature; as manifested in Mind and Matter. 8vo. 15*s*.

MODERN DOMESTIC COOKERY. Founded on Principles of Economy and Practical Knowledge. *New Edition*. Woodcuts. Fcap. 8vo. 5*s*.

MONGREDIEN (AUGUSTUS). Trees and Shrubs for English Plantation. A Selection and Description of the most Ornamental which will flourish in the open air in our climate. With Classified Lists. With 30 Illustrations. 8vo. 16*s*.

MOORE (THOMAS). Life and Letters of Lord Byron. *Cabinet Edition*. With Plates. 6 Vols. Fcap. 8vo. 18*s*.; *Popular Edition*, with Portraits. Royal 8vo. 7*s*. 6*d*.

MORESBY (CAPT.), R.N. Discoveries in New Guinea, Polynesia, Torres Straits, &c., during the cruise of H M S. Basilisk. Map and Illustrations. 8vo. 15*s*.

MOTLEY (J. L.). History of the United Netherlands: from the Death of William the Silent to the Twelve Years' Truce, 1609. *Library Edition*. Portraits. 4 Vols. 8vo. 60*s*. *Cabinet Edition*: 4 Vols. Post 8vo. 6*s*. each.

——— Life and Death of John of Barneveld, Advocate of Holland. With a View of the Primary Causes and Movements of the Thirty Years' War. *Library Edition*. Illustrations. 2 Vols. 8vo. 28*s*. *Cabinet Edition*. 2 vols. Post 8vo. 12*s*.

MOSSMAN (SAMUEL). New Japan; the Land of the Rising Sun; its Annals and Progress during the past Twenty Years, recording the remarkable Progress of the Japanese in Western Civilisation. With Map. 8vo. 15*s*.

MOUHOT (HENRI). Siam, Cambojia, and Lao; a Narrative Travels and Discoveries. Illustrations. 2 Vols. 8vo.

MOZLEY (CANON). Treatise on Predestination. 8vo. 14*s.*

——— Primitive Doctrine of Baptismal Regeneration. Post 8vo.

MUIRHEAD (JAS.). The Vaux-de-Vire of Maistre Jean Le Houx Advocate of Vire. Translated and Edited. With Portrait and Illustrations. 8vo. 21*s.*

MUNRO'S (GENERAL) Life and Letters. By REV. G. R. GLEIG. Post 8vo. 3*s.* 6*d.*

MURCHISON (SIR RODERICK). Siluria; or, a History of the Oldest rocks containing Organic Remains. Map and Plates. 8vo. 18*s.*

——— Memoirs. With Notices of his Contemporaries, and Rise and Progress of Palæozoic Geology. By ARCHIBALD GEIKIE. Portraits. 2 Vols. 8vo. 30*s.*

MURRAY'S RAILWAY READING. Containing:—

WELLINGTON. By LORD ELLESMERE. 6*d.*
NIMROD ON THE CHASE, 1*s.*
MUSIC AND DRESS. 1*s.*
MILMAN'S FALL OF JERUSALEM. 1*s.*
MAHON'S "FORTY-FIVE." 3*s.*
LIFE OF THEODORE HOOK. 1*s.*
DEEDS OF NAVAL DARING. 3*s.* 6*d.*
THE HONEY BEE. 1*s.*
ÆSOP'S FABLES. 2*s.* 6*d.*
NIMROD ON THE TURF. 1*s.* 6*d.*
ART OF DINING. 1*s.* 6*d.*
MAHON'S JOAN OF ARC. 1*s.*
HEAD'S EMIGRANT. 2*s.* 6*d.*
NIMROD ON THE ROAD. 1*s.*
CROKER ON THE GUILLOTINE. 1*s.*
HOLLWAY'S NORWAY. 2*s.*
MAUREL'S WELLINGTON. 1*s.* 6*d.*
CAMPBELL'S LIFE OF BACON. 2*s.* 6*d.*
THE FLOWER GARDEN. 1*s.*
TAYLOR'S NOTES FROM LIFE. 2*s.*
REJECTED ADDRESSES. 1*s.*
PENN'S HINTS ON ANGLING. 1*s.*

MUSTERS' (CAPT.) Patagonians; a Year's Wanderings over Untrodden Ground from the Straits of Magellan to the Rio Negro. Illustrations. Post 8vo. 7*s.* 6*d.*

NAPIER (SIR WM.). English Battles and Sieges of the Peninsular War. Portrait. Post 8vo. 9*s.*

NAPOLEON AT FONTAINEBLEAU AND ELBA. A Journal of Occurrences and Notes of Conversations. By SIR NEIL CAMPBELL, C.B. With a Memoir. By REV. A. N. C. MACLACHLAN, M.A. Portrait. 8vo. 15*s.*

NARES (SIR GEORGE), R.N. Official Report to the Admiralty of the recent Arctic Expedition. Map. 8vo. 2*s.* 6*d.*

NASMYTH AND **CARPENTER.** The Moon. Considered as a Planet, a World, and a Satellite. With Illustrations from Drawings made with the aid of Powerful Telescopes, Woodcuts, &c. 4to. 30*s.*

NAUTICAL ALMANAC (THE). (*By Authority.*) 2*s.* 6*d.*

NAVY LIST. (Monthly and Quarterly.) Post 8vo.

NEW TESTAMENT. With Short Explanatory Commentary. By ARCHDEACON CHURTON, M.A., and ARCHDEACON BASIL JONES, M.A. With 110 authentic Views, &c. 2 Vols. Crown 8vo 21*s.* *bound.*

NEWTH (SAMUEL). First Book of Natural Philosophy; an Introduction to the Study of Statics, Dynamics, Hydrostatics, Optics, and Acoustics, with numerous Examples. Small 8vo. 3*s.* 6*d.*

——— Elements of Mechanics, including Hydrostatics, with numerous Examples. Small 8vo. 8*s.* 6*d.*

——— Mathematical Examinations. A Graduated Series of Elementary Examples in Arithmetic, Algebra, Logarithms, Trigonometry, and Mechanics. Small 8vo. 8*s.* 6*d.*

NICHOLS' (J. G.) Pilgrimages to Walsingham and Canterbury. By ERASMUS. Translated, with Notes. With Illustrations. Post 8vo. 6*s.*

——— (SIR GEORGE) History of the English Poor Laws. 2 Vols. 8vo.

NICOLAS' (SIR HARRIS) Historic Peerage of England. Exhibiting the Origin, Descent, and Present State of every Title of Peerage which has existed in this Country since the Conquest. By WILLIAM COURTHOPE. 8vo. 30*s.*

NIMROD, On the Chace—Turf—and Road. With Portrait and Plates. Crown 8vo. 5s. Or with Coloured Plates, 7s 6d.

NORDHOFF (Chas.). Communistic Societies of the United States; including Detailed Accounts of the Shakers, The Amana, Oneida, Bethell, Aurora, Icarian and other existing Societies; with Particulars of their Religious Creeds, Industries, and Present Condition. With 40 Illustrations. 8vo. 15s.

NORTHCOTE'S (Sir John) Notebook in the Long Parliament. Containing Proceedings during its First Session, 1640. From the Original MS. in the possession of Sir Stafford Northcote, Bart. Edited, with a Memoir. By A. H. A. Hamilton. Crown 8vo. 9s.

OWEN (Lieut.-Col.). Principles and Practice of Modern Artillery, including Artillery Material, Gunnery, and Organisation and Use of Artillery in Warfare. With Illustrations. 8vo. 15s.

OXENHAM (Rev. W.). English Notes for Latin Elegiacs; designed for early Proficients in the Art of Latin Versification, with Prefatory Rules of Composition in Elegiac Metre. 12mo. 3s. 6d.

PALGRAVE (R. H. I.). Local Taxation of Great Britain and Ireland. 8vo. 5s.

——— Notes on Banking in Great Britain and Ireland, Sweden, Denmark, and Hamburg, with some Remarks on the amount of Bills in circulation, both Inland and Foreign. 8vo. 6s.

PALLISER (Mrs.). Brittany and its Byeways, its Inhabitants, and Antiquities. With Illustrations. Post 8vo. 12s.

——— Mottoes for Monuments, or Epitaphs selected for General Use and Study. With Illustrations. Crown 8vo. 7s. 6d.

PARIS' (Dr.) Philosophy in Sport made Science in Earnest; or, the First Principles of Natural Philosophy inculcated by aid of the Toys and Sports of Youth. Woodcuts. Post 8vo. 7s. 6d.

PARKMAN (Francis). Discovery of the Great West; or, The Valleys of the Mississippi and the Lakes of North America. An Historical Narrative. Map. 8vo. 10s. 6d.

PARKYNS' (Mansfield) Three Years' Residence in Abyssinia: with Travels in that Country. With Illustrations. Post 8vo. 7s. 6d.

PEEK PRIZE ESSAYS. The Maintenance of the Church of England as an Established Church. By Rev. Charles Hole—Rev. R. Watson Dixon—and Rev. Julius Lloyd. 8vo. 10s. 6d.

PEEL'S (Sir Robert) Memoirs. 2 Vols. Post 8vo. 15s.

PENN (Richard). Maxims and Hints for an Angler and Chess-player. Woodcuts. Fcap. 8vo. 1s.

PERCY (John, M.D.). Metallurgy. 1st Division.—Fuel, Wood, Peat, Coal, Charcoal, Coke. Fire-Clays. *New Edition.* With Illustrations. 8vo. 30s

——— 2nd Division.—Copper, Zinc, and Brass. *New Edition.* With Illustrations. [*In the Press.*

——— 3rd Division.—Iron and Steel. *New Edition.* With Illustrations. [*In Preparation.*

——— 4th Division.—Lead, including part of Silver. With Illustrations. 30s. [*Ready.*

——— 5th Division.—Silver. With Illustrations. [*Nearly Ready.*

——— 6th Division.—Gold, Mercury, Platinum, Tin, Nickel, Cobalt, Antimony, Bismuth, Arsenic, and other Metals. With Illustrations. [*In Preparation.*

PHILLIPS' (John) Memoirs of William Smith. 8vo. 7s. 6d.

——— (John) Geology of Yorkshire, The Coast, and Limestone District. Plates. 2 Vols. 4to.

——— Rivers, Mountains, and Sea Coast of Yorkshire. With Essays on the Climate, Scenery, and Ancient Inhabitants. Plates. 8vo. 15s.

PHILLIPS (SAMUEL). Literary Essays from "The Times." With Portrait. 2 Vols. Fcap. 8vo. 7s.

POPE'S (ALEXANDER) Works. With Introductions and Notes, by REV. WHITWELL ELWIN. Vols. I., II., VI., VII., VIII. With Portraits. 8vo. 10s. 6d. each.

PORTER (REV. J. L.). Damascus, Palmyra, and Lebanon. With Travels among the Giant Cities of Bashan and the Hauran. Map and Woodcuts. Post 8vo. 7s. 6d.

PRAYER-BOOK (ILLUSTRATED), with Borders, Initials, Vignettes, &c. Edited, with Notes, by REV. THOS. JAMES. Medium 8vo. 18s. *cloth*; 31s. 6d. *calf*; 36s. *morocco*.

PRINCESS CHARLOTTE OF WALES. A Brief Memoir. With Selections from her Correspondence and other unpublished Papers. By LADY ROSE WEIGALL. With Portrait. 8vo. 8s. 6d.

PUSS IN BOOTS. With 12 Illustrations. By OTTO SPECKTER. 16mo. 1s. 6d. Or coloured, 2s. 6d.

PRIVY COUNCIL JUDGMENTS in Ecclesiastical Cases relating to Doctrine and Discipline. With Historical Introduction, by G. C. BRODRICK and W. H. FREMANTLE. 8vo. 10s. 6d.

QUARTERLY REVIEW (THE). 8vo. 6s.

RAE (EDWARD). Land of the North Wind; or Travels among the Laplanders and Samoyedes, and along the Shores of the White Sea. With Map and Woodcuts. Post 8vo. 10s. 6d.

—— The Country of the Moors. A Journey from Tripoli in Barbary to the City of Kairwan. With Illustrations. Crown 8vo. 12s.

RAMBLES in the Syrian Deserts. Post 8vo. 10s. 6d.

RANKE (LEOPOLD). A History of the Popes of Rome during the 16th and 17th Centuries. Translated from the German by SARAH AUSTIN. 3 Vols. 8vo. 30s.

RASSAM (HORMUZD). Narrative of the British Mission to Abyssinia. With Notices of the Countries Traversed from Massowah to Magdala. Illustrations. 2 Vols. 8vo. 28s.

RAWLINSON'S (CANON) Herodotus. A New English Version. Edited with Notes and Essays. Maps and Woodcut. 4 Vols 8vo. 48s.

—————— Five Great Monarchies of Chaldæa, Assyria, Media, Babylonia, and Persia. With Maps and Illustrations. 3 Vols. 8vo. 42s.

—————— (SIR HENRY) England and Russia in the East; a Series of Papers on the Political and Geographical Condition of Central Asia. Map. 8vo. 12s.

REED (E. J.). Shipbuilding in Iron and Steel; a Practical Treatise, giving full details of Construction, Processes of Manufacture, and Building Arrangements. With 5 Plans and 250 Woodcuts. 8vo.

—— Iron-Clad Ships; their Qualities, Performances, and Cost. With Chapters on Turret Ships, Iron-Clad Rams, &c. With Illustrations. 8vo. 12s.

—— Letters from Russia in 1875. 8vo. 5s.

REJECTED ADDRESSES (THE). By JAMES AND HORACE SMITH. Woodcuts. Post 8vo. 3s. 6d.; or *Popular Edition*, Fcap. 8vo. 1s.

REYNOLDS' (SIR JOSHUA) Life and Times. By C. R. LESLIE, R.A. and TOM TAYLOR. Portraits. 2 Vols. 8vo.

RICARDO'S (DAVID) Political Works. With a Notice of his Life and Writings. By J. R. M'CULLOCH. 8vo. 16s.

RIPA (FATHER). Thirteen Years' Residence at the Court of Peking. Post 8vo. 2s.

ROBERTSON (CANON). History of the Christian Church, from the Apostolic Age to the Reformation, 1517. *Library Edition.* 4 Vols. 8vo. *Cabinet Edition.* 8 Vols. Post 8vo. 6s. each.

ROBINSON (Rev. Dr.). Biblical Researches in Palestine and the Adjacent Regions, 1838—52. Maps. 3 Vols. 8vo. 42s.

——— Physical Geography of the Holy Land. Post 8vo. 10s. 6d.

——— (Wm.) Alpine Flowers for English Gardens. With 70 Illustrations. Crown 8vo. 12s.

——— Wild Gardens; or, our Groves and Shrubberies made beautiful by the Naturalization of Hardy Exotic Plants. With Frontispiece. Small 8vo. 6s.

——— Sub-Tropical Gardens; or, Beauty of Form in the Flower Garden. With Illustrations. Small 8vo. 7s. 6d.

ROBSON (E. R.). School Architecture. Being Practical Remarks on the Planning, Designing, Building, and Furnishing of School-houses. With 300 Illustrations. Medium 8vo. 18s.

ROME (History of). *See* Liddell and Smith.

ROWLAND (David). Manual of the English Constitution. Its Rise, Growth, and Present State. Post 8vo. 10s. 6d.

——— Laws of Nature the Foundation of Morals. Post 8vo. 6s.

RUNDELL (Mrs.). Modern Domestic Cookery. Fcap. 8vo. 5s.

RUXTON (George F.). Travels in Mexico; with Adventures among the Wild Tribes and Animals of the Prairies and Rocky ountains. Post 8vo. 3s. 6d.

SALE'S (Sir Robert) Brigade in Affghanistan. With an Account of the Defence of Jellalabad. By Rev. G. R. Gleig. Post 8vo. 2s.

SCEPTICISM IN GEOLOGY; and the Reasons for It. By Verifier. Crown 8vo. 6s.

SCHLIEMANN (Dr. Henry). Troy and Its Remains. A Narrative of Researches and Discoveries made on the Site of Ilium, and in the Trojan Plain. With Maps, Views, and 500 Illustrations. Medium 8vo. 42s.

——— Discoveries on the Sites of Ancient Mycenæ and Tiryns. With 500 Illustrations, Plans, &c. Medium 8vo. 50s.

SCOTT (Sir G. G.). Secular and Domestic Architecture, Present and Future. 8vo. 9s.

——— (Dean) University Sermons. Post 8vo. 8s. 6d.

SCROPE (G. P.). Geology and Extinct Volcanoes of Central France. Illustrations. Medium 8vo. 30s.

SHADOWS OF A SICK ROOM. With a Preface by Canon Liddon 16mo. 2s 6d.

SHAH OF PERSIA'S Diary during his Tour through Europe in 1873. Translated from the Original. By J. W. Redhouse. With Portrait and Coloured Title. Crown 8vo. 12s.

SMILES (Samuel). British Engineers; from the Earliest Period to the death of the Stephensons. With Illustrations. 5 Vols. Crown 8vo. 7s. 6d each.

——— George and Robert Stephenson. Illustrations. Medium 8vo. 21s.

——— Boulton and Watt. Illustrations. Medium 8vo. 21s.

——— Life of a Scotch Naturalist (Thomas Edward). With Portrait and Illustrations. Crown 8vo. 10s. 6d.

——— Huguenots in England and Ireland. Crown 8vo. 7s. 6d.

——— Self-Help. With Illustrations of Conduct and Perseverance. Post 8vo. 6s. Or in French, 5s.

——— Character. A Sequel to "Self-Help." Post 8vo. 6s.

——— Thrift. A Book of Domestic Counsel. Post 8vo. 6s.

——— Industrial Biography; or, Iron Workers and Tool Makers. Post 8vo. 6s.

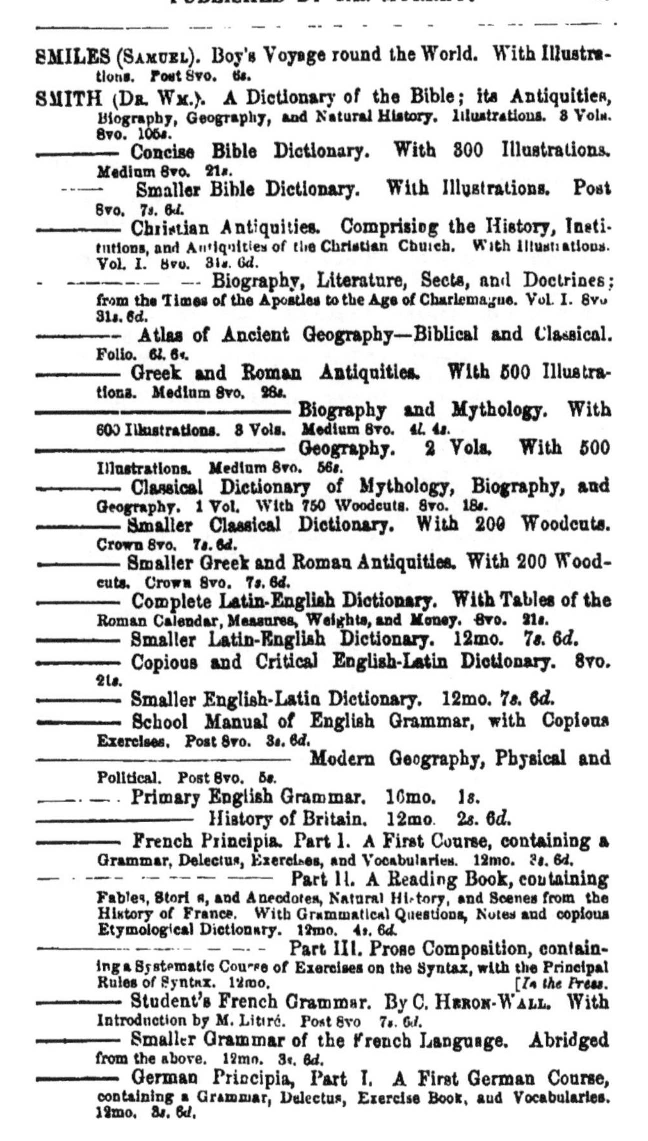

SMILES (SAMUEL). Boy's Voyage round the World. With Illustrations. Post 8vo. 6s.

SMITH (DR. WM.). A Dictionary of the Bible; its Antiquities, Biography, Geography, and Natural History. Illustrations. 3 Vols. 8vo. 105s.

——— Concise Bible Dictionary. With 300 Illustrations. Medium 8vo. 21s.

——— Smaller Bible Dictionary. With Illustrations. Post 8vo. 7s. 6d.

——— Christian Antiquities. Comprising the History, Institutions, and Antiquities of the Christian Church. With Illustrations. Vol. I. 8vo. 31s. 6d.

——— Biography, Literature, Sects, and Doctrines; from the Times of the Apostles to the Age of Charlemagne. Vol. I. 8vo 31s. 6d.

——— Atlas of Ancient Geography—Biblical and Classical. Folio. 6l. 6s.

——— Greek and Roman Antiquities. With 500 Illustrations. Medium 8vo. 28s.

——— ——— Biography and Mythology. With 600 Illustrations. 3 Vols. Medium 8vo. 4l. 4s.

——— ——— Geography. 2 Vols. With 500 Illustrations. Medium 8vo. 56s.

——— Classical Dictionary of Mythology, Biography, and Geography. 1 Vol. With 750 Woodcuts. 8vo. 18s.

——— Smaller Classical Dictionary. With 200 Woodcuts. Crown 8vo. 7s. 6d.

——— Smaller Greek and Roman Antiquities. With 200 Woodcuts. Crown 8vo. 7s. 6d.

——— Complete Latin-English Dictionary. With Tables of the Roman Calendar, Measures, Weights, and Money. 8vo. 21s.

——— Smaller Latin-English Dictionary. 12mo. 7s. 6d.

——— Copious and Critical English-Latin Dictionary. 8vo. 21s.

——— Smaller English-Latin Dictionary. 12mo. 7s. 6d.

——— School Manual of English Grammar, with Copious Exercises. Post 8vo. 3s. 6d.

——— ——— Modern Geography, Physical and Political. Post 8vo. 5s.

——— Primary English Grammar. 16mo. 1s.

——— ——— History of Britain. 12mo. 2s. 6d.

——— French Principia. Part I. A First Course, containing a Grammar, Delectus, Exercises, and Vocabularies. 12mo. 3s. 6d.

——— ——— Part II. A Reading Book, containing Fables, Stories, and Anecdotes, Natural History, and Scenes from the History of France. With Grammatical Questions, Notes and copious Etymological Dictionary. 12mo. 4s. 6d.

——— ——— Part III. Prose Composition, containing a Systematic Course of Exercises on the Syntax, with the Principal Rules of Syntax. 12mo. [*In the Press.*

——— Student's French Grammar. By C. HERON-WALL. With Introduction by M. Littré. Post 8vo 7s. 6d.

——— Smaller Grammar of the French Language. Abridged from the above. 12mo. 3s. 6d.

——— German Principia, Part I. A First German Course, containing a Grammar, Delectus, Exercise Book, and Vocabularies. 12mo. 3s. 6d.

DILKE (SIR C. W.). Papers of a Critic. Selected from the Writings of the late CHAS. WENTWORTH DILKE. With a Biographical Sketch. 2 Vols. 8vo. 24s.

DOG-BREAKING, with Odds and Ends for those who love the Dog and Gun. By GEN. HUTCHINSON. With 40 Illustrations. Crown 8vo. 7s. 6d.

DOMESTIC MODERN COOKERY. Founded on Principles of Economy and Practical Knowledge, and adapted for Private Families. Woodcuts. Fcap. 8vo. 5s.

DOUGLAS'S (SIR HOWARD) Life and Adventures. Portrait. 8vo. 15s.

——— Theory and Practice of Gunnery. Plates. 8vo. 21s.

——— Construction of Bridges and the Passage of Rivers in Military Operations. Plates. 8vo. 21s.

——— (WM.) Horse-Shoeing; As it Is, and As it Should be. Illustrations. Post 8vo. 7s. 6d.

DRAKE'S (SIR FRANCIS) Life, Voyages, and Exploits, by Sea and Land. By JOHN BARROW. Post 8vo. 2s.

DRINKWATER (JOHN). History of the Siege of Gibraltar, 1779-1783. With a Description and Account of that Garrison from the Earliest Periods. Post 8vo. 2s.

DUCANGE'S MEDIÆVAL LATIN-ENGLISH DICTIONARY. Translated and Edited by Rev. E. A. DAYMAN and J. H. HESSELS. Small 4to. [*In preparation.*

DU CHAILLU (PAUL B.). EQUATORIAL AFRICA, with Accounts of the Gorilla, the Nest-building Ape, Chimpanzee, Crocodile, &c. Illustrations. 8vo. 21s.

——— Journey to Ashango Land; and Further Penetration into Equatorial Africa. Illustrations. 8vo. 21s.

DUFFERIN (LORD). Letters from High Latitudes; a Yacht Voyage to Iceland, Jan Mayen, and Spitzbergen. Woodcuts. Post 8vo. 7s. 6d.

DUNCAN (MAJOR). History of the Royal Artillery. Compiled from the Original Records. With Portraits. 2 Vols. 8vo. 30s.

——— The English in Spain; or, The Story of the War of Succession. 1834 and 1840. Compiled from the Letters, Journals, and Reports of the British Commissioners with Queen Isabella's Armies. With Illustrations. 8vo. 16s.

EASTLAKE (SIR CHARLES). Contributions to the Literature of the Fine Arts. With Memoir of the Author, and Selections from his Correspondence. By LADY EASTLAKE. 2 Vols. 8vo. 24s.

EDWARDS (W. H.). Voyage up the River Amazons, including a Visit to Para. Post 8vo. 2s.

EIGHT MONTHS AT ROME, during the Vatican Council, with a Daily Account of the Proceedings. By POMPONIO LETO. Translated from the Original. 8vo. 12s.

ELDON'S (LORD) Public and Private Life, with Selections from his Correspondence and Diaries. By HORACE TWISS. Portrait. 2 Vols. Post 8vo. 21s.

ELGIN (LORD). Letters and Journals. Edited by THEODORE WALROND. With Preface by Dean Stanley. 8vo. 14s.

ELLESMERE (LORD). Two Sieges of Vienna by the Turks. Translated from the German. Post 8vo. 2s.

ELLIS (W.). Madagascar Revisited. Setting forth the Persecutions and Heroic Sufferings of the Native Christians. Illustrations. 8vo. 16s.

ELLIS (W,) Memoir. By His Son. With his Character and Work. By Rev. Henry Allon, D.D. Portrait. 8vo. 10s. 6d.

—— (Robinson) Poems and Fragments of Catullus. 16mo. 5s.

ELPHINSTONE (Hon. Mountstuart). History of India—the Hindoo and Mahomedan Periods. Edited by Professor Cowell. Map. 8vo. 18s.

—— (H. W.) Patterns for Turning; Comprising Elliptical and other Figures cut on the Lathe without the use of any Ornamental Chuck. With 70 Illustrations. Small 4to. 15s.

ENGLAND. See Callcott, Croker, Hume, Markham, Smith, and Stanhope.

ESSAYS ON CATHEDRALS. With an Introduction. By Dean Howson. 8vo. 12s.

ELZE (Karl). Life of Lord Byron. With a Critical Essay on his Place in Literature. Translated from the German. With Portrait. 8vo. 16s.

FERGUSSON (James). History of Architecture in all Countries from the Earliest Times. With 1,600 Illustrations. 4 Vols. Medium 8vo.

Vol. I. & II. Ancient and Mediæval. 63s.

Vol. III. Indian and Eastern. 42s.

Vol. IV. Modern. 31s. 6d.

—— Rude Stone Monuments in all Countries; their Age and Uses. With 230 Illustrations. Medium 8vo. 24s.

—— Holy Sepulchre and the Temple at Jerusalem. Woodcuts. 8vo. 7s. 6d.

—— The Temple at Jerusalem, and the other buildings in the Haram Area, from Solomon to Saladin, with numerous Illustrations. 4to.

FLEMING (Professor). Student's Manual of Moral Philosophy. With Quotations and References. Post 8vo. 7s. 6d.

FLOWER GARDEN. By Rev. Thos. James. Fcap. 8vo. 1s.

FORD (Richard). Gatherings from Spain. Post 8vo. 3s. 6d.

FORSYTH (William). Life and Times of Cicero. With Selections from his Correspondence and Orations. Illustrations. Crown 8vo.

—— Hortensius; an Historical Essay on the Office and Duties of an Advocate. Illustrations. 8vo. 12s.

—— History of Ancient Manuscripts. Post 8vo. 2s. 6d.

—— Novels and Novelists of the 18th Century, in Illustration of the Manners and Morals of the Age. Post 8vo. 10s. 6d.

FORTUNE (Robert). Narrative of Two Visits to the Tea Countries of China, 1843-52. Woodcuts. 2 Vols. Post 8vo. 18s.

FORSTER (John). The Early Life of Jonathan Swift. 1667-1711. With Portrait. 8vo. 15s.

FOSS (Edward). Biographia Juridica, or Biographical Dictionary of the Judges of England, from the Conquest to the Present Time, 1066-1870. Medium 8vo. 21s.

FRANCE (History of). See Markham—Smith—Student's.

FRENCH IN ALGIERS; The Soldier of the Foreign Legion—and the Prisoners of Abd-el-Kadir. Translated by Lady Duff Gordon. Post 8vo. 2s.

FRERE (Sir Bartle). Indian Missions. Small 8vo. 2s. 6d.

—— Eastern Africa as a field for Missionary Labour. With Map. Crown 8vo. 5s.

STUDENT'S OLD TESTAMENT HISTORY; from the Creation to the Return of the Jews from Captivity. Maps and Woodcuts. Post 8vo. 7*s.* 6*d.*

——— NEW TESTAMENT HISTORY. With an Introduction connecting the History of the Old and New Testaments. Maps and Woodcuts. Post 8vo. 7*s.* 6*d.*

——— ECCLESIASTICAL HISTORY. A History of the Christian Church from its Foundation to the Eve of the Reformation. By PHILIP SMITH, B.A. Post 8vo. 7*s.* 6*d.*

——— MANUAL OF ENGLISH CHURCH HISTORY, from the Reformation to the Present Time. By Rev. G. G. PERRY, Prebendary of Lincoln and Rector of Waddington. Post 8vo. 7*s.* 6*d.*

——— ANCIENT HISTORY OF THE EAST; Egypt, Assyria, Babylonia, Media, Persia, Asia Minor, and Phœnicia. Woodcuts. Post 8vo. 7*s.* 6*d.*

——— ——— GEOGRAPHY. By REV. W. L. BEVAN. Woodcuts. Post 8vo. 7*s.* 6*d.*

——— HISTORY OF GREECE; from the Earliest Times to the Roman Conquest. By WM. SMITH, D.C.L. Woodcuts. Crown 8vo. 7*s.* 6*d.*

*** Questions on the above Work, 12mo. 2*s.*

——— HISTORY OF ROME; from the Earliest Times to the Establishment of the Empire. By DEAN LIDDELL. Woodcuts. Crown 8vo. 7*s.* 6*d.*

——— GIBBON'S Decline and Fall of the Roman Empire. Woodcuts. Post 8vo. 7*s.* 6*d.*

——— HALLAM'S HISTORY OF EUROPE during the Middle Ages. Post 8vo. 7*s.* 6*d.*

——— HALLAM'S HISTORY OF ENGLAND; from the Accession of Henry VII. to the Death of George II. Post 8vo. 7*s.* 6*d.*

——— HUME'S History of England from the Invasion of Julius Cæsar to the Revolution in 1688. Continued down to 1868. Woodcuts. Post 8vo. 7*s.* 6*d.*

*** Questions on the above Work, 12mo. 2*s.*

——— HISTORY OF FRANCE; from the Earliest Times to the Establishment of the Second Empire, 1852. By REV. H. W. JERVIS. Woodcuts. Post 8vo. 7*s.* 6*d.*

——— ENGLISH LANGUAGE. By GEO. P. MARSH. Post 8vo. 7*s.* 6*d.*

——— ——— LITERATURE. By T. B. SHAW, M.A. Post 8vo. 7*s.* 6*d.*

——— SPECIMENS of English Literature from the Chief Writers. By T. B. SHAW. Post 8vo. 7*s.* 6*d.*

——— MODERN GEOGRAPHY; Mathematical, Physical, and Descriptive. By REV. W. L. BEVAN. Woodcuts. Post 8vo. 7*s.* 6*d.*

——— MORAL PHILOSOPHY. By WILLIAM FLEMING, D.D. Post 8vo. 7*s.* 6*d.*

——— ——— BLACKSTONE'S Commentaries on the Laws of England. By R. MALCOLM KERR, LL.D. Post 8vo. 7*s.* 6*d.*

SUMNER'S (BISHOP) Life and Episcopate during 40 Years. By Rev. G. H. SUMNER. Portrait. 8vo. 14*s.*

STREET (G. E.) Gothic Architecture in Spain. From Personal Observations made during several Journeys. With Illustrations. Royal 8vo. 30*s.*

——— ——— Italy, chiefly in Brick and Marble. With Notes of Tours in the North of Italy. With 60 Illustrations. Royal 8vo. 26*s.*

STANHOPE (EARL) England from the Reign of Queen Anne to the Peace of Versailles, 1701-83. *Library Edition*. 8 vols. 8vo. *Cabinet Edition*, 9 vols. Post 8vo. 5s. each.

———— British India, from its Origin to 1783. 8vo. 3s. 6d.

———— History of "Forty-Five." Post 8vo. 3s.

———— Historical and Critical Essays. Post 8vo. 3s. 6d.

———— French Retreat from Moscow, and other Essays. Post 8vo. 7s. 6d.

———— Life of Belisarius. Post 8vo. 10s. 6d.

———— Condé. Post 8vo. 3s. 6d.

———— William Pitt. Portraits. 4 Vols. 8vo. 24s.

———— Miscellanies. 2 Vols. Post 8vo. 13s.

———— Story of Joan of Arc. Fcap. 8vo. 1s.

———— Addresses on Various Occasions. 16mo. 1s.

STYFFE (KNUTT). Strength of Iron and Steel. Plates. 8vo. 12s.

SOMERVILLE (MARY). Personal Recollections from Early Life to Old Age. With her Correspondence. Portrait. Crown 8vo. 12s.

———— Physical Geography. Portrait. Post 8vo. 9s.

———— Connexion of the Physical Sciences. Portrait. Post 8vo. 9s.

———— Molecular and Microscopic Science. Illustrations. 2 Vols. Post 8vo. 21s.

SOUTHEY (ROBERT). Lives of Bunyan and Cromwell. Post 8vo. 2s.

SWAINSON (CANON). Nicene and Apostles' Creeds; Their Literary History; together with some Account of "The Creed of St. Athanasius." 8vo. 16s.

SYBEL (VON) History of Europe during the French Revolution, 1789—1795. 4 Vols. 8vo. 48s.

SYMONDS' (REV. W.) Records of the Rocks; or Notes on the Geology, Natural History, and Antiquities of North and South Wales, Siluria, Devon, and Cornwall. With Illustrations. Crown 8vo. 12s.

THIBAUT'S (ANTOINE) Purity in Musical Art. Translated from the German. With a prefatory Memoir by W. H. Gladstone, M.P. Post 8vo. 7s. 6d.

THIELMANN (BARON) Journey through the Caucasus to Tabreez, Kurdistan, down the Tigris and Euphrates to Nineveh and Babylon, and across the Desert to Palmyra. Translated by CHAS. HENEAGE. Illustrations. 2 Vols. Post 8vo. 18s.

THOMS (W. J.). Longevity of Man; its Facts and its Fiction. Including Observations on the more Remarkable Instances. Post 8vo. 10s. 6d.

THOMSON (ARCHBISHOP). Lincoln's Inn Sermons. 8vo. 10s. 6d.

———— Life in the Light of God's Word. Post 8vo. 5s.

TITIAN'S LIFE AND TIMES. With some account of his Family, chiefly from new and unpublished Records. By CROWE and CAVALCASELLE. With Portrait and Illustrations. 2 Vols. 8vo. 42s.

TOCQUEVILLE'S State of Society in France before the Revolution, 1789, and on the Causes which led to that Event. Translated by HENRY REEVE. 8vo. 14s.

TOMLINSON (CHARLES); The Sonnet; Its Origin, Structure, and Place in Poetry. With translations from Dante, Petrarch &c. Post 8vo. 9s.

TOZER (Rev. H. F.) Highlands of Turkey, with Visits to Mounts Ida, Athos, Olympus, and Pelion. 2 Vols. Crown 8vo. 24s.

——— Lectures on the Geography of Greece. Map. Post 8vo. 9s.

TRISTRAM (Canon) Great Sahara. Illustrations. Crown 8vo. 15s.

——— Land of Moab; Travels and Discoveries on the East Side of the Dead Sea and the Jordan. Illustrations. Crown 8vo. 15s.

TWISLETON (Edward). The Tongue not Essential to Speech, with Illustrations of the Power of Speech in the case of the African Confessors. Post 8vo. 6s.

TWISS' (Horace) Life of Lord Eldon. 2 Vols. Post 8vo. 21s.

TYLOR (E. B.) Early History of Mankind, and Development of Civilization. 8vo. 12s.

——— Primitive Culture; the Development of Mythology, Philosophy, Religion, Art, and Custom. 2 Vols. 8vo. 24s.

VAMBERY (Arminius) Travels from Teheran across the Turkoman Desert on the Eastern Shore of the Caspian. Illustrations. 8vo. 21s.

VAN LENNEP (Henry J.) Travels in Asia Minor. With Illustrations of Biblical Literature, and Archæology. With Woodcuts. 2 Vols. Post 8vo. 24s.

——— Modern Customs and Manners of Bible Lands, in illustration of Scripture. With Maps and 300 Illustrations. 2 Vols. 8vo. 21s.

WELLINGTON'S Despatches during his Campaigns in India, Denmark, Portugal, Spain, the Low Countries, and France. Edited by Colonel Gurwood. 8 Vols. 8vo. 20s. each.

——— Supplementary Despatches, relating to India, Ireland, Denmark, Spanish America, Spain, Portugal, France, Congress of Vienna, Waterloo and Paris. Edited by his Son. 14 Vols. 8vo. 20s. each. *** An Index. 8vo. 20s.

——— Civil and Political Correspondence. Edited by his Son. Vols. I. to V. 8vo. 20s. each.

——— Vol. VI., relating to the Eastern Question of 1829. Russian Intrigues, Turkish Affairs, Treaty of Adrianople, &c. 8vo.

——— Speeches in Parliament. 2 Vols. 8vo. 42s.

WHEELER (G.). Choice of a Dwelling: a Practical Handbook of Useful Information on Building a House. Plans. Post 8vo. 7s. 6d.

WHITE (W. H.). Manual of Naval Architecture, for the use of Officers of the R. N. and Mercantile Service, Yachtsmen, Shipowners, and Shipbuilders. Illustrations. 8vo. 24s.

WILBERFORCE'S (Bishop) Life of William Wilberforce. Portrait. Crown 8vo. 6s.

WILKINSON (Sir J. G.). Manners and Customs of the Ancient Egyptians, their Private Life, Government, Laws, Arts, Manufactures, Religion, &c. A new edition, with additions by the late Author. Edited by Samuel Birch, LL.D. Illustrations. 3 Vols. 8vo.

——— Popular Account of the Ancient Egyptians. With 500 Woodcuts. 2 Vols. Post 8vo. 12s.

WOOD'S (Captain) Source of the Oxus. With the Geography of the Valley of the Oxus. By Col. Yule. Map. 8vo. 12s.

WORDS OF HUMAN WISDOM. Collected and Arranged by E. S. With a Preface by Canon Liddon Fcap. 8vo. 3s. 6d

WORDSWORTH'S (Bishop) Athens and Attica Plates. 8vo. 5s.

YULE'S (Colonel) Book of Marco Polo. Illustrated by the Light of Oriental Writers and Modern Travels. With Maps and 80 Plates. 2 Vols. Medium 8vo. 63s.

BRADBURY, AGNEW & CO. PRINTERS, WHITEFRIARS.